Rock music

ROCK MUSIC

Culture, aesthetics and sociology

PETER WICKE

Translated by Rachel Fogg

CAMBRIDGE UNIVERSITY PRESS

Published by the Press Syndicate of the University of Cambridge
The Pitt Building, Trumpington Street, Cambridge CB2 1RP
40 West 20th Street, New York, NY 10011–4211, USA
10 Stamford Road, Oakleigh, Melbourne 3166, Australia

Originally published in German as *Rockmusik: zur Ästhetik und
Soziologie eines Massenmediums*
by Verlag Philipp Reclam jun. Leipzig 1987
and © 1987
First published in English by Cambridge University Press 1990 as
Rock music: Culture, aesthetics and sociology
English translation © Cambridge University Press 1990
Reprinted 1993, 1995

Printed in Great Britain by Athenæum Press Ltd, Gateshead, Tyne & Wear

British Library cataloguing in publication data

Wicke, Peter
    Rock music : culture, aesthetics, and sociology
    1. Rock music – Sociological perspectives
    I. Rockmusik. *English*   II. Title
    306′.484

Library of Congress cataloguing in publication data applied for

ISBN 0 521 36555 4 hardback
ISBN 0 521 39914 9 paperback

WG

Contents

v

90483

About the author

Peter Wicke was born in Zwickau in 1951 and is currently head of the centre for popular music research at the Music Faculty of Berlin's Humboldt University. He completed his music studies in Berlin in 1974. Since then he has been a member of the teaching staff at the Music Faculty at Humboldt University, lecturing on the history, aesthetics and theory of popular music. He received his PhD in 1980 for a thesis on the aesthetics of popular music, and in 1986 he received his Dr. sc. phil. He has published many articles in his native country and abroad on theoretical, historical and cultural-political problems of popular music, and his work has been translated into English, French, Italian, Spanish, Swedish, Finnish, Czech, Bulgarian and Russian. He is the co-author, with Wieland Ziegenrücker, of *Rock Pop Jazz Folk. Handbuch der populären Musik*. He has visited many foreign universities on lecture tours, including, as part of the preparation for this book, London, Liverpool, Manchester and Birmingham. He is a member of the International Association for the Study of Popular Music and has held the post of General Secretary of the Association since 1987.

Preface

Batteries of spotlights pick out the band in multi-coloured light against the darkness of the stage. The hall trembles under the thunderous noise of the fans. The singer steps up to the front of the stage. The music begins to the stamping rhythm of the drums ... Scene change: the shadows of young people dance frenetically in the flickering lights of a discotheque. The noise level is deafening. Nothing disturbs their abandonment to the music. The energy which keeps their bodies moving seems inexhaustible ... Scene change: a fourteen-year-old boy, eyes closed, wears the booming headphones of a stereo system. The walls around him are papered from top to bottom with posters and stickers. A record revolves on the turntable. Only a light rhythmical rocking of his upper body gives away his absorbed involvement in what is reaching him via connector and cable ...

Rock music – who can fail to recognise these descriptions of young fans which are so inextricably bound up with it? But what is it that actually lies behind these descriptions? What does the fascination with this music, reflected in such scenes, consist of? What experience of reality is to be found in the music? What significance and what cultural values are locked up in the hammering, motoric rhythms and the often shrill sounds that are transmitted to a mass audience through the songs?

This book attempts to provide an answer to these questions. It seeks to investigate the social and cultural origins of rock music in order to reconstruct the contexts in which its very diverse musical styles have arisen, and which, at each point in its development, have become the carriers of very specific meanings, embodying values which reach deep into the lives of its fans. The book seeks to penetrate to the social roots of rock music, de-mystifying its history and making clear the social movements which it reflects. The central concern of the book is to expose and to make comprehensible and meaningful those levels of rock music which lie hidden beneath its musical surface, behind its styles and ways of playing. Records and songs are not isolated objects; they are the symptoms of an extensive overall cultural context which owes its existence in equal measure to social and political relations as well as to the particular environment of its listeners.

Nothing has changed this context, or the music culture of the twentieth century, more fundamentally than the meteoric rise to fame of the Beatles. Around eighty per cent of the music currently available on sound media represents one or other branch of rock music, using the term rock music in its widest sense. In Britain and the USA alone, rock's classic countries of origin, a total of around ten thousand singles and eight thousand LPs are released in this field each year; if we assume ten tracks per LP, this gives a total of one hundred thousand songs every year. The rock'n'roll programme 'Aloha from Elvis in Hawaii', featuring Elvis Presley, was beamed across the world in January 1973 from the International Center in Honolulu; demographers estimate it reached about one third of the world's population. The satellite broadcast of the sixteen-hour 'Live Aid' double concert from Wembley Stadium in London and the John F. Kennedy Stadium in Philadelphia (with contributions from Sydney, Moscow, Tokyo, Peking, Cologne and Vienna), is said to have united nearly two thousand million viewers from 150 countries in front of the television screen. Therefore to see rock music simply as an exclusively 'teenage music', just linked to the phase of adolescence, misses the point altogether, even though young people – the age group with the most intensive contact with music – do form the central social group related to rock. In fact, the upper age limit of this group is continually rising and it has, for a long time, included young adults up to the now forty-five-year-old Beatles generation.

Merely by virtue of its numerical significance in current music production, rock music imposes conditions and has cultural consequences which allow it to become a symptom of much more far-reaching and fundamental changes. These changes cannot be reduced to the problem of 'youth', but rather amount to the formation of a new everyday culture, influenced by the media. Thus it is valid to see in rock music the prospect of a development which may be ignored or resisted, but which will definitely not be halted. By linking music, showmanship, lighting, poetry, politics and image a new art praxis has been created. On the basis of the technology of modern mass communication this praxis also validates a new kind of artistic self-awareness, which cannot be dismissed merely by alluding to the putative musical and content nonsense of commercial business-mindedness. It is more the case that it is part of the peculiar nature of rock music to involve itself uncompromisingly with the technical and economic conditions of the cultural mass processes organised by the media, and in doing this it becomes a communications medium itself. Rock music is not an object of a contemplative enjoyment of 'art' separate from everyday life; rock songs are not subjects for contemplation, their meaning is not given to the 'form' by a hidden 'content'. Rock music is a mass medium through which cultural values and meanings circulate, through which social experiences are passed on which reach far beyond the material nature of the music.

The 'content' of rock songs cannot be reduced to what is directly played or even what appears to be expressed in the lyrics. For its listeners these aspects only form the medium of which they themselves make *active* use. They integrate them into their lives and use them as symbols to make public their own experiences, just as, seen from another angle, these aspects give the experience of social reality a cultural form conveyed by the senses and thereby influence that reality. However, this does not mean that lyrics and music are now to be entrusted to the whim of an arbitrary use or that they are in the end to be interchangeable in their concrete form. Just as in a jigsaw puzzle each individual piece is only partly defined by its shape and form, while the context of the whole picture and the place of the piece in it is equally important, the 'content' of rock music is not merely grounded in the musical form of the songs. On the one hand this 'content' is determined by the contexts which its fans give it, and on the other hand it is also preconditioned by the social relations of its production and distribution together with the institutional contexts in which these stand. In other words, these contexts become a component of the lyrics, a component of a cultural text formed from cultural symbols of the most varied kind (images, technology, fashion, leisure objects, the everyday materials of the consumer society), and the music is the medium for the formulation of this cultural text. Because of this, rock music is a very complex cultural form in which dance forms, the mass media, media pictures, images and styles of dress are included as well as music. This cultural form is a social environment produced by means of music for cultural activities of the most diverse nature. Its musical and stylistic homogeneity corresponds at any given time to different social contexts, in which rock music appears with changing meanings, always defined through different characteristics, functions and methods of use. This makes it impossible to bind rock music to a rigidly delineated musical definition.

In what follows therefore, rock music itself will be allowed to speak, unburdened by the systematisation of concepts and categories. The purpose of this is to achieve a portrait of rock, of its significant characteristics as revealed in the diversity of its stylistic forms and the breathtaking dynamics of its development. The most suitable form of presentation for this is the essay, which is able to concern itself with detail while keeping the whole in view, piecing together an overall picture from the individual aspects rather like a mosaic. Of course, this does not mean that instead of offering verifiable statements I have taken flight into the twilight of metaphorical vagueness and inaccuracy, or escaped into the journalistic superficiality so common in rock literature. What I am offering are a variety of attempts at a theoretical, reflective approach to the subject, each encapsulated in a self-contained study which considers the subject from a different viewpoint, studies which can only produce a valid model of this music when combined. A form of music that is still changing so much and which, because of the dynamic nature of its own development, escapes any systematic approach, can hardly be dealt with in any other way. Because of this and because of the plethora of individual releases, dates, facts, names, styles and trends (which are in any case no longer entirely clear), I have not attempted to include everything, nor do I believe such an attempt to be necessary. What is far more important is the uncovering of those questions to which the development of rock provides an answer, the reconstruction of the cultural factors, social circumstances and contradictions to which it owes its existence.

The terms 'aesthetics' and 'sociology' in the subtitle of this book represent approaches which define the nature of the way of looking at the problem. Anyone who is led by this to expect a theory-intensive construction of categories, normative value criteria or a richness of empirical–statistical data will be disappointed. A 'theory of rock music' must be developed from the reality of the music, and this reality comprises the musical, cultural and social contexts out of which (and together with the diversity of its performance styles) it arose and out of which it has always evolved new forms. This approach admittedly demands a correspondingly complex viewpoint, for which, as scientific disciplines, aesthetics and sociology provide suitable theoretical apparatus. However, it is not the use of these disciplines that is under discussion here, but rather what I have discovered with their aid. The consideration of rock from a sociological standpoint makes it possible to regard its development as part of its fans' everyday lives and leisure and to understand it as such. The theoretical apparatus of aesthetics, on the other hand, helps to decipher the noisy sounds, the colourful facial expressions and the often obscure disguises, tracking down the code by which personal and collective experiences are recast into songs. But even if the reader's attention is directed in this way to more complex connections than would be the case from the mere description of the musical events and their chronology, even this cannot and will not deliver a really comprehensive explanation. This too is nothing more than an *attempt* to understand and to make understandable what has really been created with this music.

Just as the music itself is constantly changing, so is its terminology. The term 'rock music' means many different things and its meaning has changed at practically every stage in its development. The boundaries between it and other classes of popular music and other fields of music culture are fluid and are constantly changing. A few years ago the description 'beat music' was understood and widespread in German-speaking countries, but has since become a technical term which can now only be applied to the British rock development of the early sixties and to those groups directly influenced by it. The shortform 'rock', derived from the American term 'rock'n'roll', only came into general use in the mid-sixties, losing in the process the specific meaning that it had previously had as a description of those musical styles directly derived from rock'n'roll. Meanwhile rock music is nurtured from very diverse musical sources – even sources from quite different traditions, like the music of Philip Glass or Steve Reich, Edgar Varese or John Cage, or the music of non-European cultures or European 'classical' music. Amongst these different sources rock'n'roll plays, as before, a dominant, but no longer an exclusive, role. The term itself goes back to the language of the blues and to the slang of North American blacks, in which *to rock* is both a harmless metaphor for dancing as well as a quite obscene euphemism for the sexual act. Incidentally, this background ambiguity has remained in many lyrics right up to the present day, even if the obvious sexual meaning has in the meantime been neutralised.

In any case many different terms also exist – pop, pop music, rock & roll (in contrast to rock'n'roll) etc. – which provide a rich source of confusion, since they are partly synonyms but partly used with more or less independent meanings. This is only of relevance to the following presentation in so far as all these terms appear in perfect harmony in the works of the quoted authors and musicians. In the context of quotations their use is always synonymous with the term rock music.

The conversations and discussions which I had the opportunity to take part in stimulated many important ideas; I am also grateful to all those who have supported me with material, information and contacts in my, often very time-consuming, research. I owe my thanks equally to musicians and representatives of the music industry and also to fans, who listened patiently to me and answered my 'strange' questions, thereby often opening up broad vistas into their thoughts and everyday lives.

I would like to thank the following here for their help and support: Moe Armstrong, Clarence Baker, Chris Bohn, Iain Chambers, Chris Cutler, Geoff Davies, Monika Doering, Simon Frith, Reebee Garofalo, Larry Grossberg, Charles Hamm, Nick Hobbs, Peter Hooten, David Horn, Mike Howes, Robert Lloyd, Paul McDonald, Greil Marcus, Richard Middleton, Charles Shaar-Murray, Paul Rutten, Mark E. Smith, Philip Tagg, Geoff Travis, John Walters, Paul Willis, Tony Wilson – as well as all those whom it is not possible to mention here.

Berlin-Pankow, April 1986

1

'Roll Over Beethoven': new experiences in art

When rock music made its first appearance with American rock'n'roll in the early fifties, using the word 'art' in this context would doubtless have seemed sacrilegious. Even today the claim that rock music is an art form still provokes heated discussion and intense resistance, although in the meantime rock has aspired to academic honours and the Beatles count as its 'classics'. If to some people rock music signals a new musical creativity in the age of the mass media, to others it equally represents the mere substitution of commerce for art. Now we could just leave it at that without further observation. It is irrelevant to the actual effect of rock whether it is honoured with the description of 'art' or not. Since its real status in contemporary music culture hardly needs this sort of justification, such arguments are futile and unproductive.

However, if we want to understand what it is that rock evokes in its listeners and why this music has become in quantitative terms such a phenomenon in present-day music culture, we must start from the assumption that it should be regarded not only as the expression of general social relationships and economic mechanisms, but primarily as what it is to its young fans above all else – music. The significance that it holds, the values that it embodies and the pleasure that it provides are linked to its role as aesthetically relevant sound material. Even if it cannot be reduced to this level, but represents instead a very complex form of cultural activity (including, perhaps, dress and hair fashions, dance styles and poster collecting), the basis on which everything else rests is the music. As Michael Lydon quite correctly states: 'There's a million theories about rock'n'roll, what it is and what it means, but what is most obvious is most overlooked: it's music.'[1] However trite such a conclusion may appear, it is

1

anything but self-evident. If rock music is really to be understood in its cultural dimension it must be taken seriously as music and be accepted as a legitimate art form.

This only becomes a problem if it leads to the conclusion that those criteria of musical appreciation should apply for which Beethoven serves as a symbol, a conclusion which argues that the true meaning of music is encapsulated in Beethoven and his tradition. Although not always stated in quite such categorical terms, the majority of the countless misunderstandings that have accompanied the development of rock music are rooted in the transformation of this concept of music into an absolute standard. Measured against this, rock music would indeed be nothing but a meaningless noise, invented by a gigantic commercial enterprise to satisfy its profit requirements and made attractive to susceptible teenagers by an appealing exterior. However, this view can be countered by the fact that music is not defined by its means of expression – loud or soft, simple or extremely complex – but primarily by the effects which these achieve. The assumption that relevant and differentiated content, value and meaning can only be expressed by those musical means developed in the tradition of Beethoven and his successors not only contradicts the facts, but presents an equally ahistorical and mechanistic view of art. Artistic means of expression can never be considered separately from their cultural and functional context. There are a number of factors which affect this significantly – the question of whether music is more genuinely realised in the concert hall or in the mass media, the particular everyday activities, lifestyles and needs which music affects, the particular conditions of its production and distribution – and these factors have led not only to historical changes in the conception of music, but also to quite different perceptions of music. This has always been the case, but previously these differing perceptions did not clash as directly as they do today, when this process even intrudes into family life, creating discord between parents and children.

Thus, in order to take rock seriously as music, we need to investigate the conception of music which underlies it rather than apply aesthetic criteria and musical models that are completely alien to its cultural origins.

It is, however, rock's champions themselves, musicians,

journalists and publicists, who have contributed significantly to this confusion. They have applied socially established views of music to rock in order to create a respect for it corresponding to its cultural status. In 1963, for example, Richard Buckle in *The Sunday Times* described the Beatles as: 'the greatest composers since Beethoven'.[2] A greater misunderstanding is scarcely imaginable, for such deep-seated differences exist between these two musical worlds that the one simply cannot be measured by the standards of the other. No less misleading is the opposing theory that would have rock music understood as a form of folk music, as expressed by the American rock historian Carl Belz, who starts from the premise 'that rock is a part of the long tradition of folk art in the United States and throughout the world'.[3] Rock music is organised according to principles that are neither those of folk music nor those of bourgeois art music. In trying to measure rock against either of these we fail to recognise its musical individuality and significantly distort the perspective from which we view it. Paradoxically, it was precisely the same originality which made rock stand out from the conventions of the traditional pop song and which led falsely to the attempt to subsume it in the genre of folk music or to declare it to be 'art' according to the standards of Beethoven.

In contrast, the conception of music which is genuinely at the centre of the development of rock music − even though rock has developed in many often opposing directions in the wake of stylistic differences − was formulated at a very early stage and quite unmistakably in the music itself. It was in 'Roll Over Beethoven',[4] the Chuck Berry song that appeared in 1956, that the musical self-awareness of the rock'n'roll craze, then at its height in the USA, found a provocative and challenging expression, one which has remained something of a leitmotif. In the song the fascination of this music is compared with fever and illness, whose inevitability is taken as a metaphor for the overwhelming effect rock had at that time. Not without irony, while claiming the same status and cultural relevance, rock music appears self-consciously juxtaposed to an artistic appreciation, represented by the names of Beethoven and Tschaikowsky, for which we cannot imagine greater contrasts than a jukebox and a self-sufficient sensuousness. There is, no doubt, more to this than the simple provocation of adults by a pointed lack of respect for their musical gods. What the black singer and guitarist Chuck Berry was screaming to his fans in this song, in his breathless 'Roll Over Beethoven', heralded a conception of music which had become aware of its own novelty and which challengingly contrasted this with all other musical traditions.

What was really new about rock was its relationship with the means of mass communication – record, radio, television and film. American rock'n'roll found its basic conditions of existence in these media and accepted this fact without compromise as a prerequisite for artistic creativity. Its commercial effectiveness, which no other form of music before it had possessed, was not attributable, as is usually claimed, to the supposed exotic nature of its Afro-American roots. Even in the swing era more than two decades earlier black musicians and bands had been acclaimed by a white audience, just as there had been exchanges between 'black' and 'white' music even before this, in spite of assertions to the contrary. The assumption of a completely separate development of Afro-American and European-American music is more a racist argument that (still) legitimises the established barriers between the races by accepting a real cultural contrast between 'black' and 'white' based on skin colour, a contrast first overcome by rock'n'roll. The relationship between the Afro-American minority in the USA and white Americans, against the background of arbitrarily established barriers between the races, is far more complex than such simplistic 'black/white' thinking makes clear.

The reason for the swift and spectacular spread of rock'n'roll lay, instead, in the fact that it was so much a part of the mass media, which developed explosively after 1945. Rock'n'roll was the first form of music to be distributed in mass quantities on record, the first form of music whose development was linked to radio, film and television. It is true that in the thirties records had already been so successful that an independent industry was established on the basis of this success. But its products still went mostly to jukebox installers or were reserved for the rather more exclusive body of classical music purchasers. In the early fifties this situation changed in the wake of a number of innovations in media technology which led to a rapid reduction in the price of records.

In 1948 CBS (Columbia Broadcasting System) introduced the

high fidelity long-playing record (LP), which was made possible by reducing the playing speed from 78 to 33⅓ revolutions per minute using vinyl plastic (with its twin advantages of low noise characteristics and great strength) instead of shellac. Not long after this RCA (Radio Corporation of America) brought out the 45 r.p.m. single, based on the same technology, as their answer to the competition's LP. The single was aimed at the new teenage market and was priced within reach of teenagers' pocket money. But probably the most far-reaching development in the realm of media technology was the introduction, directly after the Second World War, of magnetic tape for recording music. This replaced the costly electrical recording method in record production and created the necessary technical conditions to allow recordings to be corrected afterwards. In 1947 the swing guitarist Les Paul was already using the so-called sound-on-sound method for producing backing tracks, copying a finished recording together with an additional section onto a second tape. In multi-track recording – first used in 1954 with two separate recording tracks (the two-track method) and then developed step by step to the current standard of 24, 32 or 64 tracks – this principle became the basis of studio music production, with far-reaching consequences for musical performance. Up to this point, developments in media technology had never interfered directly with the structure of music. They had remained external, merely allowing the performance to be stored or reproduced, although even this did not leave music completely unaffected. Harvey Fuqua, lead singer in the fifties with the Moonglows – one of the hundreds of vocal rhythm & blues ensembles around at that time – and now a producer and manager, recalled those times in 1978 and offered a vivid description of how things were done in the studios before the introduction of multi-track recording:

It wasn't like they've got 32 and 64 tracks to play with like today. They'd put the microphone right in the middle of the room and everybody stood round it, the band, the singers, everybody. If you wanted more of an instrument or a singer you'd have to move either back or forward. And you didn't necessarily use drums then; you could use a telephone book and slap it. It was wild.[5]

This meant that in theory there was virtually no difference between the recording and the live music played on stage, although in practice the playing time of the record and the recording characteristics of the microphone already imposed constraints which had to be considered when songs were conceived. But while these remained exterior constraints, multi-tracking techniques literally revolutionised musical performance from within. It was now possible to separate the music into individual parts which were then put back together in the final mixing process. Instead of the reproduction of an acoustic totality, or musical snapshot, a sort of montage principle developed. The consequence of this was that the musical result became divorced from the actual performance and feedback between the two was only partially possible. As George Harrison once said: 'Nobody knows what the tunes sound like till we've recorded them, then listened to them afterwards.'[6]

It was no longer absolutely necessary for musicians to play together at recording sessions, indeed they no longer even needed to know one another in order to produce music together; the individual parts of the music could now be recorded at distant locations and at different times. Paul Simon's description of the production of 'The Boxer',[7] his first real success with Art Garfunkel, provides a classic example: 'It was recorded all over the place – the basic tracks in Nashville, the end voices in New York St Paul's Church, the strings in New York Columbia Studios and voices there too.'[8] Music created in this way naturally demanded different principles of performance and followed new structural and organisational rules. Rock music was based on far-reaching changes in music production. The foundations for these were laid in the fifties and first came to fruition in rock'n'roll. The impact of these new developments has lasted to the present day, changing the traditional relations of popular music production and distribution (previously dominated by the mighty music publishers of Tin Pan Alley) just as much as people's contact with music in their daily lives. Yet the musical basis for this was already present in rock'n'roll, which has constantly served as a reference point for the vast majority of rock groups and rock musicians.

Two other innovations in media technology were to have equally important consequences: television and the portable radio, the latter made possible by transistor technology. Radio, which had previously been the most important means of distributing music, lost its audience to television, which was introduced at the end of the forties and was quickly accepted as the new family entertainment medium. Television also offered new prospects for the distribution of music, although at first its effect was indirect. Cinemas, coming under pressure from the unwelcome competition, reacted by orienting themselves to a young audience which was trying to escape the new family ritual in front of the television screen. Rock'n'roll was the perfect aid in this. Film, already important in the thirties in the development of hits, film hits, once again began to play a decisive role in the music business, except that the films now revolved around musical stars – whose acting often left something to be desired – and their songs. The worldwide success of a song like 'Rock Around the Clock' would have been unthinkable without the assistance of film, where it appeared more than once as a dramatic set piece – in *The Blackboard Jungle* (1955),[9] as well as in *Rock Around the Clock* (1956)[10] and *Don't Knock the Rock* (1957).[11] In fact, when the record was first released in 1954 its sales were anything but good.

With the introduction of programmes for teenagers, television also proved to be an ideal platform for the spread of rock'n'roll, even if at first rock's appearance provoked argument. The commercial status of a programme like *American Bandstand* – started in 1952 in Philadelphia by WFIL-TV and, from 1957 on, transmitted every Saturday morning across the whole of America by the ABC-TV network – with more than twenty million viewers every week can hardly be overstated. There can scarcely be a famous rock group or musician, from Chuck Berry through the Beatles and the Rolling Stones to Bruce Springsteen, who has not appeared on it during the thirty-plus years of the programme's history. Video technology and above all the introduction in 1981 by the Warner-Amex Group (a joint undertaking of Warner Communications and American Express) of Music Television (MTV) on one channel of its cable network, playing hit performances in the form of video clips nonstop, around the clock, have made television a tremendously important factor in the development of music.

Radio had found itself in a vacuum after the loss of its traditional audience and responded by focussing on specialist musical interests and target groups that could be defined as closely as possible. Through programmes reserved exclusively for rock and pop, radio became the teenager's daily companion. When the first battery driven and relatively cheap portable radios came on the market in the USA in 1954, teenagers held in their hands a medium that was out of reach of parental control and influence. From the mid-fifties in the USA alone some ten million radios were sold every year. With these radios, teenagers for the first time had a fully independent access to the media through which they could assert their own musical interests. This was to prove the decisive precondition for the shaping of age-specific music needs, and rock developed in this environment. It was no coincidence that the worldwide spread of rock'n'roll coincided everywhere with the introduction of the 45 r.p.m. single and the portable radio.

This explosive development of the mass media heralded a radical change in the conditions of production, distribution, reception and effect of music, a change which first took place in the industrially highly developed USA, a country not faced with the devastating destruction of the Second World War. Chuck Berry's 'Roll Over Beethoven' reflected this change quite precisely, not only the superficiality of the rock'n'roll craze which was fanned by commercial interests, but even more the feeling that against this background *all* established musical conventions could be called into question. The development of rock'n'roll, with the technology of audio-visual mass communication and the social changes within the culture which it provoked, did in fact literally roll over the aesthetic maxims of Beethoven and the great bourgeois musical tradition. The changes were far-reaching.

The bourgeois musical tradition is grounded in an essentially contemplative mode of listening in the concert hall, immersed in the structural detail (of the music) and requiring 'understanding'. It is not at home in a media reality which slots music into as many contexts as possible. Via the media, reception of the same piece of music can vary from the intensive, demanding concentrated attention, to the partial, switching between listening and not listening, or even to the casual, since music is continually present in different everyday contexts, from homework to housework. The traditional criteria of bourgeois musical appreciation were bound to come into conflict with such a complex web of relationships. In parallel with this, the relevance of the Tin Pan Alley hit, the 'pleasant, universal, well-constructed song'[12] of the pop music tradition, linked to the great New York publishing empires and the printing of music, was increasingly called into question. These hits had become meaningless mechanical music which followed patterns of success preserved over decades, at odds with the everyday experiences to which the media were attempting to link music in an increasingly complex fashion. Above all, however, the possibilities of mass media studio production went beyond the limits of what could be set down in musical notation, which soon put these studios beyond the use of the composers and music publishers. Both traditional songwriters and music publishers became less and less relevant in the process of music production.

The conception of music which was beginning to develop in this context was forced to differ significantly from all earlier ones. For it was faced with continuing changes in the conditions of music production and distribution, due to the new technical media, as well as changes in the way music was received and had its effect, now that most people's contact with music was via record, radio and television. Rock music was the product of the social processes provoked by these changes, social processes which signalled a radical alteration in the social conditions (of existence) of music culture. Commenting on this period, Kurt Blaukopf spoke correctly of a 'mutation of musical behaviour within the social totality'.[13] This mutation became apparent first and most clearly in the way teenagers made use of music, since they were the age group with the most intense involvement with music.

Of course this is not the only explanation for the change in the position of musical culture which took place with the blossoming of the mass communications media. The more direct cause of this change was the change in living and working conditions after 1945 in all the countries of developed capitalism, resulting from the scientific and technical intensification of production processes. Probably the most significant indication of this is a comprehensive shift in value from work to leisure, where those things which could no longer be found in work – a purpose in life, opportunities for personal realisation and personal values – were increasingly sought. The growing automation of industrial production finally destroyed the traditional ties of the working class to its work. The division of work into routine operations, within the framework of capitalist exploitation, offered a declining opportunity to identify with work as the central purpose in life. The changing structure of production, with its tendency to polarisation between machine-run, depersonalised manual work on the one hand and a highly qualified technical specialist class on the other, excluded the possibility of individual promotion just as much as the naked attitude of exploitation itself did, an exploitation which could no longer be circumvented by the traditional craft ethics of work, by pride in individual skills and their realisation in the finished piece of work. Work degenerated completely to a mere money-earning activity, to an interchangeable 'job', which was only encouraged by the trend towards a mobile and flexible workforce in this type of production. In this way, all the ideals of life were transferred to leisure, a transfer that gradually took place in all social classes and which was accompanied by an extensive expansion of the consumer goods sector within capitalist production industry. The slogan 'consumer society' was coined. This term concealed an idolisation of leisure and consumption, which saw in these twin pursuits the only important realm of human fulfilment and believed the loss of purpose at work to be compensated by an increase of purpose in leisure. But even David Riesman, who in the fifties constructed one of the most influential cultural theories of his time in his book *The Lonely Crowd*, later had to admit: 'that the burden put on leisure by the disintegration of work is too huge to be coped with; leisure itself cannot rescue work, but fails with it, and can only be meaningful for most men if work is meaningful'.[14] In spite of this, the process of increasing the value of leisure proved to be a cultural phenomenon with almost unlimited implications whose consequences were not restricted to the change in attitudes to work and the compensation in leisure for deficits in meaning and experience. The evolution of leisure into a field of personal development, experienced as increasingly important, also spawned cultural demands. This not only gave the mass media a new function, but finally led to a new type of involvement with art, which was then reduced to the level of the various forms of mass media entertainment.

Rock'n'roll also broke the conventional functional pattern of popular music forms. Before, popular music had mainly been based on dance and entertainment. Rock had a non-specific accompanying and background function for all possible activities. American teenagers did not merely lay claim to rock as 'their' music, but discovered at the same time that music could be more than a general acoustic background or a mere motoric stimulation to movement while dancing. They conferred upon rock a central significance within the structure of their leisure and projected onto it the problems of their situation. Simon Frith was able to generalise this as follows: 'The truth of youth culture is that the young displace to their free time the problems of work and family and future. It is because they *lack* power that the young account for their lives in terms of play, focus their politics on leisure.'[15]

With rock'n'roll, popular music appears for the first time within a cultural system of reference which allows it to become a *fundamental* experience, conveying meaning and significance in a manner which before this had been reserved for the 'serious' arts. Records and portable radios not only allowed music to become ubiquitous in teenagers' daily lives, they also gave it a function which tore down the barriers between the formerly separate spheres of art and everyday life. Chuck Berry's 'Roll Over Beethoven' is therefore anything but blasphemy. Rock'n'roll had the same cultural relevance for its young fans as Beethoven and Tschaikowsky had for adult music lovers. The fact that this was suspected even at the time is demonstrated by the vehemence with which the educational authorities and public opinion took to the field against this new fashion in music. It was, after all, not just a fashion which was trickling out from the loudspeakers in the background. Rock'n'roll, with all the forms of rock music that followed, represented to its young listeners a significant and essential experience of art. It was not the rebellious sounds themselves that were provocative. That sort of thing had existed in jazz and was simply part of popular music forms. What was so shocking was the fact that this music was now being taken seriously by a rising generation of young people. Quite apart from all the aesthetic debates over art, mass culture and 'highbrow' and 'lowbrow' standards which rock'n'roll had already provoked in the fifties, with this music art was translated into daily life as part of those ordinary experiences which give people meaning and pleasure. Or as Iain Chambers put it:

Existing beyond the narrow range of school syllabuses, 'serious' comment and 'good taste', popular concerns broke 'culture' down into the immediate, the transitory, the experienced, and the lived. It revealed a constructed, contradictory and *contested* history of producing viable daily experiences: ones that make 'sense', that contain pleasures, that are livable.[16]

Rock music stands at the end of this process which led to the intermingling of the experience of art and the experience of everyday life, and represents a new and emerging concept of music.

Fifties American rock'n'roll was the starting-point for this. The changes that were linked to it, in people's involvement with music as well as in the technological basis of its production and distribution, intruded deeply into the internal organisation of music-making, into the internal structure of music itself. Although rock music was fed from the traditions of popular music, from the conventional pop song as well as primarily from the blues and rhythm & blues of the Afro-Americans, and thus hardly represents a completely new beginning in musical development, it is nonetheless based on an innovative concept of music, which can be traced back to the media reality which had arisen. Thus the specifically artistic experiences linked to rock music appear in a form completely different from those suggested by bourgeois artistic norms. Not only is that experience of art which is mediated by technical means distinguished by its own rules, but it always concerns those experiences which are significant and applicable within the structure of many people's everyday lives. It is no coincidence that the meaning and significance hidden in everyday things – as well as sensuousness, pleasure and fantasy – play a central role in rock music. At the same time, the musical realisation of these factors followed certain principles which were increasingly strongly influenced by the technology of mass communication. Technical processes became musical opportunities. Indeed, rock music owes its aesthetic and musical nature in large part to technology.

With records forming the central means of distribution for rock'n'roll and rock music, it became possible to create music in ways other than those allowed by musical notation. 'We didn't write songs, we wrote records',[17] said Jerry Leiber and Mike Stoller, the songwriting and producing team to whom Elvis Presley in particular owed many of his early hits. The distinction between writing songs and sketching the charts for the track sessions for a record is indeed an important one. Only an abstract framework of music can be reproduced in musical notation. Accordingly, conventional pop songs, the Tin Pan Alley hits, existed primarily within such musical parameters as melody, harmony and formal structure, which could best be worked out in musical notation. In contrast, the human voice with its timbre and register, the niceties of intonation and phrasing, the sound characteristics of the instruments and the physical presence of metre and rhythm could now be controlled by technical means and could therefore be used increasingly consciously as a separate plane of expression. It was not only the aesthetic appeal of these factors that was discovered; they were also linked to more and more complex meanings. The sound of a guitar, which almost seemed to 'speak' when used in conjunction with special-effects equipment – as by Jimi Hendrix, for example – was now able to express much more than the melodic pattern which it was actually playing. What was interesting about the voice of a rock singer was not so much its ability to handle different melodic forms, but rather its sound, the colouring of its particular accent and its physical expressiveness. Now that it was possible to manipulate the sound properties of both instruments and voice and reproduce them precisely, the focus of musical performance gradually shifted from the written parameters, pitch, dynamics and formal development, from the melodic and harmonic aspects, to the reproducible details of the expression of sound. Thus, sound became the central aesthetic category of rock music.

Now that sound had become the key factor, technical equipment and processes acquired a more decisive role. They were increasingly used as musical material. Even their disadvantages – feedback, for instance – were transformed into an integral part of the performance. The English group Pink Floyd was one of the first rock groups to manage almost entirely without the traditional complement of instruments. The extent to which the process of creating music became an engineering and technical task is vividly evoked in this description of the building up of the sound of a single guitar by Chris Tsangarides, the British hard rock producer who has worked with, among others, Thin Lizzy and Gary Moore:

For instance, if we're doing a hard rock act and we're going to go for a basic rhythm guitar sound, I like to set up loads of amplifiers. All makes, all sizes, all over the place and then spend a long time getting them all linked up together, getting rid of all earth hums and what have you. Then I like to put the amps in various positions in the studio and screen them off from each other. Then I'll use effects on each one – maybe a chorus on one, a distortion on another, a delay on something else. Then I get a picture from all that lot once it's set up, then listen to it with the microphones in close and distant positions. As a rule I put all the close mics on one side of the stereo and all the distant mics on the other side, then I mess around with those microphone levels just to find the sound that I wanted. If I use eight amplifiers in the studio, I might only put close mics on two. But I wouldn't turn off the others because I'd let the spill from those go down the ambient microphones.[18]

In this way each producer has developed his own methods, often carefully concealed from the competition, which allow him to become a creator of equal standing, if not the dominant pole, in the artistic production process. His function is not merely restricted to the sound concept of the instruments. That is left mostly to the studio engineers and technicians, while the producer decides the basic questions of the correct technical realisation of a song for record production, questions which naturally have quite a bearing on the musical context. The song, recorded first as a number of separate tracks, is only a semi-finished musical product to which further layers of sound can be added, tracks deleted or rerecorded. But, most importantly, it is possible to work on the sound of each separate recorded track afterwards and finally to fit it into its proper place in the track that is being created in the mixing process, whether as a part filling in a section of the sound, as an accompanying part, or even as the central part which supports the song musically. The producer, together with the sound engineers and technicians he has available, is no less creatively involved in this process of musical formulation than the musicians. As Glyn Johns, who produced the hit album *Desperado*[19] for the Eagles, said: 'So, when everyone's gone home you then take what you recorded and completely change it.'[20] Trevor Horn, who in 1983 adapted a highly technical concept of sound to the English group Frankie Goes to Hollywood so precisely that 'Relax'[21] became one of the biggest successes in the history of the British music business, went even further: 'All of this equipment means you can basically do anything with sound and you don't even need musicians. But without musicians, you'd lose the performance, you'd lose the feeling. You'd lose the only thing that has any magic to it.'[22] Just what could be achieved in the studio was demonstrated by Trevor Horn more than by any other producer. From the basic recorded material he produced a total of seventeen different versions of 'Relax', which in some cases differed quite substantially, and then released these one after the other. In this way the history of rock music has also been written by the producers. And even sound engineers like Steve Lipson from Trevor Horn's studio, or Alan Parsons, who with producer Chris Thomas was among those responsible for Pink Floyd's *The Dark Side of the Moon*,[23] long ago stepped out of their anonymous supporting roles.

In other words, the process of musical performance has become so complex through its links with technology that it can no longer be mastered simply by a musician, let alone be set down in musical notation by a composer as it used to be. Rock music is created on foundations which, as the result of the technology of studio production, have a necessarily collective character. For a live performance studio conditions are simply made as portable as possible, served by the group's own technical crew. In this context music as the individual expression of an outstanding artistic personality is *de facto* impossible. Rock is a collective means of expression, to which the individual musician can only contribute in a collective activity with others, with technicians, producers and, of course, with other musicians. This collective nature is not at all altered by the fact that in the context of commercial exploitation there is an additional personalisation, pushing forward a 'frontman', behind whom the collective relationships seem to disappear. The shift from a hierarchical model of music – with the composer at the top and all the other participants merely following the instructions he has set down in the score – to a collectively organised form is the crucial conceptual change which began with rock'n'roll. Music became

the medium of expression for collective experiences, emotions
and ideas. It became involved in relationships of a collective
nature, both in the production process and within the structure of
teenagers' leisure. The form of music created within the mass
media finally refuted the idea that music laid bare the inner
thoughts of its creator, that its reception happened as a private,
almost intimate, dialogue, with the message carried by the sound,
which aroused purely personal feelings rooted in the individual
biography of the listeners. Michael Naumann and Boris Penth
were correct in their observation concerning the reception of
rock: 'Although devotion to the music often takes place in an
individual manner, the process of its consumption is shot
through with group experiences; the role of fan gives rise to a
spiritual context.'[24] Here the whole reference system within
which music exists, in which it maintains meanings and embodies values, has changed. Music is not only distributed
by the mass media, it has itself now become a form of mass
communication.

In musical terms rock's emergence as a form of mass communication was signalled by the radical re-orientation of the
development of pop music towards the traditions of Afro-
American music in the USA. Even Chuck Berry's 'Roll Over
Beethoven' was really nothing more than Afro-American rhythm
& blues. Elements of form and style from Afro-American music
had served to enliven the music industry since at least the end
of the nineteenth century, with cakewalk and ragtime and then
with the jazz dance fashion. These elements were adopted by
white musicians, denuded of their original significance and
adapted to the dominant European tastes in music. Even in jazz,
although musicians with Afro-American origins played an
important role, until the Second World War it was ultimately
European musical habits which dominated – in the New York
Dixieland version of early New Orleans jazz, in the Chicago style
and above all in swing. Rock'n'roll appeared to lie in the same
line of development but in fact brought with it a significant
change. Elvis Presley or Bill Haley were no longer merely taking
set pieces from blues and rhythm & blues and imposing them as
superficial effects on quite different musical categories. Their
popularity was founded precisely on the fact that they were
copying Afro-American music with all its characteristic features,

including the performance style of black musicians, as closely as possible. What was happening was a complete reversal of the earlier situation. Whereas before, white musicians had adapted elements of the Afro-American musical tradition to their own aesthetic ideas, now they were trying to suit their performance to the aesthetics of Afro-American music, until ultimately black singers and musicians like Chuck Berry, for instance, were themselves able to appear as millionaire pop stars. This was not merely chance, nor could it simply be attributed to the gradually changing position of the Afro-American minority within American society after 1945, which found expression in comprehensive politicisation and growing resistance within the framework of the developing civil rights movement. It was more that, as a result of the centuries-long social isolation of black people, even in the environment of the modern city and the ghetto, blues and rhythm & blues had largely retained the collective character of music which is part of all authentic folk music. Chris Cutler has correctly traced the origins of this unusual quality back to the particular social situation of black people in the USA, linked as it was to the separation of the races: 'They had lived, in a sense, through an accelerated transition to Capitalism without having been part of the process − as "outsiders". Thus it was that they were uniquely able to experience and express the alienation at the heart of Capitalist society without having been ideologically incorporated into it. And still speaking with the voice of a Community.'[25]

Remote from 'whites only' society, banished to the black districts of the city, Afro-American music preserved all those features that link music to a collective and communal experience, to the shared experience of suppression. Thus the subjectivity of the musician, his emotions and his ideas, were simply the medium through which the collective fate of all black Americans was given expression. In this music the performance drew the listener in, demanding his active participation and direct involvement. The musical means which were used to achieve this proved to be so well-suited to the new mass media production conditions that the status of Afro-American music in commercial music production changed almost at a stroke. Up to this point it had merely been copied as a fashionable effect without any real understanding of its musical features, except by the purists among white jazz musicians who hardly reached mass audiences. Now, as a sign of a novel and more contemporary aesthetic of pop music, both white musicians and producers tried to adopt these features in as pure a form as possible. Alongside the social and cultural factors which paved the way for the attraction of Afro-American music, particularly to teenagers from the broad American middle classes (we will come back to these factors in due course), it was the music's collective nature that gave it such a high status, and allowed it to become the musical point of origin for everything that followed in rock'n'roll and rock music. For right from the start rock'n'roll was nothing more than black music performed by white musicians. And even the great successes of rock often turn out on closer inspection to be white cover versions of Afro-American blues and rhythm & blues songs, if indeed after the mid-fifties they were not brought directly into rock'n'roll by black singers such as Chuck Berry, Fats Domino, Little Richard or Bo Diddeley, when at least the outward semblance of racial barriers finally fell in the music business. Even the song that gave Elvis Presley his commercial breakthrough in 1956, 'Hound Dog',[26] had already been released three years earlier by the blues singer Willie Mae Thornton.[27] Bill Haley owed his popularity to a song by the black musician Joe Turner, 'Shake, Rattle and Roll'.[28] Such instances could be listed more or less indefinitely. And even after this it has always been cover versions of Afro-American blues and rhythm & blues songs which have appeared like a leitmotif throughout the history of rock music. Even if the forms and playing styles of Afro-American music have lost much of their expressiveness in their often very superficial imitation by white musicians, they provided the decisive impulse for the changes in musical performance necessitated by the constraints of technical production.

The rhythmic complexity of Afro-American music, probably its most prominent feature running as it does through all its forms and styles, played the decisive role in this change. Rhythm is the central musical component which acts as the disciplining factor and organises the course of the music and the playing of the musicians. What appears to be mere repetition of unchanging formulas and patterns is in fact the detail of a total rhythmic texture put together from individual musical elements. Built up on the relationship between short set phrases, patterns, which are there not merely for their own sakes but make musical sense in their rhythmic relationship to one another, the collectivity of this process is one of the most important aesthetic foundations of Afro-American music. The rhythm does not consist of the chronological course of a linear, self-contained sequence of notes, but is translated into the spatial dimension, giving each musician an equal opportunity to play in relation to the basic metrical pulse, the beat (whether felt or actually played) so that ultimately the rhythmic structure is the result of the superimposition of all the levels of playing. Thus, through these more or less spontaneous reactions, a collective musical event is created in which the listeners are also included. Their reactions are taken up by the musicians, translated into their playing and included in the music. The whole is a result of the action of musicians and audience on each other, as well as amongst themselves, synchronised by the beat, which unfolds into a rhythm that is converted into movement and back again. Music simply forms a framework for this process, in which there is no question of a self-contained and fixed musical result separable from the actual playing. Equally, in this type of music 'expression' is not a function of a specific aesthetic code or of conventional principles of construction, according to which content is transposed into musical structures and translated back again by the listener, assuming he has understood it. Expression operates by means of the sensory directness of rhythm, sound, gestures and above all the human voice. The ability of the human voice both to portray emotional states directly by means of a husky, strained sound, from a toneless guttural grunting to an ecstatic cry, and also to communicate these forcibly to the listener by the naturally appealing character of this physiological process, stands at the centre of the aesthetics of Afro-American music. This use of the voice has its counterpart in the instrumental techniques which largely rest on the imitation of the effects of the human larynx, reproducing emotional expressions with grinding 'dirty tones'. For this reason it would be more accurate to speak about 'presentation' than 'expression'. The essential nature of Afro-American music is to be found in the collective presentation of emotions, postures and gestures.

Once technology made it possible to record music in its 'sound' form (rather than as notes on a stave) and to reproduce it at will, this collective principle of performance produced the necessary conditions for it to undergo an almost organic growth on the basis of the existing technology of music production in the studios of the mass media. The collective presentation of musical content in rhythmically structured sound, performance based on the emotional effects of the sound structures (moreover, without being bound to musical notation), an inner musical structure open to spontaneity and constant changes in detail without calling the whole into question – these characteristics corresponded ideally to the montage-like method of production in the recording studios. Of course, rock'n'roll and rock music were not a straight-line development of Afro-American music. In a quite different context, created by teenagers' leisure needs and the social, economic and cultural laws of the mass media, only those musical possibilities of this style which suited the prevailing technical possibilities of studio music production were developed further. The original rhythmic complexity of Afro-American music was vastly simplified in rock'n'roll. A hammered, rigid basic rhythm replaced a flexible swinging one. Subtlety of sound gave way to a noisy and aggressively insistent playing. The emphasis (in Afro-American music) was on the sensory presence of rhythm and sound, often loud enough to suggest physical contact. In rock music it was above all the tonal aspects of this that were modified. What was left, however, was the arrangement of the parts over a metric-rhythmic basic pattern, constructed as the sum of all the parts played and held together by the drums. The function of sound as a direct sensory and physical means of representation was also retained, and emotional fulfilment, 'feeling', was the key to this. Rock music also represented its content in those musical dimensions that are realised collectively – rhythm and sound. But in rock music this corresponded to a musical concept based on a novel understanding of music oriented towards the technology of mass communication.

In this respect rock music stands at the end of a historical process, in the course of which the functions of music were split up, step by step, by a division of labour, so that music obtained a quasi-collective character. Even at the turn of the century the composer often delivered only the rough draft of a pop song, leaving the detail of its performance to the routines of the arrangers, who cut it to suit different casts, uses and publications.

At the beginning of the twenties the personal relationship between the composer and the lyricist also collapsed, with lyrics for the prototype songs being provided later by writers specialising in this work. The increasingly reckless production policies of the great American music publishers, such as the film company Metro-Goldwyn-Mayer's Robbins Music Corporation, the Warner Brothers Company's publishing group Harms, Witmark & Remick or the publishing houses of Shapiro-Bernstein and Buddy Morris, oriented as they were towards mass sales, compelled them to rationalise as much as possible by promoting specialisation on the basis of a division of labour. At the end of this process in the early fifties, 'most pop songs were written in music publishers' offices in New York (hit factories) by a task force of writers, who were generally treated like assembly line workers'.[29]

However, even these methods still did not alter the conventional song concept. In spite of all the changes within the composition process the songs were still taken as personal expressions of their creator, even though the term 'composer' was nothing more than a legal title which secured the intellectual property rights in the musical idea. The singer had to offer his personality as a substitute for this personal feeling and add, in terms of subjective facial expressions, enough to maintain the fiction that the songs were communicating a personal dialogue with the listener. The gesture 'especially for you' thus became a calculated ideology of the trade. And when the efforts of the performers finally only represented the result of a collective work process in the recording studios, this song concept became completely hollow.

The functions of musical performance, divorced from one another on the basis of a song concept that had embraced industrial production methods in music, were brought together again by rock music, thus opening up new musical dimensions. In this context Simon Frith has pointed out the status of rock's Afro-American roots in a discussion of the vocal techniques of rock singers: 'Black singers used these vocal techniques to develop a song form that combined individual and collective expression. In traditional pop songs, by contrast, crooners appeared to direct their messages to individual listeners only – the white pop ideal was to make mass communication feel like a private conversation

rather than a public event.'[30] The contradiction between the
aesthetic foundations of musical performance, at the level to
which it was reduced in the ideal expression of the traditional pop
song, and the real conditions of production and distribution, as
they existed in connection with the media, was resolved by rock
music. Rock not only affected the processes of musical
performance and its aesthetic foundations, but also the image of
the musician himself. It was rock that first opened the studios
to the broad wave of amateurs. The specialised professionalism
of the old style, the routine of composers and arrangers and
musicians trained to read music no longer fitted into the new
conditions, which amateurs learnt to adjust to much more
quickly and simply. A new category of musician sprang up. As
Chris Cutler put it:

Recording has done more though than just reunify existing categories,
it has brought into being a new, previously unthinkable category,
consisting of those who come to the new medium not as Musicians, nor
as Composers, but as something new; who will use the new medium
in a new way, who are not part of the old institutions and do not share
the outlook of those institutions; who are, in fact, *created by the new
medium*.[31]

The rock musician represents a type of musician for whom
creative involvement with technology, with amplifiers, microphones, special-effects machines and computer-controlled
synthesisers has become increasingly characteristic. Rock
musicians often do not learn to play their instruments in the
traditional way, but learn to control them, exhaust their tonal
possibilities and to work creatively with them, often using
unconventional methods. For such musicians the studio is no
longer the pinnacle of a successful musical career, but the starting
point.

These musicians were the first to get involved, with a naive
lack of concern, in the synthetic, artificial and vulgar. They
entered the bizarre and gleaming world of post-1945 mass culture
without trying to hide their involvement with it and without the
embarrassed quasi-artistic behaviour of the traditional pop ideal.
Because of the criticism of unrestrained commerce which this
world of colour magazines, advertising, film, television, detective
serials, records, Coca-Cola and hot dogs brought with it, it has
often been overlooked that at the same time an aesthetic code

for the mass experience of everyday events was born. This code suited the technical production of art and the use of art oriented towards transience, as mediated via channels of the mass media, far better than the pseudo-individual expression of 'soul' and 'feeling' of the conventional pop song did. Particularly by its intellectual champions, rock music has always been seen as an artistic contrast to commercial mass culture, a viewpoint which has always exposed it to the same misunderstanding. With the intention of taking rock seriously as a cultural phenomenon in its actual sphere of influence and, by doing this, to prevent the conclusion being drawn – on the basis of both the inescapable commodity character of rock and the commercial spectacle that it too represents – that it was worthless in artistic terms, an aesthetic code was constructed around this music, which rock songs actually only rarely corresponded to. Jon Landau, one of the most influential American rock critics and also a famous rock producer, made the point that: 'To me the criteria of art in rock is the capacity of the musician to create a personal, almost private, universe and to express it fully.'[32]

Behind Landau's comment lie the academic dogmas of the ideology of the 'work of art'. According to these too 'authentic rock' should be distinguished from mere commerce, and it is contrasted with the 'synthetic' evidence of mass culture, but not with the real rock experience. John Lennon, whose songs are often used as proof of this thesis, in his numerous interviews used to reject vehemently the 'deeper meaning' which was always being read into his songs:

To express myself ... I could write 'Spaniard in the Works' or 'In His Own Write', the personal stories which were expressive of my personal emotions. I'd have a separate songwriting John Lennon who wrote songs for the sort of meat market, and I didn't consider them – the lyrics or anything – to have any depth at all. They were just a joke.[33]

Lennon's comments on those people who pounced on his songs with the ambitious concepts of an artistic aesthetic are even clearer:

There's a bloke in England, William Mann, who writes for *The Times* and who wrote the first intellectual article about the Beatles, and after this people began to talk about us in intellectual terms ... He uses a whole lot of musical terminology and he's a twit. But he made us acceptable to the intellectuals ... But he is still writing the same rubbish. But he also did us a whole lot of good, because all the intellectuals and middle-class people were suddenly saying 'Ooh'.[34]

Lennon's brusque tone should not be allowed to hide the fact that he is absolutely correct here. Rock songs are not art songs, whose hidden meaning should be sought in their form and structure. It was only those people who believed they had to defend these songs against their real character as a popular art form who ever viewed them in this way.

The reality is that rock music stands right in the middle of the commercial whirlpool of mass culture, of the undifferentiated circulation of cultural assets, messages, images and sounds. It is a synthesis of the fragments which were left over from this whirlpool; but a synthesis that was able to follow its own laws of aesthetics in the context of media communications, precisely because it only met fragments of this and that, rather than being weighed down with the millstone of tradition. Even rock'n'roll was in fact nothing but a commercial conglomeration of playing styles and traditions torn from their original contexts – from the Afro-American blues and rhythm & blues tradition as well as from different regional dance music styles of country music. Later, in rock, Indian raga met northern English, Scottish and Irish folk music traditions; reggae, dub, rap and New York scratch, the street music of American city ghettos, met the tonal experiments of the European avant-garde. But the commercial mixing of all this was at the same time a process of distillation, which liberated those elements which suited an experience of art linked to the media, an aesthetic code of everyday life. To the prevailing bourgeois concept of art, anti-technical and shamefully overlooking its own economic basis, this mixture of elements in rock was nothing more than a perfect example of commercial barbarism, a destruction of all moral and artistic values by the naked calculation of market interests. As a result the constructive side of this process, spawning an everyday aesthetic, has always been overlooked. And in any case, rock music was not only compromised by being fitted into market strategies and by having its reception made part of a commercial calculation. It might indeed have submitted to the ruling interest of capital, whose goal was not only to maximise profits but also to maintain its own system; but the social and cultural mass processes provoked by this had for a long time not been completely under the control of the economic mechanisms belonging to capital interests. In his study of the cultural activities of British rockers and hippies Paul Willis drew attention to the fact that interaction with objects in the world of commerce is not fully determined by their economic form:

Though the whole commodity form provides powerful implications for the manner of its consumption, it by no means enforces them. Commodities can be taken out of context, claimed in a particular way, developed and repossessed to express something deeply and thereby to change somewhat the very feelings which are their product. And all this can happen under the very nose of the dominant class – and with their products.[35]

To see young rock fans merely as passive puppets dancing on the economic and ideological apron strings of the capitalist music industry is a gross oversimplification of the problem. This thesis refuses to recognise the cultural potency of class conflict and the struggle over meaning and value in relation to the popular arts which results from the social contradictions of capitalism. Rock fans are not an undifferentiated mass of manipulated consumers. Their relationships with this music, with the values that it embodies and with the meanings which circulate in it follow socially very diverse everyday experiences which even the music industry must go along with up to a point, making a similar distinction between social groups, if it wants to market its products successfully. The dividing line is not drawn between 'commercial' rock production and the so-called 'authentic' rock song. It is more that rock music stands in the middle of a cultural and ideological field of conflict which cannot be understood by making a simplistic comparison between what is more or less 'commercial'.

The origin of such a comparison is a fundamental lack of understanding of the aesthetic strategies which support an experience of art embedded in everyday life. Rock is not received through the critical apparatus of contemplation, of consideration by visual and aural means; its reception is an active process, connected in a practical way with everyday life. Rock songs are not objects of contemplation, to be assessed according to how much hidden meaning they reveal in their innermost structures. Their banality and superficiality, their shrill, colourful and trivial nature, are not flaws, the missing deeper meaning is not artistic weakness and the obvious nonsense not without significance. Popular art forms are never pure, never to be taken as self-contained aesthetic creations in whose construction a deep-lying meaning is enclosed. Seen in this light they are dreadfully banal and rock's noisy, shrill and stamping sound structures, driven by computerised rhythms, indeed appear to be the deafening flattening of each even slightly different experience of reality. All the attempts to find a deep significance in the structure of rock songs do not change this. These attempts were in any case only felt to be necessary by rock's intellectual interpreters or at least they remained a matter of the verbal message of the song. Rock songs are *cultural* texts, which circulate in the profane language of gestures, images, fashionable ideas and sounds, linked to the unprepossessing elements of everyday life, to the 'events without prestige' as the French sociologist Henri Lefebvre called them.[36] Transported by the media 'in the geography of a *particular* and individual reality',[37] here in everyday life these elements are redimensioned, expanded by dimensions which are readable neither in the lyrics nor in the music but which find a kind of framework in them. What counts in the end is not the musical and verbal 'message'. The songs form a moveable coordinate system for everyday cultural activities and leisure, that is open to different opportunities for use, for imparting meaning, for fun, for sensuousness and for pleasure. This does not exclude the fact that the lyrics or musical structure of the song could be transformed by an understanding of art which might make them an explicit 'message'. The lyrics of Bob Dylan, for instance, undoubtedly belong in this category. But even in such cases the songs are placed in a context of use developed by teenagers themselves, even then they are fragmented and made relevant, have their fixed structures of meaning broken up again for other, new, ones and for the individual possibilities of involvement with them. Thus, behind the verbal and musical structure of the songs lies a very complex and continually active cultural process which has many often fleeting and transient links with reality. The attempt to express these links as content poured into the musical form, according to the simple scheme of the aesthetics of art, must therefore fail. If this view is taken of their content, rock songs often appear to be of a quite grotesque banality, since their true links with reality are not reflected in this view. Iain Chambers wrote quite correctly: 'To attempt to explain fully such references would be to pull them back under the contemplative stare, to adopt the authority of the patronising academic mind that seeks to explain an experience that is rarely his or hers.'[38]

These are new experiences of art, linked to the technology of mass communication and mediated in the daily lives of their recipients. These experiences have resulted in a concept of music for which the conceptual stance of the aesthetics of art is unsuitable. They have robbed the academic art expert of his authority, because in this social model of art, the popular art form, everyone is an expert. This is the deeper truth of Chuck Berry's fifties rock'n'roll song –

ROLL OVER BEETHOVEN!

2

'Rock Around the Clock': emergence

It was the Eisenhower era, from 1953 to 1960, which shaped the everyday experiences to which rock'n'roll was linked; the era of the cold war, a period which saw the conservative restoration of American capitalism and its seemingly limitless economic growth. The Second World War had dragged the USA out of the depression of the thirties. The victory over fascist Germany and its Axis partners Italy and Japan had been an overwhelming one. It had been a just victory, so that these days we are no longer surprised at the glorification of this victory afterwards. The returning war veterans had a right to be feted as national heroes. They now wanted nothing more than a little peace and to catch up on what they had missed: earning money, family life, the dream of prosperity. Against this background their relationship with the ideas of liberalism and bourgeois democracy, for which they had fought in the war, was bound to become increasingly uncritical. The result was an anachronistic nationalism which became the dominant ideology. According to David Pichaske: 'What the golden fifties were really about was the unnatural prolongation of World War II heroism and mindset, both of them narrow and atavistically barbarian during the war years, both of them narrow and anachronistically barbarian in the fifties.'[1]

This environment was also the breeding-ground for the anti-communist excesses of McCarthyism. In March 1950, in a speech to the American Congress lasting more than five hours, Senator Joseph R. McCarthy had discussed a supposed 'communist infiltration' of the United States. Following this the domestic political climate succumbed to wild hysteria. Julius and Ethel Rosenberg were presented to the now hysterical public as Soviet nuclear spies and, in an unprecedented act of judicial murder, were sent to the electric chair by an American court. The Korean war became the bloodbath of American democracy. Hearings before the Congress committee set up to investigate 'un-American' activities (the House Un-American Activities Committee – HUAC) reached their high point. On the basis of the Loyalty Order more than 2.5 million government employees were subjected to screening. The McCarran Act, which stipulated the registration of communists and communist organisations, legalised comprehensive spying activities by the FBI. The search was not only on for putative signs of 'communist conspiracy'; the snooping also covered drinking and sexual 'aberrations'. In the writer Bernard Malamud's gloomy opinion of this period: 'The country was frightened silly of Alger Hiss and Whittaker Chambers, Communist spies and Congressional committees, flying saucers and fellow travelers, their friends and associates, and those who asked them for a match or the time of day. Intellectuals, scientists, teachers were investigated by numerous committees and if found to be good Americans were asked to sign loyalty oaths.'[2] This explains the cultural emptiness, the social rigidity, the conservatism in post-war America. Conformity became the essential feature of social behaviour.

Because of this, it was teenagers more than any other age group who were confronted at home and at school with a monstrous propaganda campaign for 'American values', for the American way of life. The pressure to conform and to achieve within the American education system grew in proportion to the excesses of McCarthyism and became an essential social experience for this post-war generation. This left its most lasting mark on the high school, the type of school which smoothed the path to social advancement and was a preparation for a college or university education. With slowly rising prosperity in fifties America (at least for the white majority) – the average family income rose by 15 per cent and the average wage by as much as 20 per cent[3] – this became the classic educational course for lower-middle-class teenagers:

The importance of a college education was inculcated in the mind of every young middle-class American from an early age, partly because Americans have the childish belief that every problem can be solved if only the potential solver has the right credentials and partly because

a college education for all one's children was like a barbecue or a
new Chrysler, just another suburban status symbol.[4]

Thus an increasing number of young Americans worked towards
high school entry. Here the fourteen to seventeen year olds
were subjected to conventions which nurtured a particular
sort of social organism and formed the social background for the
rock'n'roll experience.

At that time the American high school still thought of itself
as an educational institution in the traditional manner. As well,
it also wished to be a model of social life, motivating its students
with the concept of dynamic, flexible and high quality achievement and, as far as outward appearance went, moulding neatly-
dressed, middle-ranking employees who would later be a true
credit to their firms. These educational institutions more or less
formed the centre of local cultural life, particularly in the
countless small towns, with their obligatory sporting events,
their diverse cultural activities and the high school balls, prepared
as the culmination of the year's activities. The conventions
which regulated daily life in the classroom indulged the most
conservative ideas of middle-class respectability. The following
excerpt from one of the many handbooks which instilled the
fundamental rules of suitable behaviour in the students, the *High
School Student Handbook* of Springfield High School in Springfield, Pennsylvania, may serve as an illustration:

One thing you may always count on in Springfield is the fine appearance
and good conduct of your classmates. Any time we make a field trip, have
visitors in our assembly programs, or go before the public in any fashion,
the boys wear coats and ties and the girls 'dress-up' a little more than
usual. As a representative of Springfield High School, you must at all
times keep your best foot forward both in and out of school.[5]

With its rules of dress, its stylised manners, its team spirit, with
all the *petit bourgeois* trappings of social programmes, school
clubs and its own newspaper, this was a world all of its own. The
American sociologist Arthur Coleman described the high school
student of this period as: ' "cut off" from the rest of society,
forced inwards towards his own age group. With his fellows, he
comes to constitute a small society, one that has its most
important interactions within itself, and maintains only a few
threads of connections with the outside adult society.'[6]

This was in precise accordance with the educational concept of the high school. The artificiality of this school world was intended to mould those personal characteristics which would be a feature of the future government or senior lower-ranking employee, without needing to restrict the students' hallowed 'individual freedom' in any way to make them fit this standard office worker template. Each individual was programmed to abide by these rules in high school; thereafter he only had to function according to these and was able to consider this as the expression of his 'individual freedom'.

The reason why this well-organised educational perfectionism encountered growing resistance at the beginning of the fifties, suffering from a lack of discipline, until ultimately even vulgar, noisy rock'n'roll arrived in its hallowed halls, lay to a not inconsiderable extent in its own nature. The oppressive, claustrophobic atmosphere of conservatism which held sway in the high schools may have suited the political climate of the time, but had for a long time no longer corresponded to the real experiences of the teenagers who were threatened with suffocation in it. The traditional values of a high school education being promoted could simply no longer withstand the social reality. These values were upheld only by hypocrisy. The paradise promised as a reward for successfully completed school examinations and for achieving the best marks proved to be an insipid prosperity which was no longer an adequate goal, because it had become a prosperity founded on credit, a mere facade, unreal through and through. American capitalism, which was radically modernising its methods of production, no longer offered acceptable professional prospects even for those who had completed a higher education. Do-it-yourself capitalism was over and done with. What was required was a host of technical employees who could be deployed at will either to sit out the day in the office or to supervise the automatic production lines; unless, of course, there was the possibility of qualifying for the creative elite of top-ranking scientists in the technological field. This latter was in any case only a prospect for the exceptionally gifted with suitably wealthy parents, for places to study for these qualifications cost astronomical sums because of the necessary expenditure on technical equipment. The lack of a common purpose in life therefore became the basic experience of this generation.

In the material gathered by American sociologists studying this phenomenon the point is emphasised often enough. One teenager interviewed said that she did not want to be like everyone else. She felt that all the moulds were just hanging there waiting for her to be poured into them – marry an engineer, live in a model house in a decent well-to-do middle-class suburb, produce 2.3 children, pay your taxes, sleep with your legally espoused husband twice a week, wind yourself up every morning with the little key in the small of your back like a Japanese toy, go through life without thinking, feeling or doing anything on your own initiative, let yourself be carried along by the current and take things as they come. No thank you very much, she felt, not me, not ever.[7]

If these feelings called into question the educational goals followed in high school, then the commercial world of mass culture – flickering on the television screens, streaming out of the transistor radio and juke box loudspeakers, pictured on the shiny pages of magazines and on cinema screens – did its best to put an end to the conservative educational fervour in these institutions. A flood of opportunities to consume surrounded teenagers and offered them, as a stimulation to further consumption, the model of a boundless hedonism, of pleasure as the purpose and content of life. The whole system of advertising, with its cunningly calculated sales psychology, was in the final analysis geared to nothing more than the promotion of consumption for its own sake. Justifying consumption required a suitably strong motive in the paying customer: the pleasure of consuming. The continually varied theme of advertising came down to the simple statement that pleasure was the essential purpose in life. Unlike any previous generation, teenagers were now exposed to the enticing picture world of advertising through radio and television programmes and films produced specifically for them and through the up and coming 'youth' magazines. This advertising was aimed at a leisure market which served their needs, composed of fashion accessories, clothes and, of course, music. And again unlike previous generations, it was particularly those teenagers collected together in high school on the basis of their social origins who had the opportunity to indulge in the promoted pleasure of consumption, especially since they themselves were not yet in the position of having to pay for it.

Thus pleasure became a conscious and essential content of their leisure activities and achieved a central value in their behaviour. The outward signs of this were the car, the party, the petticoat and the pony-tail.

It is not surprising that this emphasis on pleasure conflicted with the conservative educational demands of the high school as well as with parental views on upbringing. Behind this conflict lay a deepening contradiction between the social conditioning of the workforce – undertaken in school and oriented towards asceticism and a renunciation of consumption, which was supposed to ensure the highest possible achievement at work for the lowest possible wage – and, opposed to this, the economic formation of a suitable model consumer for the expanding consumer goods industry, a consumer who was required to have precisely the opposite characteristics. The renunciation of consumption which was indirectly required of the former – the industrious employee, loyal to his firm and abstaining from all extravagance – proved in the latter to be the greatest obstacle to the economic functioning of the capitalist society. Outside the production environment what was required was a consumer who would buy on impulse and who would be ready to go along with every extravagance in the range of goods available. During the post-war development of the USA this conflict intensified through on the one hand the reactionary conservatism of McCarthyism with its appeal to the preserved pattern of American capitalism (continued in the policies of Eisenhower) and on the other hand increasing economic prosperity, which gave rise to the term 'consumer society'.

High school teenagers experienced this conflict as a clash between the completely opposed value systems of school and leisure, with the whole might of the social forces involved behind it. As a result parental and school authority unavoidably lost credibility; the values which they were promoting no longer seemed to correspond to 'real life' outside school. But teenagers' dependence on parents and school grew proportionately. Was it not parental prosperity which made possible the various pleasures of leisure, such as cars, dancing, parties and the continual acquisition of fashionable new clothes? Was it not the high school diploma which offered the prospect of earning a large enough salary to afford a similar lifestyle in the future as well? The consciousness of this dependence strengthened the alternative function of leisure even more and made it a refuge, which at least for a short time allowed teenagers to fulfil their own youth. Thus, for these teenagers leisure became an alternative world to that of school and the parental home; their daily lives swung between these poles. This contradictory existence also formed the background experience for rock'n'roll, formed a basic pattern which returned time and again in its lyrics. Chuck Berry's 'School Day',[8] for example, expressed this in a very characteristic manner.

The contrast between school and leisure expressed in 'School Day' defined a genuine experience quite commonly observable in the self-awareness of adolescents, but an experience which achieved an additional dimension in the American high schools of the fifties. It was this experience which began to reflect the gaping inner contradictions of a capitalist lifestyle. The central significance which rock'n'roll had for high school students was linked to the fact that in rock'n'roll they could establish and enjoy the meaning and values of their concept of leisure. Their relationship with music exerted a decisive influence on rock'n'roll. Their everyday problems determined its content. Ultimately, through the media, their behaviour became the model for the leisure behaviour of teenagers from the other social classes.

Music has always been linked most directly to the experience of growing up. This was already true when, at the beginning of the century, the first dance fashions flooded American cities. Jazz, in particular, had an enormous appeal as dance music for the younger generation of that period. But in the case of jazz, what young people experienced above all was the delight of already being adult, of equal and independent participation in adult pleasures, produced by and for adults. In contrast, rock'n'roll was a direct product of the fusion of the self-awareness of teenagers and popular music as it developed in the wake of the post-war discovery of their purchasing power in the record market. Until then popular music had been taken more or less for granted. It was part of the regular high school festivities and simply provided an opportunity for dancing and the social framework for meeting a partner. Rock'n'roll made popular music a medium which was consciously and actively shaped by teenagers to be the embodiment of the structure of significance which they had developed for their leisure. Dancing and music were no longer only popular and welcome distractions. They acquired a quite characteristic significance, fixing the central cultural values of teenagers' leisure, adopting these values, absorbing them and passing them on. In the context of their leisure activities popular music experienced a social change in meaning. Together with the record player, autographed postcards and posters, popular music marched into the teenager's bedroom (recently proudly refurbished from its nursery status) where it was taken unbelievably seriously, changing from a casual amusement to an essential element of leisure. Instead of just accepting passively what their parents considered to be 'good music', which had provided the background for dancing lessons when they were learning the rules of 'good behaviour', teenagers now actively chose 'their' music, looking for the sort of music which could incorporate the values and significance of their leisure and develop them creatively. Of course, what teenagers considered to be 'their' music was already in existence and hardly changed: Afro-American rhythm & blues, a post-war development of the city blues idiom and country music from the rural south. The only thing that was new about it was its description – rock'n'roll. Greil Marcus is quite right to point out that: 'Most of the first rock'n'roll styles were variations on black forms that had taken shape before the white audience moved in.'[9]

It took the music industry a long time to come to terms with the fact that this new market of teenage record buyers, which it had recently discovered with such high hopes, could not be supplied according to the existing rules of commercial logic. This caused a tremor in the foundations of the music business which ultimately threatened to make its carefully calculated sales categories – popular music for their national market, country music for the regional market and rhythm & blues for the Afro-American market – completely absurd. But before this could happen and make the music business – always very risky – completely uncontrollable, the strategists of the music industry carried out a new segmentation of their market. Rock'n'roll was now the name given to that sales category in which the products on offer, and any calculations concerning these, met the needs of teenage record buyers. However, the music industry found it was no longer able to rely on any such calculations because of the way that teenagers' involvement with music had become active and was now part of a context of use developed by teenagers themselves.

At the beginning of the fifties noticeable changes in the musical tastes of high school teenagers were already beginning to emerge, spreading from the urbane and provincial southern USA. Instead of continuing to follow such public darlings as Frank Sinatra or Frankie Laine, the saucy ballads of Rosemary Clooney or the gentle swaying of Patti Page's 'Tennessee Waltz',[10] they became fascinated by the energy-laden rhythms of Afro-American dance music. In 1950, Fats Domino's *The Fat Man*[11] was one of the first rhythm & blues records to be bought by both black and white purchasers. In fact this was a conventional 8-bar blues, which went back to the 1940 recording *Junker Blues*[12] by the coloured musician Champion Jack Dupree from New Orleans. And what had changed conditions so that this music could penetrate the massive racial barriers to white teenagers at all was radio.

Radio stations which focussed on the Afro-American population of the USA as the target group for their advertising, attracting it through a suitable choice of music – blues, jazz, gospel and the stylistic variations of the up and coming rhythm & blues – existed in increasing numbers even during the war. Even this target group had become of interest to radio advertisers because of its rising income due to the growing need for workers in branches of the armaments industry. Commercial radio stations built up the target audiences for their advertising through music programmes. These programmes were compiled from precisely the sort of music which would appeal to the advertisers' potential customers. This was done on the basis of a regularly reviewed 'playlist', which listed all the songs which could be played during programmes. By the beginning of the fifties the rhythm & blues stations which had grown up in this way had spread across the whole country. And since it was impossible to maintain racial segregation on the airwaves as well, all people needed to do to listen to these stations' music and the breathtaking 'hot' style of their disc jockeys was to turn the tuning knob. Then the trend towards television led the national radio stations of 'white America', linked together in trans-regional chains, to focus on the local area as well, so that they could remain competitive with the country-wide television networks by offering a slightly different programming slant. Had they not done this they would have lost their paying advertisers to television altogether, which would have left them facing bankruptcy. Because of this trend the most diverse regional styles of country music once again achieved a higher status on radio programmes.

Rhythm & blues – a description which covered the playing styles of the city blues idiom, Afro-American dance music and the black hits of gospel-influenced vocal ensembles like the Inkspots or the Drifters – and country music were made up of a huge breadth of divergent musical styles. Teenagers, who now had access to both via the radio, ruthlessly selected and accepted just the particular music which suited their leisure values. This was music which was rebellious and provocative in style, which offered a sensuous pleasure and which suited their world of parties, rendezvous, boastful car rides, dreams and longings. Elvis Presley's first single combined both musical styles, with a cover version of a blues number on the A-side of the record and a country song on the flip side. Bill Haley's origins were in a country music variation of swing rooted mainly in Texas and Oklahoma, an adaptation of swing standards in the style of the folk music string bands of that region. His band, in which from 1947 he worked as a singer before he took over as leader, was still calling itself The Four Aces of Western Swing until 1947. Only a few years before his great hit with 'Rock Around the Clock', an advertisement for the radio station WPWA in Chester, Pennsylvania, where he was also employed as a disc jockey, had tried to launch him into the business as 'the nation's singing and yodeling cowboy star'.[13] Chuck Berry came from the Chicago blues scene where he had worked for a few years in the southside bars of the city until in 1955 he had a success with 'Maybellene',[14] a song which fascinated white as well as black teenagers. Berry succeeded as the first black rock'n'roll star to be accepted by the media as well as the public, but he did not remain the only Afro-American musician in the rock'n'roll business. Fats Domino, Little Richard and Bo Diddeley played equally important roles.

Both apparently fundamentally different musical directions, country & western and rhythm & blues, had common features which, in spite of their pronounced musical diversity, allowed them to offer something substantially similar to high school teenagers – a pure expression of genuine experience. Both musical styles went back to a folk music source – to the blues tradition and to the songs and dances of the white country dwellers respectively – which represented the outcasts and outsiders of twentieth-century America, black people and 'poor white trash', the farm workers and small farmers. Despite the fact that by the early fifties rhythm & blues and even more so country music represented variations of their original folk music traditions which had long since become commercial, and despite the fact that they were in sales categories sharply divided and separated by racial barriers, their origins were not as far apart as the music industry, with its stark contrast of 'white' country music and 'black' rhythm & blues, would have had people believe. John Grissim's description of country music as 'white man's blues'[15] is therefore entirely correct. Both musical styles exhibited a naturalism in content which was poles apart from the fantasy world of Broadway. Unlike the latter, both examined the real experiences of real people in often rather graphic word images and represented something genuine and unspoilt in a world which no longer seemed to be dominated by anything but money and consumption. Rudi Thiessen's description of blues points this out very clearly: 'The experience of blues is first and foremost the utopia of an undistorted experience.'[16] And Bill Malone described country music in these terms: 'More than any other form, country music became the naturalistic mode of expression within American music, dealing with the problems of drink, divorce, infidelity, marital problems and tragedy.'[17] In musical terms too there were parallels between country music and blues at least in one respect. Both were founded on an aesthetic of sound which made emotional qualities sensorily direct and immediately translatable in vocal expression; in country music by a sharp and rather nasal tone, in blues by a broken, physically expressive singing style.

In spite of these similarities, the social positions of the white and black rural populations in the American south, where both these forms of music had their roots, were still so different that, apart from these common features and leaving aside the mutual influences, their musical forms of expression remained funda- mentally different. These differences only deepened in the process of their commercial exploitation. Blues lived in the collective experiences of the black minority and developed with its changing circumstances. Blues adapted to the lifestyle in the city ghettos and found new means of expression there which reflected the thoughts and feelings of the black industrial proletariat and, as rhythm & blues, answered its need for at least one element of carefree everyday pleasure. In contrast, country music had hardly reacted to social change at all. It was shaped by the individualism of the American pioneering period, but was rooted in the loser's experience, nevertheless deeply based on trust in God and hard work, seeing in these the eternal values of the human condition. Its typical feature was an often narrow-minded conservatism. This was reinforced as it was gradually commercially exploited with the growth of radio in the twenties. In the fifties country music stood for the imagined values of an 'original American' natural way of life, nostalgically contrasted with the hectic bustle of the city. It projected the pioneering spirit of the land acquisition period into the sober business world of industrial capitalism, carrying the size and expanse of America into the bourgeois narrowness of its social structures.

The conservatism of country music on the one hand and the rebellious energy of rhythm & blues on the other became the essence of rock'n'roll, revealing an ambivalence which exactly suited the way high school teenagers felt about life. Wanting to do everything differently from their parents and yet wanting to be exactly the same, seeing prosperity and consumption as the essential conditions of a meaningful life, but no longer believing in such a life; this was the nature of the inner conflict with which this generation of teenagers struggled. Rock'n'roll reduced this to a musical formula, expressing both the noisy rebellion and the secret conformity. Thus, it could become the medium which was able to grasp, to absorb and to pass on the contradictory experiences of teenagers.

The first explicit expression of this inner conflict was in the recordings made for the small Sun label of the Memphis Recording Service in July 1954 by a young man completely unknown at the time, a truck driver with Crown Electric Company – Elvis Presley. The Memphis Recording Service was one of those one-man companies hoping at some point to strike gold in the music market. One of its sources of income, apart from recordings of

the unknown blues singers of the region which it then sold on
to the large record companies, was a record making service for
anyone who wanted to use it. For just a few dollars anyone could
go into the studio and have a record made for his own private use.
When Elvis Presley first tried out his singing skills here at his own
expense in the summer of 1953, he had just left Humes High
School in Memphis and, faced with rather modest results in his
final examinations, had nothing more in mind than a job as a
driver. Up to this point his development had in many ways been
typical of the teenagers of his generation in small-town America.
Born in 1935 in Tulepo, Mississippi into an impoverished lower-
middle-class family – his father had been a self-employed truck
driver before working for a trucking firm – and growing up in
Memphis where he finally succeeded in entering high school, he
had direct experience of the dreary everyday reality of lower-
middle-class life and of the overwhelming conformity of the time.
Elvis' reaction was indifference and a deep reluctance to accept
any responsibility which might have forced him to submit to the
constraints of being a proper young man, which was what high
school had tried to make of him and his contemporaries. His first
encounter with music dated back to his pre-school days and the
church choir of the Pentecostal First Assembly of God church in
Memphis. At the age of ten he won a prize in a school singing
competition at the Mississippi-Alabama Fair and Dairy Show. He
played the guitar a little – his parents had given him a guitar for
his eleventh birthday – listened to the radio for hours on end and,
like all his contemporaries, developed a preference for the
earthiness of rhythm & blues and the rough ballads of country
music. In this respect his home city of Memphis offered a
fascinating spectrum of the South's musical traditions. There was
an independent local blues development, dating back to the early
twenties, a distinctive gospel tradition in the black churches and
an extensive selection of country music in the boorish hillbilly
style. Memphis had the first black-run radio station in the USA
and famous blues musicians like Howlin' Wolf and Sonny Boy
Williamson had their own programmes on the local radio.

In the summer of 1954 the Memphis Recording Service
finally gave in to Presley's insistence and produced a commercial
record with him. Like all the following five singles on the
in-house Sun label it consisted simply of a selection from this

musical spectrum, oriented towards the musical tastes of his former high school classmates. 'That's All Right (Mama)' by the blues singer Arthur Big Boy Crudup on the A side was coupled with 'Blue Moon of Kentucky', which Bill Monroe had made a country music classic.[18] This combination matched the mood of the time exactly, especially since Presley sang both songs completely unpretentiously with the spontaneity of the amateur, quite unconcerned about their original stylistic characteristics. 'That's All Right', for example, is unsophisticated conventional blues, easy to sing and simple in style. Presley's voice – with its rather nasal tone far removed from the sensuous expressiveness of Afro-American blues singing – together with the rhythm guitar marking the beat by strumming chords, with the crude bass moving in simple tone steps and the melody guitar supporting the singer, gave this song an absolutely unmistakable character, which sought to make up for its obvious clumsiness with an almost movingly comic enthusiasm. Nothing seemed to go together properly: the voice did not suit the conventional style of the song, the country-style strumming of the rhythm guitar did not suit the blues-style melody guitar, and the unbridled enthusiasm did not suit the banality of the lyrics. But it was precisely these factors which gave the song as a whole its irrepressible image of rebellion. Teenagers felt the singer was one of them. He was someone who had succeeded and with his unprofessional musicality had really shown the others, the adults, what teenagers could achieve. No, they were not failures simply because they tried to reject the conformity, the norms, the rules and the discipline of high school or at best bowed to them with a show of reluctance. They just wanted to be *different*, admittedly without quite knowing *how*; but basically they were not questioning the rules of the society they lived in. To them Elvis Presley was significant because, representing them all, he had succeeded in penetrating a particular social sphere – the music business – and making himself respected there without accepting its norms. This was quite clear in his records, in their naive dilettantism, measured against the professional standards of the time, and in the provocative impudence with which they displayed this naivety. Paul Willis' opinion is very accurate.

The assertive masculinity of the motor-bike boys also found an answering structure in their preferred music. Elvis Presley's records were full of aggression. Though the focus was often unspecified and enigmatic, the charge of feeling was strong. In the atmosphere of the music, in the words, in the articulation of the words, in his personal image, was a deep implication that here was a man not to be pushed around. His whole presence demanded that he should be given respect, though, by conventional standards, the grounds for that respect were disreputable and anti-social.[19]

Elvis Presley embodied the uncertain and consuming desire of American high school teenagers in the fifties, the desire somehow to escape the oppressive ordinariness which surrounded them without having to pay the bitter price of conformity. His quick success seemed to be the proof that, in principle, escape was possible. Even though his songs were simply cover versions of songs which had been around for a long time – and not a few songs in Elvis Presley's repertoire belonged in this category – they thus acquired an additional dimension. Presley finally made these songs 'their' music, for he was one of them. It was no longer an alien cultural identity which spoke through these songs, the identity of outlaws, of the Afro-American and white 'fringe groups' from the lower end of the social scale, but their own. Teenagers had integrated this music into the context of their lifestyle, accompanied by the derogatory remarks of adults, threatened by parental bans and school disciplinary measures. Through Elvis Presley this context was now public, sanctioned by the music business. The whole commercial fuss about him was their social justification. The effect of this was overwhelming. The country singer Bob Luman later described the effect Elvis had at a time when, shortly after the release of his first single, he was still going from one Southern high school ball to another:

This cat came out in red pants and a green coat and a pink shirt and socks, and he had this sneer on his face and he stood behind the mike for five minutes, I'll bet, before he made a move. Then he hit his guitar a lick, and he broke two strings. I'd been playing ten years, and I hadn't broken a *total* of two strings. So there he was, these two strings dangling, and he hadn't done anything yet, and these high school girls were screaming and fainting and running up to the stage, and then he started to move his hips real slow like he had a thing for his guitar. That was Elvis Presley when he was about 19, playing Kilgore, Texas.[20]

What Bob Luman was describing was not at all the mystical effect of a charismatic personality, which was how the music industry tried to promote Elvis, neither was it the supposed 'ecstatic' effect of rock music, an effect attributed to rock because of these sorts of scenes. It was far more a reaction to the social phenomenon of Elvis Presley, to the mere fact of his existence in the musty conservative atmosphere of the Eisenhower era. And the more the media turned this reaction into an anti-American threat, the more it gained in strength. In the fact that, with Elvis Presley, for the first time one of them was on stage – someone the same age as them, with the same experiences and someone who was precisely as outrageous and provocative as they would at least have liked to be – his young audience experienced its social power. And the more the media blew this up into an attack on America, the more colossal this power seemed. 'Reactionaries and patriots saw in the demonstrably rebellious music cult a malicious attempt by the communists to undermine American society through its young people.'[21] The public anti-rock'n'roll campaigns in America, stirred up and accompanied by internal arguments in the music industry – the Broadway publishing empires correctly foresaw the danger to their existence which the victorious progress of rock'n'roll represented – could only hide for a short time the fact that Elvis Presley and rock'n'roll did not stand for a rejection of the American way of life. They stood for a different, more up-to-date and less conservative version, a version which American capitalism itself had ultimately given birth to. Greil Marcus wrote later: 'The version of the American dream that is Elvis' performance is blown up again and again, to contain more history, more people, more music, more hopes; the air gets thin but the bubble does not burst, nor will it ever. This is America when it has outstripped itself, in all of its extravagance.'[22]

Admittedly this does not exclude the possibility that, in spite of all this, high school teenagers did take rock'n'roll as an alternative to the official cultural models, career plans and thought patterns of the conservative fifties and integrate it as such into their lifestyle. Merely the obscure origins of rock, the suggestiveness it conveyed in veiled hints and its boundless light-heartedness must have acquired a sensational explosive force in an environment where even Shakespeare was only permitted for use in reading assignments in a shortened, censored version. 'Rock'n'roll presents a fairly succinct and radical critique of fifties life, along with an equally coherent alternative.'[23] In contrast to the conservatism and conformity of Eisenhower's America, rock'n'roll offered a philosophy of pleasure, a philosophy tied up with dancing, erotic necking, the legendary dates of the American teenager (with their strict conventions of behaviour), car rides and, of course, the fun to be had from the music itself. Rock'n'roll formed a sort of matrix, an invisible but clear framework for the leisure activities of high school students. It provided a context of significance made up of values and meanings which could then be developed further. Rock'n'roll offered a cultural coordinate system on which the boring procedures of the daily high school routine could also be plotted. Of course, this did not actually change anything; high school remained the central focus of teenagers' real daily lives. But now their daily routine had been expanded in leisure and, with rock'n'roll, by cultural dimensions which changed the whole structure of their lives, which added individual everyday relationships to those prescribed by high school and the family.

It was Bill Haley's 'Rock Around the Clock'[24] which, not incorrectly, epitomised these changes. Written by Jimmy DeKnight and Max C. Freedman, this song was originally created as a boogie for Sonny Dae and his Knights,[25] a version which was a total failure. In Bill Haley's version it became a classic expression of rock'n'roll, even though it only achieved this success at the second attempt when it was rereleased a year after its first appearance. Like most rock'n'roll songs it is based on the conventional 12-bar blues form. What differentiates it clearly from rhythm & blues songs with quite similar structures is the dominant motoric movement which runs through this song. The insistent racket of the drums and the stuttering repeated thirds from guitar and saxophone give the song its individuality, which stresses the feeling of movement even more. The 'beat' is played loudly in the foreground over the dotted triplet shuffle rhythm, and is consistently accentuated against the conventional beats in the bar, on what would normally be the upbeat. Even the singing is more like a rhythmic utterance of short melodic particles than conforming to the bourgeois concept of singing. The whole sound is consciously unbalanced and noisy. Literally every bar seems to signal rebellion. Yet this is only one aspect of this song. Far more importantly, in its musical form it encompasses essential leisure values of American high school teenagers.

The musical construction of 'Rock Around the Clock' is completely geared to movement. The only suitable way of relating to this song is through dancing, through action and reaction in movement. This movement conveys a particular sensuous experience of a quite forceful directness which corresponds to the music. Both the element of movement and the sensuous quality contained within it here stand for more general cultural aspects of the lifestyle around which teenagers organised their leisure. The status enjoyed by those leisure activities involving movement must not be overlooked. The cult of the motorcar occupied joint first place with dancing. And in its turn this merely expressed the translation into leisure of the real experience of increasing mobility, of the injection of dynamism into life through the forces of highly developed capitalism, which in fifties America, particularly in the high schools, conflicted with social rigidity and conservatism. The same was true of the pleasure-oriented sensuousness which had established its position so spectacularly in rock'n'roll and yet was nothing other than an element of the capitalist lifestyle, adapted by teenagers, but which in advertising, for example – in the product-aesthetic featuring of consumer goods – was presented as having long been generally accepted. In Bill Haley's 'Rock Around the Clock' the cultural contexts of which rock'n'roll was a part were now included in the music itself.

But this song probably became the epitome of the total phenomenon above all because it gathered together all these elements in a handy verbal expression which offered a clear, if basically misunderstood, clue to the cultural meaning of rock'n'roll, and which could be hurled against the distraught educators, parents and school alike, like a battle cry. The incantation of the ecstasy of dancing around the clock portrayed in the lyrics of 'Rock Around the Clock', points to a central aspect of teenage leisure behaviour, one which gave an important dimension to their cultural activities – the unimportance of time. The repeal in leisure of strictly decreed, ordered and planned time slots – later to be called 'dropping out', but which here was still fixed on dancing – at least appeared to abolish the prescribed power of the structured activities of daily life as expressed in the daily schedule and therefore offered the possibility of re-ordering these activities as the basis of an individual strategy for life. This is nothing more than the necessary process of their acceptance, only in a cultural form. But if these lyrics are taken in terms of the aesthetics of the 'work of art' as the 'message', as the real 'content' of the song and if this song is taken literally, as if it were suggesting anti-social behaviour to teenagers, suggesting that they accept dancing round the clock as a real purpose in life, this fact is fundamentally misunderstood. As Michael Naumann and Boris Penth remarked:

When he [Bill Haley] promoted 'Rock Around the Clock', this did not mean that the teenagers who received it enthusiastically now agreed, as might be thought from the words, that the whole purpose of life was to dance wildly and freely on the dance floor and that this was the sum total of happiness ... This song and others like it, indeed rock'n'roll altogether, acted as a trigger of chains of association and fantasies, which embraced teenagers' *whole* context of life and reinterpreted it.[26]

Rock'n'roll formed a new cultural context around teenagers' daily lives, around their obligations at school and at home, which included the diversity of leisure activities linked to this music. This expanded the existing structures of daily life, made them more relative and changed their power, but at the same time made them acceptable and integratable.

Chuck Berry described this phenomenon very nicely in 'Sweet Little Sixteen'[27] which appeared in 1958. (In fact, the most intelligent and most precisely observed lyrics in rock'n'roll have always come from him.) Like no other singer he understood his audience and generalised their experiences in his songs. In 'Sweet Little Sixteen', the enthusiasm for rock'n'roll of a sixteen-year-old girl begging her parents to be allowed to go out is contrasted with the role which she must and does play again the next morning, namely that of the 'sweet-little-sixteen-year-old' at the school desk. This song rests completely and utterly on the basis of traditional behaviour. Chuck Berry's 'Sweet Little Sixteen' is not protesting or even rebelling against the need to ask permission before she goes out. She abides by the norms of the family home and begs for her little piece of freedom, cleverly using the influence a daughter has on her father so that he may defend her from motherly strictness. But then the most important thing to her is to get dressed up in lipstick and high-heeled shoes, the outward signs of being grown-up, which through and through fits with a conventional understanding of her role. And the next morning she will be the 'sweet-little-sixteen-year-old' again, doing her best in high school. This song grasps the inner connection of the contrast between leisure and school. Only the final acceptance of the norms of family, home and school make possible the leisure world which has arisen as an alternative to these, but which in its function is not nearly as alternative as it was thought. It simply provides a context in which the behaviour models which have been raised to the status of norms are made acceptable to young people so that ultimately these can also be adopted.

In this song Chuck Berry addressed a very important element. However rebellious and provocative rock'n'roll appeared and however much it conflicted with the conservative and conformist pressure in the high schools at the time, it was nothing more than the cultural form in which the teenagers in fifties America accepted their real conditions of life. Its significance lay precisely in the fact that it gave a complex cultural form to this process, one which was conveyed through music and linked to the media, which could take up the separate experiences of young people and feed them back. Here music no longer consisted of the interchangeable reproduction of popular melodies which only had to fulfil their purpose as dance music. Music now existed in a context which opened up completely new prospects for it.

3

'Love Me Do': the aesthetics of sensuousness

Rock'n'roll contained the seeds of a development which was to advance into new musical dimensions in the sixties. The foundations of this development were laid in British beat music. Although rock'n'roll had turned music into a collectively used teenage cultural leisure form, the beginnings of a basic change in popular music which could be seen in this failed, ultimately because of production conditions in the mass media. Rock's musical roots – the traditions of Afro-American music and country music – were still influenced far too much by their folk music origins to allow them to be easily transformed into an aesthetic created on the basis of a relationship with the media. The growing significance of the mass media – particularly records – for music, shifted the internal relationships of musical performance further and further in the direction of the musical potential of studio production. Rock'n'roll styles were simply not flexible enough and they increasingly lost their original individuality. The connection between the music and the context in which American teenagers had used it had at first been very immediate, but this trend caused it to dissolve again. The missing element was rock's firm establishment in the process of music production, which had so far remained untouched by it. The change of meaning which rock'n'roll had brought to popular music was of no interest to the record companies and recording studios. The use of new production methods, for which suitable forms of music could easily be found, did not change in the slightest the conventional view of popular music which the media worked to, i.e. an easily sold entertainment product. Indeed, the media eroded rock'n'roll from the inside. Elvis Presley's 1956 release 'Love Me Tender'[1] provides a perfect example of this. In David Pichaske's opinion:

48

It is difficult to find a simpler, thinner, less professional piece than 'Love Me Tender', Elvis' first number-one ballad: lean, acoustic guitar accompaniment, tenth-grade barbershop harmony, voice coming at you as through a long tunnel, delivery accentuating the jog trot meter of pure doggerel: 'Love me tender, love me true, / Never let me go. / You have made my life complete, / And I love you so.' A complete embarrassment; next to 'Aura Lee', from which it stole its tune, an abomination. The perfect example of rock-n-roll's rejection of prettiness, overrefinement, academic orchestration and lyrics, smoothness, even subtlety.[2]

The self-perception of media producers was focussed on a professionalism which stamped its mark on the norms of the traditional pop song. Thus, the particular characteristics of rock'n'roll were formalised according to the old patterns of the music industry and were ultimately turned against rock'n'roll itself. By the end of the fifties there was nothing left of rock'n'roll except 'a soft drizzle for budding teenagers'.[3] In any case the interchangeable nature of teenage stars such as Frankie Avalon, Paul Anka, Annette, Bobby Vee or Ricky Nelson, taking over from one another in increasingly quick succession, and the sound-oriented rock'n'roll of the vocal groups, the Drifters, Shirelles, Marcels and Platters, now made it very clear that the emphasis of music production had shifted away from the musicians to the record producers.

In contrast British beat music penetrated even music production itself, establishing within it an aesthetic which suited both the cultural contexts of use which had evolved as well as the technical creation of music. The first song which made this clear was the Beatles' 'Love Me Do'; a song which, not least because of this, became a legend. Twenty years after its first release in October 1962 it even reappeared in the British top forty.

'Love Me Do', with 'P.S. I Love You' on the flip side, was the Beatles' first official single.[4] The song itself is not particularly exciting, nor is it difficult to identify its precursors. Carl Perkins' country ballad 'Sure to Fall',[5] already quite an old song, provided the musical framework. The model for John Lennon's harmonica insertions was 'Hey Baby' by the American pop singer Bruce Channel.[6] (The Beatles, together with Howard Casey and The Seniors, The Big Three and The Four Jays – the local matadors of the Liverpool 'scene' at the time – had competed for the honour of being the supporting band for Channel's Liverpool concert in October 1962.) The song itself consists of a constant repetition of its rather thin basic elements: a scant rhythm-set phrase in the backing vocals, a short melodic motif and the repeated 'Love, love me do, you know I love you'. The arrangement, with three guitars and drums as well as the harmonica, could hardly be any simpler. The bass guitar swings back and forth between the roots of the three chords used while the rhythm guitar adds the regularly strummed triads and the lead guitar simply follows the melody line. Beneath this is a stereotyped drum pattern which marks the beat. The interplay of Paul McCartney's vocals, supported by George Harrison and John Lennon, with the harmonica insertions is the only distinctive element of the song, and even that was copied.

What is it then that makes a song like this legendary? How does it mark a cultural turning point of such significance that George Melly actually considered it the starting point of a 'revolution'?[7] After all, its musical substance hardly seems to justify this, even according to the standards of the time. Dave Harker may have found the answer to these questions when, in his analysis of Melly's theory of the beginning of a 'revolution' he wrote about the Beatles' productions up to the mid-sixties: 'Only – and it's a big only, mind – the music of their early singles retains any of its freshness after a decade and a half; and we're left wondering whether even that contribution would have seemed so epoch-making had not the commercial competition been so miserable as it was in the early 1960s. Nostalgia apart, I think not.'[8] It is true that in the British hit parade, where it reached a respectable seventeenth place, this record found itself in a musical environment in which it was not difficult to attract attention. And it is no less true that this song was the first to bring a quite different basic conception of popular music into the hit parade which was what gave it its much praised 'freshness', however simply, even naively, this was presented.

In any case, the remarkable thing about this recording was that it had audibly broken consistently maintained professional standards in music production. The young men who had stood in the studio were pure dilettantes in the eyes of the professional musicians. The material they played no longer came from the desks of the professional songwriters of London's Denmark Street – the home of the great British music publishers – but had been confirmed by their audience a long time ago in countless live appearances. It was impossible to work with studio musicians which, even in rock'n'roll, was otherwise customary with new groups, since the songs were arranged for the instruments which the group themselves played. And the way they played those instruments, with their naive lack of concern and their enthusiastic greenness, contradicted every norm. The appearance of this record in the official channels of the British music business signalled the break with a concept of professionalism which had dominated the British music industry until then. And this happened under the aegis of the most important producer of popular music in Great Britain, EMI (Electrical & Musical Industries) – the 'biggest record producer in the world' as a slogan on every record which carried the EMI logo self-consciously declared.

Of course the Beatles were not by any means the only group playing this kind of music at the time. They were not even the first to be immortalised on record. The cellar clubs and pubs across the country, but particularly in the northern industrial cities, were full of amateur bands with their three guitars and drums trying to assert themselves with an exclusively young audience of fourteen to eighteen year olds. There are supposed to have been 400 groups in Liverpool alone.[9] Even before the Beatles, Howard Casey and The Seniors from Liverpool released several songs on Fontana, a small subsidiary label of Phonogramme Records, which belonged to the Dutch company Philips. In comparison with the explosive rock'n'roll of Howard Casey and The Seniors the Beatles' 'Love Me Do' seems rather worthy and conventional. But in spite of this, thanks to their clever manager Brian Epstein, the Beatles were the first band to sign a contract with one of the large market-leading record companies. At the time it was like opening a floodgate and this was what gave this song its legendary significance. 'Love Me Do' was the first song coming out of the broad amateur music movement of the time which achieved unlimited media presence, which was on national radio and which was available in the large record shops. Only a few months later there was hardly one of those amateur bands who had not been put under contract, just as a precaution. Bill Harry, a close friend of John Lennon at the Liverpool College of Art and from 1961 to 1965 the publisher of the magazine *Mersey Beat*, later wrote:

Looking back, at a time when Rock music is so firmly established, it is hard for many people to realise how difficult it really was for a group from the British provinces to become successful and maintain success. The music scene was firmly controlled by a few moguls in London and Pop was a truly manufactured music. The Beatles not only gave their music to the world, they broke down barriers and opened the floodgates to those who were to follow.[10]

Looked at more closely, 'Love Me Do' represented not only the beginning of a structural change within the music industry which resulted in pop music being taken out of the hands of a small group of professional songwriters, but also a different conception of popular music, one which showed the basic form of rock.

The first obvious break with the traditional aesthetic communication model of pop music was the fact that it was now the whole group who were the focus of identification for the audience, not an individual singer. What had been concealed in rock'n'roll – seen from outside it appeared to be the same as the conventional pop song, simply in another musical form – here became quite clear. The Beatles' 'Love, love me do, you know I love you' no longer concealed the stylised role play of the languishing lover undertaken for the entertainment of the audience. Sung by more than one person this no longer made any sense. Thus, this song was spared the theatricality which the traditional pop song had acquired from its roots in the musical stage entertainment of the nineteenth century – operetta, music hall and later the talking picture. And this inevitably shifted the aesthetic coordinates of the music, which could no longer be taken as a code representing individual expression and the emotions which the singer personified. The idea that a pop song should be constructed like a conversation between singer and audience, that the singer should give a personal significance to the music, finally collapsed with this change. There was no longer a romanticised 'I' behind the Beatles' songs but, visibly, a collective 'we', and this lifted the music out of a communication pattern in which it was understood as the musical symbol of personal emotions. Instead of expressing emotions with great feeling, which the text of 'Love Me Do' actually suggested, and for which a suitable reservoir of musical means were available in the conventional pop song, this song was, by way of complete contrast, totally unsentimental in style.

The intensity of 'Love, love me do …' was created in a very genuine way, without following the conventions which always necessitated the musical expression of great love in 'great' melodic phrases. In the construction of this song the rhythmic organisation dominated all other musical factors. Even the vocal part did not have a particularly original or concise melody, in fact had no individual melodic form, but was nothing more than one element of a rhythmically constructed whole. The act of listening to this song was coordinated with a rhythmically organised progression of movement, one which seemed full of intensity because of its almost manic uniformity instead of merely portraying this intensity according to the conventional rules. The ceaseless repetition of the basic musical elements of the song had a rather hypnotic effect. Every dancer knows what intensity of feeling can be produced by a repeated pattern of steps and it was as dance music that 'Love Me Do' originated. In other words, instead of transposing emotions into musical structures according to a handed down aesthetic code, these emotions were *presented* in movement, a movement which demanded the active participation of the listener so that the emotions could be created in reality. In his research into Afro-American music, in which this form of music has its roots, Bram Dijkstra correctly established: 'Such movement does not actually have to happen. Just as a dancer can dance to music in his head, the seemingly passive listener always reacts mentally to the rhythmic pattern which his senses are registering, even if he is not consciously listening.'[11] The basis of what Dijkstra is describing is the direct sensuous power of music. Here musical performance takes place according to an aesthetic of sensuousness.

The force behind this concept of music was American rock'n'roll, particularly those Afro-American forms which have already been mentioned. But since in Britain this musical import from the USA encountered completely different conditions and was removed from its original context, in Britain it evolved far beyond its inherent boundaries. The key to the conception of British beat music – and all that followed – lies in the particular way in which rock'n'roll was received. It was in this context that the aesthetic of rock was created, an aesthetic which runs through all its playing styles and stylistic forms with their continually changing emphases and their new attempts at

developing its musical possibilities. The individual nature of this
aesthetic resulted from the relationships which rock'n'roll
entered in fifties Britain. Here is Dick Hebdige writing about the
British reception of rock'n'roll:

> The music had been taken out of its original context ... and transplanted
> to Britain ... Here, it existed in a kind of vacuum as a stolen form – a focus
> for an illicit delinquent identity. It was heard in the vacant lots of the new
> British coffee bars where, although filtered through a distinctively English
> atmosphere of boiled milk and beverages, it remained demonstrably alien
> and futuristic – as baroque as the juke box on which it was played. And
> like those other sacred artefacts – the quiffs, the drapes, the Brylcreem
> and the 'flicks' – it came to mean America, a fantasy continent of
> Westerns and gangsters, luxury, glamour and 'automobiles'.[12]

Here, as in the USA, rock'n'roll constituted a complex cultural
environment, although linked to different everyday experiences
and different living conditions. And it stood out radically from
the indigenous pop music. What was understood by pop music
in Britain at the time was a completely different world.

In the fifties the BBC, in its role as the British national
cultural institution, still possessed almost unlimited authority
in all questions of the nation's musical entertainment. The
only alternatives to the BBC were the English evening programmes of Radio Luxembourg and the commercial television
station Independent Television (ITV), finally approved by the
British Government in 1954 after long discussions. At that
time ITV hardly affected the development of pop music. Radio
Luxembourg on the other hand, a radio station modelled on
American radio, reached a not inconsiderable audience of young
people in England but was situated on the Continent and was
therefore only of limited interest to the British music industry.
The authority whose programming policies exercised by far
the greatest influence both on the nation's musical taste and
on the British music industry was the BBC. But the BBC was
dominated by an unparalleled conservatism which felt the
new teenage musical needs emerging in the fifties were linked
to the nightmare of the decline of culture and education in a
commercial mass culture modelled on the American experience.

The BBC considered itself a cultural educational institution.
It only granted entertainment an independent status in programming structures during the Second World War, when the

radio was used to mobilise a spirit of resistance in the civilian population as well as in the armed forces. The Light Programme was introduced in 1946 to replace the Forces Programme (introduced at the beginning of the forties for troop entertainment). To a large extent it took over the Forces Programme's view of entertainment, but was still based on a concept which did not see any difference between entertainment and education. Sir William Haley, director of the BBC, described this concept in 1946 in a pamphlet on programming entitled 'The Responsibilities of Broadcasting': 'Each programme at any given moment must be ahead of its public, but not so much as to lose their confidence. The listener must be led from good to better by curiosity, liking and a growth of understanding.'[13] The concept of musical entertainment was thus linked to the idea that the listener would be completely uncritical and have no standards of comparison, a point of view which found expression in the description of the programme allocated for this purpose as the 'Light Programme'. An official BBC document laying down guidelines for the content of this programme was based on the assumption that the listener was: 'not going to listen for more than half an hour, that he prefers orchestral sounds to the purer music sound of a string quartet, and that he is essentially not a highbrow'.[14]

The educational and instructional claims of the programme makers started from this both simplified and superficial view of the listener and they therefore completely missed the point of the real use of the media. The programme makers themselves considered 'light entertainment' synonymous with the 'light classics'. In their view the Light Programme was mainly addressed to housewives. The programmes were designed for home and family and the tastes and cultural values of the lower middle classes therefore reigned unchallenged. It is not surprising that from the mid-fifties rock'n'roll imported from America became the enthusiastically accepted alternative to all this, particularly among working-class teenagers, for they were unable to recognise themselves in the BBC's model listener.

Another factor was that the BBC was not allowed to use records on its music programmes for more than twenty-two hours per week, an anachronism remaining from the early thirties. The BBC was bound by an agreement with the British Musicians' Union which limited the so-called 'needle time', the broadcasting of records, in order to secure jobs for professional musicians in live studio music broadcasts. In addition only every third piece of music broadcast could be a piece of vocal music. Consequently the BBC clung unwaveringly to an aesthetic concept of pop music which was oriented towards the instrumental swing standards of the thirties. Because of the authority possessed by the BBC this naturally had an effect and became the norm. The journalist Jeff Nuttal recalled later: 'Popular culture was, at that time, not ours. It was the province of the young adult, contrived and modified by the promoters and impressarios and aimed at the mid-twenties age group ... this was the heyday of the vast popular dance-halls, the Mecca and the Locarno.'[15]

For a period of over thirty years in England this view of popular culture was epitomised by Victor Sylvester and his band. They were one of the most successful British dance bands, not only appearing regularly on the BBC but also selling a total of more than 27 million records – a figure that was only exceeded much later. Victor Sylvester had become famous in the twenties through his connection with a campaign by the Imperial Society of Dance Teachers, who wanted to improve the cultural standing of jazz. Along with the dance styles associated with it, jazz was considered very 'un-British' and even at that time presented a challenge to the guardians of public morality. Sylvester and his band provided the musical basis for this campaign with a variant of jazz suited to the style of European light music. His collected songs were a model for the British dance band and fifty-five editions were printed between 1928 and 1955.[16] Of course, the fact that he maintained his position unchallenged and continued to be successful was largely because until the mid-fifties there was a general ban on performances by American bands in England. Until the mid-fifties, then, British pop music was dominated by dance bands playing swing: in particular, the Victor Sylvester Orchestra and the bands of Jack Parnell, Eric Delaney, Ted Heath and Cyril Stapleton. Apart from this, there were only cover versions of the most traditional American hits. Dicky Valentine, Anne Shelton, Ronnie Hilton and Frankie Vaughan were the stars of the nation.

The large record companies, foremost among them EMI, naturally adjusted to the guidelines of BBC programming policy and only concentrated on those releases which, in view of the existing limitations of the needle time agreement, had any chance of being considered for the broadcasting playlist, one of the main tools of sales promotion. Hunter Davies, the first biographer of the Beatles, described this quite clearly:

It was like bringing out a regular monthly magazine. Each month a company like Parlophone brought out around ten new records, all planned about two months ahead, which they called their monthly supplements. They were always very strictly and fairly balanced. Out of the ten new records two would be classical, two jazz, two dance music – the Victor Sylvester sort of dance music – two would be male vocal and two would be female vocal.[17]

Like everything else this too was conservative, firmly rooted in habits whose only justification was that things had always been done that way.

Bill Haley's 'Rock Around the Clock', released in Britain in 1954 on the Decca Brunswick label, really exploded onto this soft British musical entertainment scene. The contrast could not have been greater. It was also the first single to sell more than a million copies in Britain.[18] This was the signal for a radically different style of leisure behaviour, particularly among British working-class teenagers, for as the sociologists and consumer strategists quickly found out:

the teenage market is almost entirely working class. Its middle class members are either still at school and college or else just beginning on their careers: in either case they dispose of much smaller incomes than their working class contemporaries and it is highly probable, therefore, that not far short of 90 per cent of all teenage spending is conditioned by working class taste and values.[19]

Rock'n'roll made it obvious for the first time in Britain that working-class teenagers were beginning to form cultural value patterns in their leisure which were increasingly clearly contrasted with the official cultural institutions. Just the fact that 'Rock Around the Clock' was an American production shocked the officials of British culture.

The first direct contacts with highly commercialised American mass culture were via the American forces stationed in England in 1942 and their radio station, the American Forces Network (AFN), set up as part of the troop welfare operation. Since then a massive campaign had been running in British public opinion

against the 'American influence', fearing that it would undermine British cultural traditions. Even in 1942 the British Government limited the transmission radius of the AFN stations to 10
miles in order to protect their own population from it as far as
possible. As Dick Hebdige wrote later: 'By the early 50s, the very
mention of the word "America" could summon up a cluster of
negative associations.'[20]

In order to 'prove' the corrupting influence of American
culture there was also no lack of exaggerated scandal reports in
the British press about young criminal offenders and their
rock'n'roll background. When the Bill Haley film 'Rock Around
the Clock' opened in British cinemas in 1956 playing to full
houses, the climate of public opinion suddenly became
hysterical. After the film had appeared in a London working-class
area the *Daily Express* reported civil-war-like battles between the
police and two thousand rampaging teenagers. Other newspapers
picked up the story and kept it in the public eye for weeks on end.
Since then it has become one of the standard stories about the
arrival of rock'n'roll in Britain. Ian Whitcomb later investigated
the reports and arrived at a quite different presentation of the
facts:

the picture played 300 cinemas scattered around the country (including
such tough cities as Glasgow and Sheffield) without any trouble. Then,
after a performance at the Trocadero in South London, there was some
good natured larking: a few hundred boys and girls danced and chanted
'Mambo Rock' on Tower Bridge, holding up traffic. Some cups and
saucers were thrown too. Later there were a few ten-shilling fines. One
boy was fined £1 for accidentally kicking a policeman.[21]

Despite this the film caused more conflict as cinema owners were
provoked into overreacting by the scandal which the press had
made of this particular event. They interrupted performances and
called in the police just to stop dancing between the seats. The
result was slashed cinema seats. Screenings of this film were then
finally forbidden.

In fact these arguments about rock'n'roll really concealed a
conflict of a quite different nature from the one which was pushed
into the foreground and in which people were encouraged to
believe – the danger of the 'Americanisation' of British culture.
Since the thirties, pop music in Britain had been nurtured by
American influences and the pre-war Hollywood film successes

had left deeper marks on Britain's cultural life than rock'n'roll, linked as it was mainly to working-class teenagers, could ever bring with it. Conservative Britain was far more afraid of the political consequences which might arise from an undirected commercial generalisation of the cultural needs of the masses. The real problem was a concept of mass culture which threatened to undermine the authority of the official British cultural institutions, supported by Crown and Government, a concept of mass culture which merely because of its numerical supremacy, was bound to lead to a shift in cultural processes towards the needs and lifestyle of the working class. As Iain Chambers commented: 'It was the novel and unsolicited ingression of new tastes coming from "below", and their evident powers to challenge and redraw some of the traditional maps of cultural habits, that generated many an acid but apprehensive rebuttal.'[22] Class divisions in Britain – reaching as they did deep into the structure of the cities, with their socially sharply distinct residential districts – were reinforced culturally. In people's minds working-class culture and lifestyle, once given the opportunity to develop, were linked to the spectre of the decline of the nation. In 1962 the publicist Charles Curran wrote with quite unrivalled cynicism about the lifestyle of the working classes in *Crossbow*, the international magazine of the Conservative party: 'It is a life without point or quality, a vulgar world whose inhabitants have more money than is good for them, barbarism with electric light … a cockney tellytopia, a low grade nirvana of subsidised houses, hire purchase extravagance, undisciplined children, gaudy domestic squalor, and chips with everything.'[23] What Curran expressed openly here was exactly the perception of the ruling conservative elite, which as far as it was concerned, legitimised its claim to power.

Fifties Britain also saw the conservative revitalisation of existing social relations. The collapse of the British Empire after the Second World War, when it had to relinquish sovereignty to its colonies, plunged British capitalism into a deep crisis. In order to solve this crisis all possible forces were mobilised. In 1951 the post-war Labour Government with its cautious programme of reforms gave way to a Conservative administration. The Conservatives remained in power until 1964 and from 1957 onwards, particularly under Prime Minister Macmillan, sought to remove social divisions altogether with the concept of the 'classless consumer society' and the slogan 'You've never had it so good'. While on the one hand British capital interests tried to solve the problems occasioned by the loss of markets and cheap labour in the former British colonies with a cynical contempt for the working classes, on the other hand they promoted a 'classless' consumer paradise, a superb screen for the genuine interests of capital. In order to give a certain reality to the promised 'class-lessness', without even touching real class conditions, a consumer culture was cobbled together in which social differences genuinely seemed to have disappeared. No wonder then that in the outward appearance of British cultural life an attempt was made to wipe out the last remnants of an independent working-class lifestyle and culture, even in leisure and family life. The traditional cultural infrastructure of the city working-class districts, with their traditional pubs as the focus of social gather-ings and cultural communication, was swept away. The media reflected the consumer paradise in shallow images and sounds which corresponded to the cultural ideal of the *petit bourgeois*, an ideal which had become the norm because it was the lowest common denominator of the socially differentiated cultural forms. Even the programming policy of the BBC bowed imper-ceptibly to this norm. The British nation appeared to be a single community, held together by the common aim of increasing prosperity. The fact that an atom of prosperity for some meant a thousandfold profit for others was no longer obvious, at least at first glance. And ultimately capital interests succeeded in achieving the economic prosperity and political stability which they needed for the undisturbed increase of their surplus wealth. Ian Birchall described the situation in the following terms:

Britain in the late fifties and early sixties saw an unprecedented degree of political stability and general prosperity ... But above all society was fragmented and individualistic. Improvements in living standards in a boom situation came from local bargaining and direct action – politics or identification with a social class seemed increasingly irrelevant to the real concerns of life. More and more working-class people, especially the young, told social scientists and opinion pollsters that they were not working class. Political apathy was defined, in the phrase of the distinguished historian E. P. Thompson, as 'private solutions to public problems'. For youth above all frustration and satisfaction were defined, not in social terms, but in relation to personal, and particularly sexual relations. It was this pattern of life that found its cultural reflection in the rock music of the years 1963 to 1966.[24]

At first the 'pattern of life' which Birchall describes here was linked to American rock'n'roll, which gave British working-class teenagers a medium of self-portrayal. Even if they no longer considered themselves working-class, their experiences were still class-specific. Their search for cultural forms which suited them and which differed from the official consumer model, in which they could rediscover themselves and which they could relate to their everyday experiences, was nothing more than an expression of this. Dick Hebdige is quite correct in his comments on this phenomenon:

None the less, despite the confident assurances of both Labour and Conservative politicians that Britain was now entering a new age of unlimited affluence and equal opportunity, that we had 'never had it so good', class refused to disappear. The ways in which class was *lived*, however – the forms in which the experience of class found expression in culture – did change dramatically.[25]

Rock'n'roll promoted the utopia of a distant America, an utopia which could encompass the everyday experiences of British working-class teenagers with all their longings, desires, hopes, frustrations and leisure needs. Rock'n'roll mediated a self-image to these teenagers, which – influenced by the values and leisure patterns of American high school students – was literally miles away from their actual situation, but which despite this could only find its basis in the structure of their daily lives. It took the experience of daily life in the dismal English working-class suburbs, where the cinema was the only remaining alternative to the street, to see rock'n'roll as an opportunity for cultural realisation, an opportunity which was able to break down the constricting boundaries of school, work and the family home by making them able to feel an undefined longing for something 'real' which had to exist somewhere beyond the oppressive ordinariness of life. Thus, with a provocative challenge rock'n'roll bore witness to the social and cultural claims of British working-class teenagers, even though these claims were expressed via a foreign identity. Dick Hebdige's expression, a 'stolen form',[26] neatly picks up this point.

Against this background, rock'n'roll achieved a significance in Britain which it had never possessed in America. In fifties Britain it became the cultural symbol of working-class teenagers. To conservative public opinion as expressed in the media, this situation logically represented an external attack on the supposed 'classlessness', an attack which considerably disturbed the 'social peace' of the nation. When the rise of British beat music made the argument that British culture was being swamped by American music imports untenable, reactions sharpened, thereby reinforcing the link between this music and the social problems of the working-class teenager. Music became a convenient symbol in the increasingly sharp conflict. The fact that teenagers themselves took this conflict quite personally – equating it with clashes with their parents, with school, with the world around them, with the problems of getting a job, with their superiors at work – did not change the social nature of the conflict at all. This was not the private conflict of a restless youth, the so-called 'generation conflict', but was rather concerned with the opportunities for developing a lifestyle and culture suited to the class-specific experience of the changing face of British capitalism. It is not surprising that ruling conservative opinion considered this a threat. The *New Statesman*, the opinion leader of the political establishment, in 1964 described the 'menace of Beatleism':

Both T.V. channels now run weekly programmes in which popular records are played to teenagers and judged. While the music is performed, the cameras linger savagely over the faces of the audience. What a bottomless chasm of vacuity they reveal. Huge faces, bloated with cheap confectionery and smeared with chain-store make-up, the open, sagging mouths and glazed eyes, the hands mindlessly drumming in time to the music, the broken stiletto heels, the shoddy, stereotyped, 'with-it' clothes: here, apparently, is a collective portrait of a generation enslaved by a commercial machine.[27]

Such distorted images dominated public discussion about British beat music and also formed the background which gave a song like the Beatles' 'Love Me Do' its explosive force. The contradiction that it was precisely the political apologists of a commerce-led consumer society who were complaining about the reality of such commerce is only an apparent one. Just as the powerful control centres of monopoly capital had a basic interest in maintaining the ideology of the 'classless consumer society', so the music industry, once it had discovered the commercial potential of the beat boom, had an equally direct interest in its exploitation, whether this suited the official model of a uniform consumer culture or not. The arguments were not about a socially meaningful development of mass culture, but were between two factions of the ruling power structure – the political representatives of state authority in the interests of monopoly capital and the financial empires of the culture and music industry – over control of any such development.

It was this background which gave rock'n'roll in Britain and British beat music its spectacular significance, and which allowed music to become the symbol of a deep cultural conflict. This conflict brought with it a polarisation between the class-specific cultural claims of working-class youth and the cultural representation of a supposedly classless consumer society. Within this conflict rock'n'roll, as played by young amateur groups, was transformed by an aesthetic which caused far-reaching changes in popular music. The amateur bands chose to play those rock'n'roll songs which meant something to them and their audience. However, their choice was definitely influenced in part by the context in which this music found itself in Britain. The mere fact that there was such a broad amateur music movement looking for its roots in a music form imported from abroad cannot have been pure chance.

Of course, when a new market began to appear with the rock'n'roll craze among working-class teenagers the British music industry also reacted promptly, despite the public arguments. However, right from the start the music business adapted rock'n'roll to suit its concept of 'excellent entertainment for the whole family', as David Jacobs, compere of the television programme 'Juke Box Jury', a pop music programme for teenagers, put it at the time.[28] Practically every month a new young star appeared on the record market, gushingly billed as 'Britain's answer to Elvis Presley'. Tommy Steele and Cliff Richard in particular represented the British form of soft rock'n'roll blend with their cliched 'good boy' style, a style which actually robbed rock'n'roll of precisely those elements which had initially made it an alternative to the bourgeois British pop music productions of the fifties. This ultimately resulted in young people playing rock'n'roll themselves, once the skiffle craze had made playing music fashionable. Even the Beatles, who first played the jazz clubs as a schoolboy skiffle band, only became local stars in Liverpool when they resorted to imitating American rock'n'roll and dressed in virile leather suits. Paul McCartney later recalled: 'We started off by imitating Elvis, Buddy Holly, Chuck Berry, Carl Perkins, Gene Vincent...the Coasters, the Drifters – we just copied what they did.'[29] The first press report that appeared about the Beatles – in 1961 in one of the early editions of the magazine *Mersey Beat*, by Bob Wooler, disc jockey at the Liverpool Cavern Club which later became the mecca of English beat music – still acknowledged them for their rock'n'roll qualities:

Why do you think The Beatles are so popular? Many people many times have asked me this question since that fantastic night (Tuesday, 27th December 1960) at Litherland Town Hall, when the impact of the act was first felt on this side of the River ... I think The Beatles are No 1 because they resurrected original style rock'n'roll music, the origins of which are to be found in American negro singers ... Here again, in The Beatles, was the stuff that screams are made of. Here was the excitement – both physical and aural – that symbolised the rebellion of youth in the ennuied mid 50s.[30]

Admittedly British working-class teenagers were not only interested in rock'n'roll as music and it was not only the musical attraction which ultimately led people to play it. Quite the contrary, since when rock was played on a line-up of three guitars and drums not very much remained of its original musical qualities. It was more or less reduced to noisy playing over the beat, the basic metric unifying feature, which was why it was also called beat music. The most significant effect of playing rock'n'roll was that it helped to create a leisure environment which working-class teenagers could call their own. The beat clubs which sprang up in disused cellars, former jazz clubs and pubs were their world and provided a centre for their leisure needs where only the rules that *they* made counted. They were not allowed into bars, dance halls and pubs, since these sold alcohol and were therefore barred to young people under 18. The few youth clubs which existed were under educational supervision and were usually organised by church-based charitable organisations, who not only did not have rock'n'roll in mind but considered their 'cultural' leisure activities – handicrafts circles, games and community singing – an alternative to it. In contrast to all this, playing music themselves created an independent leisure environment, supported by the way the music was used and developed by the teenagers themselves. Their leisure activities shifted away from the streets and into the beat clubs. Richard Mabey investigated this process among the Liverpool street gangs: 'As the process of producing a group from within a gang's ranks was cumulative one could feel the decline in tension in other forms of competition. What mattered now was not how many boys a gang could muster for a Friday night fight but how well their group could play on Saturday night.'[31] The bands learnt how to play from the reaction of their audience. Thus, the music developed completely unhindered in the wake of the relationship between music and its social function which had arisen when rock'n'roll had arrived. Ultimately this led to the reconstruction and reorganisation of music as a medium of expression. Simon Frith described this as follows: 'British beat emerged from musicians' attempts to solve two problems at once: on the one hand, they wanted to sound like their favourite American records; on the other hand, they had to make a living playing in clubs which meant they had to play dance music with enough loud energy and local familiarity to bring crowds back.'[32] With both these aspects a cultural context was addressed which led to a gradual change in the internal parameters of performance and which at the same time adopted the playing models taken over from rock'n'roll.

As British working-class teenagers played their favourite American records, the symbolic content which rock'n'roll had acquired in the conflicts of the fifties was realised. To the teenagers this aspect of rock'n'roll was of far greater significance than the actual content of lyrics and music. It gave the songs a second plane of expression. If the lyrics and music of rock'n'roll songs were essentially about the leisure values and pleasures of being an American high school teenager, at the same time they were also a symbol for the cultural claims of working-class teenagers in Britain, for the leisure structures influenced by their class-specific experiences. The forms of informal companionship which these teenagers experienced, with their roots in their own district and in local conditions, gave them a distinctive feeling of solidarity and belonging; the organisation of leisure as time free from work and not as an alternative to school and conservative educational norms; the robustness, directness and explicitness of their leisure behaviour as elements of a small amount of control over their own lives which was denied to these working-class fifteen-year-old school-leavers at work; the literal struggle for their own leisure opportunities against the background of the material, financial and cultural constraints which existed – in these things those class-specific experiences which had become associated with rock'n'roll in Britain were expressed quite directly. With the playing of rock'n'roll songs this plane of meaning became more and more topical, or as Rudi Thiessen put it: 'The misconception in the fact that white proletarian children consider the music of a colonised people their own, is what allows them to play it as their own music.'[33]

Because of this, alongside its musical form playing music acquired another, symbolic, form characterised by the inversion of the relationship between musicians and audience. Indeed, this second symbolic plane of meaning did not result from the performance itself nor from the actual content of lyrics and music. It resulted solely from the contexts in which the young working-class audience placed this music. In fifties and early sixties Britain American rock'n'roll announced the claims of working-class teenagers to their own opportunities for self-fulfilment through leisure, opportunities suited to their experience; but this was not something which the songs of Elvis Presley, Chuck Berry, Buddy Holly or Little Richard expressed, and actually had nothing to do with the 'messages' of these songs. And even the British beat groups did not embody this fact in the way they played when they first began to play rock'n'roll. They simply actualised this second plane of meaning which rock'n'roll already possessed quite independently of them and which had been mediated by working-class teenagers in their use of rock and confirmed by the public reaction to it. In this way a complex secondary system of meaning originated, constructed over the original meaning of lyrics and music. In this secondary system of meaning rock'n'roll songs were robbed of the original concrete determinacy which they had possessed in American high schools and in the leisure structures of American teenagers, in order to acquire an equally concrete determinacy in a symbolic form. This now became a second-order determinacy of content, in which the songs themselves were once again taken as material for expression – by the young audience now – and the musicians simply provided the raw material. But because this determinacy of content was not encoded in lyrics and music and was not developed and attached to the original meaning of these, it was unstable and lacked durability. It was a distillation of the cultural context in which this music was placed, which gained a temporary stability by virtue of the arguments about it. The spectacular effect of the appearance of the Beatles' 'Love Me Do' in the British hit parade can be put down solely to this secondary plane of meaning, which at the time, was very concrete and obvious, although today it can no longer be discerned in this song without a laborious reconstruction of the original context. When this song appeared in the British charts again in 1983 it was a symbol of something quite different, the nostalgia for the 'golden sixties' and the longing for a time long past. Both these aspects have always been more important and relevant for this song and its effect than the naive adolescent longing of 'Love, love me do, You know, I love you ...' and its musical translation into the primary immediate plane of performance.

Admittedly it does not mean that because of this rock'n'roll music was actually interchangeable or that its musical form and the content of the lyrics were completely unimportant. But form and content now followed other rules than those which correspond to the conversion of content into the dialectic of form, into the unity of lyrics and music. The most important thing about this music is no longer the wealth of emotion, the fulfilment of the content and the diversity of associations developed in the artistic structures, but rather the ability of these elements to be open to the symbolic meanings which they receive from their listeners.

Of course, the fact that British working-class teenagers in particular identified with rock'n'roll and, in playing it, developed a musical form which more directly suited their needs and the structures of meaning of their leisure, was not due to any arbitrary act nor to pure chance. In the first place this naturally had something to do with the musical qualities of rock'n'roll, and secondly it was linked to the particular musical nature of individual songs, for these songs were not played indiscriminately. Mike Howes, a producer with his own studio complex in Liverpool, was one of the working-class youngsters who crowded the beat clubs night after night, and reported: 'At that time it was black rock'n'roll that particularly appealed to us, the songs of Chuck Berry, Little Richard and Fats Domino. The bands who could play these songs best were the most popular, and the Beatles were among them. This was around 1960/61.'[34]

What was important was rock'n'roll's dance music qualities and the songs from the Afro-American tradition were the ones which suited this best. The songs which exercised the greatest influence on early British beat music were those with the most motoric energy, like Chuck Berry's 'Roll Over Beethoven'. It was not by chance that this song was in the Beatles' repertoire together with a number of other Berry songs.[35] Dancing itself was, of course, already a central element of teenage leisure activity and, together with music, created their own leisure environment. But at the same time it was the form of the literal appropriation of the rock'n'roll songs which made them open to *their* meanings and open to being *their* medium of expression. In sensuous identification with the music through bodily movement in dance the structures of the songs were dissolved into patterns and images of movement. It was not their meaning, their content, that was 'read' but their movement; they were not merely heard but rather physically deciphered. And it was exactly this which formed the basis for the construction of a second, symbolic, system of meaning over the immediate content, a system of meaning which, without being obvious in the songs and without being fixed in meaning by the lyrics and music, is nevertheless not independent of them. Teenagers stripped rock'n'roll songs of their concrete determinacy of meaning by changing them into patterns of movement while they were dancing. And as patterns of movement they could be assimilated into the structures of their lifestyle and leisure and could then themselves function as the material of a more comprehensive system of meaning, combined with other material such as clothes, hairstyles, gestures (coolness, etc.) and styles of speech (slang) as elements in a complex cultural style of behaviour. But for this to happen, the utopia of a distant America, mediated through the lyrics, was anything but unimportant.

Along with the musical qualities of rock'n'roll, the content of its lyrics also contributed decisively to making these songs stand out from the indigenous British pop music of the time.

The function of this content was to allow rock'n'roll to become part of a context in Britain in which it could become a symbol for the cultural claims of working-class teenagers. But these cultural claims did not in any way consist of a literal longing for America, for the pleasures of the American high school teenager, but rather of the search for their own opportunities for fulfilment in leisure corresponding to their own experiences. British society, with its insistence on the supposed classlessness of the evolving consumer society, denied them this fulfilment and had swept it away and suppressed it in what the media offered. The more open rock'n'roll songs were for this use, the more deeply they entered into this context through their musical and textual form – as energy-laden dance music and as provocative America-Utopia – but the more, in their connection with the problematic of high school and the leisure values of American teenagers, they remained open for British working-class teenagers to find themselves in them, the more popular they became. As a result a complex multi-dimensionality was established, both in performance and in involvement with the music, which became the foundation of rock music and which established an analogous multi-dimensional song concept for further development. The French semiotician Roland Barthes, found a very accurate model for this when he was working on similar multi-level systems of meaning in images and literary texts:

In the same way, if I am in a car and I look at the scenery through the window, I can at will focus on the scenery or on the window-pane. At one moment I grasp the presence of the glass and the distance of the landscape; at another, on the contrary, the transparence of the glass and the depth of the landscape; but the result of this alternation is constant: the glass is at once present and empty to me, and the landscape unreal and full.[36]

Even if it may perhaps seem erroneous, rock songs can be compared to the window of the car in Barthes' model. Just as the form and composition of the window determine the segment of reality which is visible through it, yet it is not the window but the scenery beyond which attracts the eye of the onlooker, so it is with rock songs. Lyrics and music anchor them in the cultural contexts of leisure, the everyday life and lifestyle in which they function, determining in the same way a particular, social, segment of reality. But beyond these contexts more comprehensive meanings are enclosed which are as equally little formulated in lyrics and music as the scenery is displayed on the window; but just as much linked with the lyrics and music of the songs as the view of the scenery remains determined by the form and composition of the window. And just as the car moves through the scenery so that new segments of reality become visible without the form and composition of the window changing – these always limit the onlooker's field of view in the same way – so rock songs can be moved through the cultural scenery, always encompassing new meanings without the lyrics and music changing. The same songs had a quite different meaning in American high schools than they did in the leisure structures of British working-class teenagers. If we focus on the songs, we become aware of their internal composition and the content formulated within this. But just as in Roland Barthes' model the form of the window and its material composition – its streaks and air bubbles, the structure of its surface – are not at all the object of interest of the person looking at the scenery; they limit his field of view and influence the colour and perspective of the visible piece of scenery and are therefore not unimportant since the window and the scenery seem to melt into one unity, so the internal composition of the songs is not in the slightest of real importance to the listener. What is of importance is the ability they have, like the window, to be transparent to the symbolic meanings lying beyond them, meanings with which they form a single unity, as the window does with the piece of scenery. If in contrast to this we focus on the leisure structures of teenagers, on that 'scenery' in which the songs are situated, then meanings become visible which are expressed not in the lyrics and music of the songs but in teenagers' total leisure behaviour, in a cultural style of behaviour which admittedly also includes a close involvement with music.

However complicated this relationship may appear, it is quite easily achieved by the musicians. They only have to succeed in providing a music with which each audience identifies. They do not have to track down the complex secondary plane of meaning which their songs receive from the audience, nor do they have to understand the open nature of their songs. Indeed, as long as they keep their relationship with their audience in mind, something which they always professed if only for commercial reasons, they may even believe that they are only expressing their own thoughts and emotions. Even the British beat groups were naturally not aware of these relationships, but they fulfilled them by playing American rock'n'roll songs. When they then went over to playing their own songs, even though these followed the same pattern, they lacked both that developed relationship with tradition which was behind rock'n'roll in the USA and also the necessary professionalism simply to continue rock'n'roll: 'What started as a pop revival, a new burst of teenage rock'n'roll, ended up, then, suggesting quite new possibilities for popular music as a form of artistic expression: rock'n'roll became rock.'[37]

These relationships constituted a song concept which was freed from the functional narrowness of traditional pop music, from its reduction to dancing and entertainment, but which on the other hand was able to realise very complex meanings without being overlooked in terms of content and without having to desert the functional planes of dancing and entertainment. This song concept needed no complex and differentiated 'significant' musical structures in order to realise those symbolic meanings. Quite the reverse, the more open the songs remained, open to different possibilities of meaning and of use, the more flexibly they followed the meanings which had developed in the teenagers' leisure behaviour. Their concrete acquisition through translation into patterns and images of movement, the sensuous development of their content of movement, in spite of everything made possible a performance that was always different, especially since to a great extent this was developed from the musicians' consciousness of their own bodies and did not simply follow some principles of construction which would have had to have been learnt and which would have required an understanding recognition from the listener. Of course, real movement was not always necessary in order to decode this music in its dimension of structuring movement. It was quite sufficient if it was merely imagined. Even the introduction of rock concerts did not push this element into the background at all, especially since they usually took place in empty halls without seats where, once again, people were able to move to the music. Rock concerts were more based on commercial motives, gathering as many paying fans as possible around the groups. Although at no point in its development was rock music ever pure 'listening' music, it was always more than dance music.

Thus there is a sensuous truth behind rock music which is not attached to the logic of the structural detail but rather to the sound of the surface characteristics of the musical form. Put together from a style-dependent repertoire from more or less fixed 'standard' playing formulas, rhythmic models and stereotyped sounds which, like the parts of a kaleidoscope, form continually changing patterns, this musical form corresponds to a mode of perception and use in which music is not taken as a form of expression similar to speech with prescribed structures of meaning but as a body-orientated sensuous experience. The Who's Keith Moon put it in this way: 'Of course we take our music seriously. But we don't give any messages. People can take what they want from our songs' [translated from German].[38] The essential nature of the rock experience does not consist of decoding the music as a structure of meaning but rather in being able to place one's own significance on the sensuous experience which it provides. Thus music is performed according to an aesthetic of sensuousness.

4

'My Generation': rock music and sub-cultures

Rock music developed as one element of a complex cultural context. Within this context, at any given time, its playing styles and stylistic forms acquire a specific significance, support meanings and values which allow it to function as a medium for the experiences of everyday life. Rock music is neither a musical reflection of reality nor mere entertainment. Together with often bizarre as well as banal everyday objects – carefully selected clothes, hairstyles, the motorbike (cultivated as an infantile symbol of masculinity), razor-sharp steel combs, pointed shoes, chains or metal-studded leather armbands – rock forms the material context of cultural leisure behaviour. It is the respective fans who, with these objects, allocate precisely defined meanings to rock, and who set in motion a dialectical relationship between musical form and cultural usage which has continually spawned new playing styles. In the words of Simon Frith: 'The rock audience is not a passive mass, consuming records like corn-flakes, but an active community, making music into a symbol of solidarity and an inspiration for action.'[1]

Because of this it is impossible to consider rock music without placing it in its social and cultural contexts. Rock music is not the musical means of expression of youth in general, swinging from one 'craze' to another according to the latest fashion. It is only in the commercial reflection offered by the music industry that rock appears like this. In fact, each of rock's stylistic forms and playing styles is linked to concrete social experiences and cultural contexts, within which it continues to exist long after the mass media have lost interest. Even while the Beatles were celebrating their great triumphs in sixties Britain, rock'n'roll, where everything had started, had not disappeared and was not forgotten. To its fans it remained what it always had been.

These fans made up the audiences of the anonymous bands who shared their passion for rock'n'roll, far from the media fuss surrounding the Beatles. It was only much later, at the end of the seventies, that this same rock'n'roll scene reappeared briefly in public view, this time under the label of pub rock (a term coined by the music paper *Melody Maker*) and represented by groups like Dr Feelgood and Lew Lewis.

Reading the history of rock music as presented by the music industry in the context of its international marketing strategy gives rise to a fundamental misunderstanding. Rock developed not through an arbitrary linear progression of styles, but organically through its respective cultural contexts of use, embedded in the concrete structures of everyday life and specific social experiences and forming a multi-layered totality composed of parallel streams and separate 'scenes' diverging more and more widely. But, in its continuing frantic search for new material, the music industry reflected rock's organic evolution as a one-dimensional process of development. Of course, the industry's stance does not mean that anything outside this context would have been left entirely to its own devices. Rock music is in any case intimately linked to the conditions of studio music production. But the industry's investment decisions, particularly expenditure on advertising, promotion and sales, have always depended on what would make the most money at any given time. Such decisions are not only influenced by which musical movement has the greatest number of potential record purchasers, but also by which of the possible target groups is prepared to spend the most money on records. But this is a completely different story from what actually takes place in the cultural use of rock. Here rock is interwoven with the structures of ordinary life as it is actually lived and with the formation of leisure, which links it to both age-specific and class-specific experiences. Only selected parts of the diverse spectrum of such links were ever commercially exploited. Thus, to a listener indifferent to this stylistic blowing hot and cold it might appear not only that one trend followed another, but also that rock music spoke, in particular, for a youth for whom the consciousness of belonging to the same generation had wiped out all social differences. In reality though, as the British youth sociologists Graham Murdock and Robin McCron have established, rock music:

'confirms and strengthens class differences instead of creating a classless youth society'.[2] And, in addition, rock music is so closely related to the social, class-specific experiences of its listeners that it only becomes comprehensible when considered as a medium for these experiences; detached from these it loses all meaning. Even the music industry has been unable to dissolve or manipulate away this context. The industry's effectiveness is in fact based on making this context more general and allowing it to manifest itself to all teenagers together. Charlie Gillett pointed out that even the phenomenal success of the Beatles in the sixties was due particularly to the fact that they presented the acceptable face of working-class teenagers, instead of denying the social origins of their music:

Their social message was rarely expressed, but hung about their heads as an aura of impatience with convention and evident satisfaction with wealth and fame, and was expressed in their carefully chosen style of bizarre clothes. Where authors had shown working-class youth as caged within a harsh physical world ..., the Beatles presented working-class youth loose and free, glad to be out, unafraid to snub pretension, easily able to settle in comfortably where a rest could be found.[3]

Of course, the media image that the Beatles supported did not change anything in the real situation of British working-class teenagers and the actual conditions of their everyday lives. The Beatles put this type of music back into working-class teenagers' usual everyday existence and gave it a particular significance in this context. Other bands followed their lead and adapted their playing to the structures of meaning being developed here, creating a new stylistic form of rock music. The result was hard rock, represented at the end of the sixties by groups like Uriah Heep, Black Sabbath and Led Zeppelin. And the cycle began again.

Thus it has always been socially determined groups of fans who, in their leisure behaviour, have developed values and meanings in relation to rock music which have been able to form the starting point for new developments. And we can therefore only agree with Lawrence Grossberg's statement:

Rock and roll is not only characterised by musical and stylistic heterogeneity; its fans differ radically among themselves although they may listen to the same music. Different fans seem to use the music for very different purposes and in very different ways; they have different boundaries defining not only what they listen to but what is included within the category of rock and roll.[4]

This has too often been overlooked and has thereby encouraged a concept of rock music which has placed it in the social no-man's-land of a classless youth culture, thereby removing it from precisely those contexts which alone make it comprehensible.

Even when, in 1965, The Who released their now famous 'My Generation',[5] it was not an expression of a comprehensive consciousness of belonging to a particular generation, even though this was how it seemed and it was often misunderstood in this way. Yet what is emphasised in the song and what, in live performances, was regularly combined with a spectacular auto-da-fé of instruments and amplifiers – systematically reducing them to firewood – simply corresponded to the self-perception of a small section of British working-class teenagers to whom involvement with rock music had become a cultural process of a quite particular kind. These teenagers called themselves Mods, a term derived from Modernists. The Who seemed to them the very incarnation of their concept of rock music, and they were also the first band to adopt in their overall appearance the pattern of cultural use of music developed by their fans instead of merely providing the musical object of this use. Peter Townshend, the leader and artistic brains of The Who, later admitted this quite frankly in an interview for the American music magazine *Rolling Stone*: 'What the Mods taught us in the band was how to lead by following.'[6]

This brought an aspect of rock music to the surface which first made it obvious that rock music is not only music per se, it also stands at the centre of cultural contexts which are created by the fans and which are materialised through a repertoire of objects, gestures and codes of behaviour which have obviously been chosen with great care. What made the Mods different from their contemporaries was not only their taste in music, which focussed on rock'n'roll's rhythm & blues roots and its development in American soul music and, diverging as it did from the commercial Beatlemania of the time, was represented in Britain above all by groups like The Who, The Kinks, the early Rolling Stones, The Small Faces or the Spencer Davis Group. The Mods' hallmarks also included a motorscooter, which had to be an Italian model, a Lambretta TV 175. With its battery of lights, horns and mirrors this recently popularised mode of transport was transformed into an obvious cult object. Fashionable, well-cut suits, the obligatory parkas to wear over them and a neat, short haircut were just as much part of being a Mod as the almost ritual arrangement of their leisure. Next to the scooter an excessive cult of dancing occupied centre stage in a Mod's leisure. The cult led them to spend every free evening in one of the West End music clubs or in the Soho rhythm & blues clubs. At the weekends these evenings would carry on into the early hours of the morning and the Mods countered the inevitable exhaustion of this continual ecstasy of dancing with pharmaceutical stimulants, amphetamines. The core of the Mods was composed of fifteen- to eighteen-year-old teenagers from the East End suburbs or the new housing estates in South London who belonged to a social milieu made up of a section of the working class which was participating, within certain limits, in the increasing prosperity of the consumer society and which had a secure basis for its livelihood. They were in training or were already working and seemed to accept without reservation the role that was intended for them, that of taking their place among the working class of a capitalism revolutionised by technology. There was nothing particularly special about them except that, with the conspicuous and exotic nature of their leisure behaviour, they provided the social basis for an important branch of British rock music.

In Britain, American rock'n'roll and the early Northern Mersey Beat had already been anchored in similar fixed structures of cultural leisure behaviour. At the time their fans called themselves Teddy Boys. Their 'DA' haircut – an elaborate quiff on the back of the head held in place with hair-cream – was a tribute to American rock'n'roll models. 'Shoestring' ties, long jackets with velvet lapels and crepe-soled shoes bore witness to the fact that a rigid code of dress was just as much a group symbol for them as for the Mods barely a decade later. The leisure behaviour of Teddy Boys also followed a series of unwritten, but definite, rules. The homage they paid to physical and practical force earned them quite a few headlines in the media, but the connection with music was not so clear. In fact, in their Liverpool years, even the Beatles found their most loyal followers among the Teddy Boys, but they themselves never belonged to this group and very quickly distanced themselves from this environment. By contrast, The Who made it obvious even to public opinion that rock music was shaped by distinct sub-cultures, acquiring from them meanings and values which the music industry merely adopted and exploited. According to the analysis of John Clarke, a British cultural studies theorist: 'the major developments in commercial Youth Culture have been derived from innovations originating *outside* the commercial world, at a "grass-roots" level. To be successful, an impetus of this kind must develop from local contexts and interactions, and satisfy local "needs", before attracting large-scale commercial involvement'.[7]

The local contexts and interactions which John Clarke mentions here are a component of sub-cultures which play a central role in the development of rock music. Behind each of rock's stylistic forms and playing styles lie complex cultural contexts of a particular type, local 'scenes' which include precisely defined variations on an involvement with music, putting these in stable relationships with the everyday lives of their fans. The Teddy Boys formed the cultural frame of reference for the early Mersey-beat, the Mods for the rhythm & blues oriented branch of British beat music, while the Rockers preserved traditional rock'n'roll. In the late sixties psychedelic rock was supported by the student hippy sub-culture, whereas hard rock and heavy metal were linked to the skinheads, another working-class splinter group. Right up to punk and new wave, the history of rock is interwoven with more or less conspicuous teenage sub-cultures. They occupy a central status in rock music, because they are composed of the very teenagers who are most intensely involved with music, representing their respective fans, thus linking the stylistic forms of rock with meanings and values which give them a particular significance in the structure of teenagers' daily lives. The fact that this process requires a framework of sharply distinguished and intensified cultural relationships, to allow the sub-cultures to stand out from their social background, is rooted in the social nature of highly-developed capitalism and the cultural processes which it sets in motion.

With the aim of maximising profits, all products in this situation are surrounded with a web of social significance right from the outset through advertising and aesthetic presentation as a further inducement to purchase, which quite overlays their actual utility value. Thus a pair of trousers is no longer just an article of clothing, but also a social symbol, promising the wearer youthfulness, sportiness or an erotic aura, making him look like a 'man of the world' or whatever else the imaginative variations of the advertising experts on the theme of 'trousers' might be. In this context Boris Penth and Günter Franzen wrote: 'everything is already possessed and overlaid with immensely powerful socially produced images'.[8] Of course, this was particularly true of music production, whose products by their very nature support meanings and which are always made up of sound *and* meaning. Increasing the meanings they support, making them a moment of an ideological total context quite independent of the direct content of the songs, is not difficult because it is far less obvious. We will consider this in more detail later.

In contrast to this the question has always been posed whether this really results in the total manipulation of rock listeners by an all-embracing ideology of consumption, whether the listeners genuinely unconditionally accept the constant ideological meanings which come with rock and whether they become spiritually enslaved to commerce. Paul Corrigan and Simon Frith formulated this question as follows: 'Certainly the agencies of pop culture (record companies and teenage magazines and clothes shops and so on) *exploit* young people (hardly a surprising aspect of capitalism); the question is to what extent they *manipulate* them.'[9] And their own answer was: 'the fact that young people are heavily involved in commercial institutions does not mean that their response is simply a determined one'.[10] Indeed quite the opposite, since they are able to replace the music in the context of their everyday life and leisure, and within this context imbue it with their own meanings and values. For, as we have already seen, rock music is based on a song concept which only reveals its significance in precisely such contexts, and merely provides its listeners with a medium which they themselves must make active use of. These listeners, therefore, always react to commercial products in a class-specific manner, linked to the background of their own social experiences which even commerce is unable to erase. And the contexts in which they place music, as part of this process, have to become more and more densely packed, the more comprehensively the music industry, for its part, surrounds rock music with a cultural context made up of fashion, magazines, media images and the aura of its stars. Thus these contexts condense into developed sub-cultures which, with their deliberate signs of being different, play an

important role in the social conflict over the cultural meaning
and value of rock music. As Iain Chambers put it: 'Clothes
become "weapons", "visible insults" in a cultural war, and
make-up becomes "face-painting".'[11] From the unconventional
conglomeration of insignificant everyday objects sub-cultures
develop a material context of cultural behaviour which is stable
enough to allow those meanings and values which the music
embodies for them to be fixed in it.

So, using mirrors, lamps and horns, the Mods made their
scooters look like apparitions from science fiction stories, like
rolling technical monsters. The way they changed a harmless
means of transport into an outwardly menacing, futuristic
symbol, seemingly both the victim and caricature of a fascination
with everything technical, clearly corresponded to the way they
used music. For them rock music was the mysterious essence of
a modernity which both opened up prospects and opportunities
and also had its menacing aspects, reflecting the rhythms of the
industrial age which literally had to be 'danced out' in order to
keep up with them. The style of their involvement with rock
music lent it the lascivious and asocial aura of the night life in
the morbid entertainment districts of capitalist cities, through
which they usually rode round and round in their scooter con-
voys. It is therefore not surprising that they indulged in a stylistic
variant of rock which linked the energy of rhythmic conciseness
with technical orgies of sound – or at least what passed for them
in those days. Rock music as the pulse of the present translated into sound, as concentrated energy, injecting tension and
vibration into body and nerves on lethargic evenings, as the
power-house of a wild devotion to leisure and as the central
element of the organisation of sensuous experience which broke
through the restricted field of experience of school, work and
domesticity in front of the television every evening – these were
the key elements of the Mods' use of music. The releases of The
Who and the Rolling Stones between 1964 and 1966 provide
almost classic testimonials to this conception of music.

And, as with the Mods, sub-cultures generally produce complex systems of meaning which manifest themselves in the
cultural leisure behaviour of the teenagers committed to them
and which are linked to the easily available profane materials of
everyday life. It is obvious that this is anything but a form of

passive consumer behaviour. Instead, it bears witness to an astonishing creative energy which only a very superficial examination could fail to expose. The fact that consumer goods industries and commercial mass culture provide the same things for everyone, the same images, the same sounds and the same everyday objects does not mean that everyone uses these in the same way. The myth of rock music as a classless youth culture only arose because it was assumed that because teenagers of all social classes were fascinated by the same songs they must all find the same meaning in them. Rock music is the object of an active cultural use which is socially very diverse and which at the same time includes those everyday objects which lend themselves to the often pithy and witty expression of particular meanings, whether these be long, short or gaudily coloured hair, trousers, jackets, shirts, socks or shoes, combs, armbands, chains or safety-pins, the modern remnants of older fashions, motorscooters or motorbikes.

The use of the concept 'sub-culture' to describe those cultural contexts which give rise to particular systems of meaning was significantly discredited at the end of the sixties when the ideology of the student movement and their sub-cultural offspring, the hippies, adopted the term and interpreted it in the sense of a 'subversive culture'. They linked this to the hope of a revolutionary explosive force, supposedly residing in these subcultures, which was to make the youth of the world the creators of a completely new society, beyond both capitalism and socialism. History has long since pronounced its judgement on this movement. The revolutionary dreams of the hippies were either vaporised in a haze of drugs or provided a small group of desperate lunatics with the justification for a campaign of urban guerilla warfare with no regard for people at all. Sub-cultures are not subversive, but are an expression of the cultural process of differentiation which is characteristic of the way of life in highly-developed capitalism, a process which begins to form at the point of contact between class-specific and age-specific experiences. The process gives expression to the social problems of life *in* the capitalist system but not to a political protest *against* it. Even the hippies considered culture and music a supposedly 'revolutionary' alternative to politics, which distinguished them from the radical sections of the student movement in American and

Western European universities. In spite of the anti-capitalist views which they expressed, they were not opposed to the capitalist organisation of society in particular, but rather to social institutions in general. They did not call for the political change of social structures, but for their removal altogether. With this approach they occupy a special place in the teenage sub-cultures of the post-war period, which places them in the tradition of the nineteenth-century bohemians. They were interested in an alternative lifestyle outside the categories of 'work' and 'leisure', of which rock music along with other forms of music, particularly Eastern ones, only formed part. They were not primarily rock fans. The teenage sub-cultures of the Teddy Boys, Mods, Rockers, Crombies, Skinheads and Punks which arose around rock music belonged to the different strata of working-class teenagers and were therefore necessarily limited to leisure. It is for this reason that music plays an important role, for it moulds an all-embracing leisure environment, including the mass media as well as local leisure facilities, discotheques, clubs and dance halls, which brings teenagers together. This is an environment in which class-specific experiences can be lived out and expressed. But this is not a protest against the social origins of such experiences, and we have to concur with John Muncie, when he writes: 'In many subcultures (certainly not in all of pop culture) there is a hidden potential for resistance and political action, but such potential is hardly ever realized partly because of lack of interest and organization and partly because of the extent of external control.'[12]

In this respect one of the most widespread misconceptions of rock music is to see it as an expression of the protest of young working-class people in a capitalist society against the constraints of their social existence. Rock music is much more closely involved with the class-specific experiences formed under these constraints. In the sub-cultures which grew up around rock music the problems of the class experiences of young working-class people find a particularly clear and age-specifically divided expression. According to Graham Murdock and Robin McCron sub-cultures: 'can therefore be seen as coded expressions of class consciousness transposed into the specific context of youth and reflective of the complex way in which age acts as a mediation both of class experience and of class consciousness.'[13]

For teenagers experience their class situation in a completely independent way. And because of this, with capitalism's increasing pace of social development, their individual opportunities in life diverge from those of their parents even though these remain structured along class-specific lines. In spite of all the differences these opportunities are still influenced, as their parents' were, by educational disadvantages, by the limit on earnings imposed by being the section of society with the smallest portion of society's wealth, by dead-end jobs and the specialisation and routines of work. The lives mapped out for them are therefore as much related to their parents' as they are different. But another part of the age-specific nature of the class experience under capitalism is that, at a formative stage of their development, working-class teenagers are exposed in school to the direct constraints of a bourgeois institution, with which they are forced to come into conflict just as much as they are with the commercial leisure opportunities provided for them. This results in age-specific reactions to problems which affect the whole working class. In teenage sub-cultures these age-specific reactions are merely condensed into a cultural form which allows them to be expressed and lived out:

In addressing the 'class problematic' of the particular strata from which they were drawn, the different sub-cultures provided for a section of working-class youth (mainly boys) one strategy for negotiating their collective existence. But their highly ritualised and stylised form suggests that they were also attempts at a solution to that problematic experience: a resolution which, because pitched largely at the symbolic level, was fated to fail. The problematic of a subordinate class experience can be 'lived through', negotiated or resisted; but it cannot be resolved at that level or by those means.[14]

Nevertheless, it is important to stress that rock music, although commercially produced and distributed, functions as an essential element of the class context of the working class under capitalism. Even Mod sub-culture, and the music of The Who, the Rolling Stones and the other rhythm & blues oriented bands which supported it, was in the mid-sixties nothing more than a class-specific reaction by working-class teenagers to the social reality of British capitalism of the time. And this social reality appeared significantly different to them than it had either to their parents or to their sub-cultural predecessors, the Teddy

Boys. The Teddy Boys had represented the unskilled section of the young working classes for whom British consumer society was never a reality. Their leisure behaviour, including their involvement with music, was never a conflict with the ideology of the consumer society, but was a form of cultural self-assertion, carried through with force if necessary. In contrast, the Mods came from a section of the working class which was able to participate in the economic growth of British capitalism in the fifties. In Britain, the years 1951 to 1964 saw 'a steadier and much faster increase (in the average standard of living) than at any other time in the century'.[15] But what remained unchanged in spite of this were both the inequality in the proportional shares in the blessings of prosperity and social injustice. That section of the young working class for which the capitalist pleasure of consumption had to some extent been available at home, but which itself had hardly had the opportunity to walk into the future on certain paths of prosperity, was now asking itself what the value of a freedom was that was reduced to the choice between a growing number of washing powders from different manufacturers. They had still to achieve living standards even comparable to their parents'. There could be no continued growth in prosperity without increasing the working class' proportional share of society's wealth. But in fact the signs pointed far more to crisis than to continued growth. In 1963 unemployment reached a level of 3.6 per cent of the population, its highest level since 1940.[16] In direct contrast to their parents these teenagers were once again becoming more clearly and directly conscious of the barriers of class allegiances. Those teenagers who reacted actively began to transform the problematic and contradictions of this experience into a cultural form, one in which they could be expressed and worked out. Charles Radcliffe described the sub-culture of the Mods, their leisure rituals, their exclusive style in clothes and their excessive involvement with music as a: 'furious-consumption programme which seemed to be a grotesque parody of the aspirations of the Mods' parents'.[17]

In fact the Mods reacted to the questionable nature of the consumer society ideology they were experiencing in a way which expressed distance through excess. Their outward appearance matched that of the dummies in department store windows down to the smallest detail. They were just a touch too neat and a touch too well dressed not to have a rather unnatural and unsettling effect. By appearing at work or at school like a walking dummy they caricatured the rituals of consumption without quite escaping them. A working-class teenager who once chooses as the focus of his leisure those city nightclubs usually reserved for the high society in-crowd drowning in boredom, is breaking out of the social role-play and is quite definitely not behaving in the way working-class teenagers are supposed to behave. This teenager has seen through the emptiness of a strategy of life bound to the forces of consumption, but without being able to find an escape. He confronts the obvious senselessness of this sort of life by behaving in a senseless manner. This was nowhere more accurately formulated than in the Rolling Stones' 1965 release '(I can't get no) Satisfaction'.[18] With their cult of modernity the Mods created a cultural form which parodied the ideology of the consumer society and at the same time expressed the lack of a concept of life with any future prospects. This was also the reason for the despairing transfiguration of their own youth which The Who formulated in 'My Generation' (Hope I die before I get old). This was the *one* possibility of escaping from the clutch of bourgeois ideology.

Thus, just as in Mod sub-culture industry's mass-produced goods were used and had their meaning altered, functioning as cultural raw material, the music industry for its part used the cultural relationships developed around music by the teenage sub-cultures as the raw material for the manufacture of their commercial product. In fact, once it became obvious that rock was far more than just music, the engine of commerce went full speed ahead. As Iain Chambers commented:

Around 1964–5 there occurred a decisive shift in the economy of public imagery surrounding pop music. Pop stopped being a spectacular but peripheral event, largely understood to be associated with teenage working-class taste, and became the central symbol of fashionable, metropolitan, British culture. It had moved from being a show business mutant to becoming a symbolisation of style.[19]

At that time the Mod sub-culture provided the ingredients for an unparalleled fashion craze, in which industry used the entwining of music in a meaningful sub-cultural context for its own complex marketing purposes. The myth of 'swinging London' was created in the fashion boutiques and record shops of London's Carnaby Street, a term which put its stamp on this period and made rock music an international cultural phenomenon. In John Clarke's words:

The whole mid-1960s explosion of 'Swinging London' was based on the massive commercial diffusion of what were originally essentially Mod styles, mediated ... into a 'mass' cultural and commercial phenomenon. The Beatles era is one of the most dramatic examples of the way what was in origin a sub-cultural style became transformed, through increasingly commerical organisation and fashionable expropriation, into a 'pure' market or 'consumer' style.[20]

Although the period from 1964 to 1966 was later linked to the Beatles, in fact the Mod heroes dominated this time. This is quite obvious even in the purely commercial categories of the charts, the weekly listing of the best-selling records. During this period only eight of the Beatles' total of eighty-two releases reached the top ten. During the same period the Rolling Stones and The Kinks made the top ten nine times, in spite of their significantly smaller output, and The Who reached the top ten six times. 'Swinging London' was moulded by the Mod concept of music and their cult bands, including, with those bands already mentioned, a number of other bands with only one, two or three top ten successes. The view of this period later shifted significantly because rock music has always been regarded as the history of individual bands and removed from the context of its cultural use. The fact that during this period the Beatles released the greatest number of songs and therefore in total also sold the greatest number of records, that in 1965 they received MBEs from the Queen and therefore doubtless had the most spectacular career of any rock group says something about their commercial potential as the object of music industry investment, but is not by any means the same thing as an analogous cultural effectiveness. Although none of the Mod cult bands achieved a similar sensational career, taken together from 1964 to 1966 they still left deeper marks than the Beatles could do as a single group. In contrast to all the myths Iain Chambers cannot be contradicted in his view: 'At the same time, with their royal premieres and MBEs, the Beatles had seemingly been absorbed into the cushioned category of "family entertainment".'[21] The extensive reflection of Mod sub-culture in the fashion market and the mass media documented the mechanics of the capitalist exploitation of sub-cultural forms, but at the same time contributed to the spread of these forms and developed new creative opportunities for them, opening up to them the technical and economic potential of the media.

Thus teenage sub-cultures with their class-specific structures and commercial mass culture, mainly produced by the media, do not form a rigid contrast to one another. They rather permeate one another, though in a highly contradictory way, and simply represent a differing application, influenced by class contrasts, of the *same* cultural objects, musical forms and institutions. This aspect is very important. Without it the contradictory dialectic of the cultural use of commercial mass products remains incomprehensible. Commercially produced mass culture on the one hand and the sub-cultures with their class-specific organisation on the other merely form differing cultural contexts and relationships around the same objects. Even rock music seems different in its relationship with the media than in the everyday lives of its fans. Rock music is always both part of a commercial product *and* an object of class-specific cultural use, whereby the one limits and conveys the other. The Who, The Kinks and the Rolling Stones only really advanced to the status of cult bands in Mod sub-culture when they were in a position to use all the technical possibilities of the transformation of musical creativity then available – including the distribution of their music over the mass media – and thus had long since lost the status of a local amateur band. Rock music is not a form of folk music, not the spontaneous product of a sub-cultural community of fans, which is then constantly merely granted the unavoidable fate of commercial status. Sub-cultures form far more around the cultural use of industrial products, of commercial mass products, whether these be articles of clothing, motorbikes or even records. It is only natural that teenagers from a class of industrial workers should also transport their class-specific experiences, if they have any at all, through those objects which they know well and are comfortable with, whose 'secrets' they know, instead of evading these issues and escaping into a 'folk art' village idyll.

Thus it is no contradiction that the creative peak of Mod sub-culture coincided with the peak in its commercial exploitation in the mid-sixties. If this was also the beginning of its decline this is only because commercial exploitation of cultural forms always means their boundless generalisation as well. The problem with commerce is not that its mechanisms want to remove music from the hands of its fans. The belief in the folk music qualities of rock, in its origins in the spontaneous creativity of the community of its fans, was always a romantic idea which never corresponded to the reality. Rock music is linked to the technical possibilities of the recording studios, and represents an industrial product, whose high technical quality is part of its cultural potency. Its commercial utility is in this respect an indispensable precondition, just as the technical and financial cost which underlies it forces upon rock an economic dimension. The only problem with this is that in the context of class contrasts it is subjected to a profit interest that has become independent, which penetrates far beyond social and even national relationships, resulting in the limitless generalisation of cultural forms of expression into a comprehensive commercial mass culture. But this robs them of their social content, formalises them and transforms them into a non-committal fashion phenomenon which quickly wears itself out.

Even Mod sub-culture trod this path eventually. For what at first corresponded to the social experiences of a particular section of British working-class teenagers was made ubiquitous in fashion boutiques, the mass media and young people's magazines, in advertising and in the record market and was redefined as a youth model. The Mods' style of dress, their music and their leisure rituals were presented in such a way as to rob them of their original class-specific context, within which they had possessed social significance. Gary Herman described this phenomenon using the example of the music programme 'Ready, Steady, GO!', introduced in 1963 by the British commercial television station, ITV. This programme quickly became the most popular of its kind and played a very important role in the British music scene. The Rolling Stones, The Who, Dusty Springfield, The Animals, The Kinks, The Moody Blues and somewhat later even Jimi Hendrix, all largely owed their popularity to this television programme. Herman wrote:

'Ready, Steady, GO!' was an enormously popular pop programme, on the lines of the earlier '6.5 Special', with a live studio audience and groups miming to their records. It was part of the vast publicity machine that ensured a profit for the producers of mod-style goods. Each member of the audience received a politely worded letter reminding him or her to dress stylishly, to dance his or her best, not to smoke and generally to behave like a credit to British youth while on show.[22]

The care taken over the preparation of this programme which Herman describes shows the mechanisms on which the commercial generalisation of sub-cultural forms and styles rested. The important thing was to release these forms from their original context, a process which was entirely conscious and planned, as the example shows. 'Ready, Steady, GO!' therefore contributed in large measure to the redefining of the hallmarks of Mod sub-culture, most of all of course their music, as a desocialised symbol for a particular generation.

When in this way Mod sub-culture had finally become commercial mass culture and had lost its social distinction, it ceased to exist as a sub-culture. At other points in the social spectrum the process of forming consistent cultural contexts around music by particular groups of teenage fans began all over again. In fact, in parallel with the commercial generalisation of Mod culture, this process had already led to a clearly different pattern of cultural leisure behaviour in the Rockers. The Rockers came from the underprivileged strata of the working class and naturally were unable to get anywhere with the caricaturing consumption fetish of the Mods. They articulated their social experiences in quite a different way, returning to original rock'n'roll like the Teddy Boys had in the fifties. The system of meaning and value which they created in their cultural leisure behaviour was then developed by their cultural descendants, the Skinheads, in a direction which offered an anchor point for the playing styles of hard rock.

Yet in spite of the significance of such sub-cultural contexts in the development of rock music and its different stylistic forms, we must not overlook the fact that these contexts are only supported by a relatively small circle of active fans. Most teenagers only have a more or less playful relationship with these, one which often changes from one sub-culture to another. Simon Frith is quite correct in pointing out that not every teenager is an active rock fan and not every teenager gives rock music such a binding status in his leisure behaviour:

Most working-class teenagers pass through groups, change identities, play their leisure roles for fun; other differences between them – sex, occupation, family – are much more significant than distinctions of style. For every youth 'stylist' committed to a cult as a full-time creative task, there are hundreds of working-class kids who grow up in loose membership of several groups and run with a variety of gangs.[23]

Of course, it is only this factor that makes possible the commercial generalisation of sub-cultural contexts and forms of expression into an all-embracing fashion phenomenon, precisely because for most teenagers music and cultural leisure behaviour never attain such a sufficiently binding nature as to no longer leave them open to other possibilities. For this group, the original context of what they encounter as a commercial product in connection with music, styles of dress, hair fashions and media images is genuinely irrelevant. It provides them with a leisure identity, limited in time, which they accept with a sense of fun without giving it a particularly high status. The rock audience is always an aggregate composed not only of teenagers from very different social origins, but also of a mixture of active fans and those teenagers for whom rock music is merely one of a number of attractive leisure possibilities. Lawrence Grossberg drew attention to the fact: 'that there is no stable and homogenous rock and roll audience except as it is constructed through the marketing practices of the dominant economic institutions'.[24]

On the other hand, the significance of the teenage sub-cultures which grew up around rock music and became the social starting-point for the different playing styles and stylistic forms lies in this, that they continually evade and break up commercial contexts and link the music with their own values and meanings which are outside the control of commerce. In the words of John Clarke and Tony Jefferson, sub-cultures are: 'being involved in a struggle fundamental to the social order – that of the control of meaning ... It is significant that in this struggle for the control of meaning, one of the most frequent adjectives used to describe disapproved of behaviour by the young is "meaningless".'[25] Because of this, rock music stands at the centre of a continuing conflict about the values and meanings associated with it, a conflict which allows it to become the object of cultural class conflict in highly developed capitalist societies. The sub-cultures of teenage rock fans are bulwarks in this conflict.

5

'Revolution': the ideology of rock

One of the myths about rock music is that it arises spontaneously out of the common experience of musicians and fans. Rock music is, in fact, an industrial product and therefore in the first instance follows the *conceptions* which both musicians and producers have of their audience and their own activities, of the demands and possibilities of music and of the relationship between rock music and society. The fact that, as part of this process, musicians always attempt to match the thoughts and feelings, the patterns of value and cultural meaning of music of their fans, that they want and need to be successful, does not mean that they merely become an instrument for fulfilling the wishes of their audience. It is more the case that they react completely independently and consciously to the demands of their audience, the more so in fact because most musicians have a completely different social background from that of their working-class fans. Most rock musicians come from the *petit bourgeois* middle classes and have never experienced the everyday life of working-class teenagers. And even those musicians who have personal experience of this way of life live, as musicians, in a world characterised not always by wealth and luxury but certainly by freedom from the routine, the uniformity and the constraints of working in a factory or going to school. Pete Townshend, one of the few rock musicians who has come to see his position as a musician in a more realistic light over the years, once commented: 'Pop audiences and pop musicians are geared to different time structures, they lead different lives entirely.'[1]

In other words, rock musicians never adopt the experiences of their audience spontaneously and directly, but fragmented by ideology, by a way of looking at things which corresponds to their social perspective and which is the result of their artistic and political self-perception. And even if involvement with rock music is a relatively independent cultural process, it is fulfilled in relation to playing styles and stylistic forms, structures of sound and visual concepts of presentation which primarily follow the musicians' value judgements and the meanings they intended. These reflect the musician's view of himself as artist as well as the aesthetic and political claims which he connects with his music. So behind rock music stands not only a complex web of contexts of use, but also a context of reflection mediated in political and ideological terms which determines the musical performance – the ideology of rock.

This ideology became particularly clear in the late sixties when both musicians and audience began to be more consciously involved with rock music. In 1967 the Beatles released their first concept album *Sgt Pepper's Lonely Hearts Club Band*[2] a song cycle composed of enigmatic collages of lyrics and music. They followed this in 1968 with 'Revolution' (on the flip side of 'Hey Jude'),[3] the first of their songs to contain an explicit political statement, which also clarified how they defined their own social role as a rock band. Only a few weeks after the release of 'Hey Jude' the Rolling Stones released their famous song 'Street Fighting Man' on the album *Beggars Banquet*.[4] Another 1968 release, Pink Floyd's *A Saucerful of Secrets*,[5] was a record which began to extend the frontiers of rock with its sound montages flowing into one another, giving up the foreground emphasis on beat and rhythm in favour of more complex sound structures and extended chains of improvisation. Both in artistic and political terms these releases, together with a whole host of others, bore witness to a significant growth in self-awareness. Simon Frith's comment on the rock music of the late sixties was that: 'Rock was something more than pop, more than rock'n'roll. Rock musicians combined an emphasis on skill and technique with the romantic concept of art as individual expression, original and sincere. They claimed to be non-commercial – the organizing logic of their music wasn't to make money or to meet a market demand.'[6]

Rock music had become 'progressive', or at least this was how musicians, as well as journalists and fans, referred to the music which distinguished itself by virtue of its artistic and political ambitions from the purely commercial products of the music market. It was Frank Zappa who at that time created the most concise definition of such music:

If you want to come up with a singular, most important trend in this new music, I think it has to be something like: it is original, composed by the people who perform it, created by them – even if they have to fight the record companies to do it – so that is really a creative action and not a commercial pile of shit thrown together by business people who think they know what John Doe and Mr Jones really want.[7]

A sharp dividing line was now drawn between rock music, released from every suspicion of commercial motivation, and the usual chart-style pop music, and the justification for this division was provided by the professional rock criticism which arose at the time. The fact that with this self-perception rock musicians distanced themselves to a significant degree from their real activity as musicians was mostly due to the desperate state of the music industry, which even then was still experiencing serious difficulties in coping with the dynamics of what was to it a new market. Although rock music brought with it an enormous increase in turnover, it remained a closed book to the market strategists. They were most successful when they simply gave musicians a free hand. This of course nourished the musicians' illusion that, in contrast to traditional musicians, they were in control of the production and distribution of their music and were not forced to make any commercial concessions. But when they began to see their music as a medium for political conflict with the authority structures of state-monopoly capitalism, it was not long before the music industry made its view clear. Jac Holzman, President of Elektra Records, one of the three pillars of the media giant WEA Communications, explained to the magazine *Rolling Stone* in 1969: 'I would like to set the record straight and explain that Elektra is not the poor dupe of some kind of revolution. We think that the revolution will be won with poetry not politics, that poets will change the structure of the world. Young people have understood this message and understood it on the best possible plane.'[8] The music industry's turnover figures left no doubt about the 'best possible plane' of artistic commitment.

Yet however illusory it may have been, the artistic and political self-awareness of musicians in the late sixties made the ideological consciousness from which this music drew its sustenance more clearly visible than at any other point in rock's development. The basic structures remained the same, even if they continually found expression in new forms. Creativity, communication and a sense of community were to become the key concepts for this process. This did not happen by chance but rather had its source in contexts which have had a lasting influence on rock music: in the American folk- and protest-song movement and the political view of music which this spawned, as well as in the intellectual environment of the British art schools. Both of these played a great role in the formulation of the demands which formed the starting-point for rock musicians' consideration of their own activity, and which offered musicians concepts of society and art into which their ideological conscious-ness was interwoven. And the basis for this was their social position as musicians, the socio-economic nature of their activity.

Rock musicians earn their living by selling a service, their ability to make music. The exact content of this service is in fact determined by the purchasers, record companies and concert promoters, who turn the musician's ability into a commercial product. The musicians themselves can only offer their abilities, the purchasing decision rests with the music industry. This simple socio-economic process leads musicians to develop a particular perspective from which they consider themselves and the whole process of rock production and distribution. Despite the fact that music production – as we have already seen – has become a very complex and increasingly collectively organised process, musicians still play their part in this process as indi-vidual vendors of an individual service. Because of this rock music seems to them to be primarily a matter of their individ-uality. Seen from their point of view, musical performance is not a process organised socially under certain conditions, controlled by record companies, promoters and agents, but first and fore-most the realisation of their own personality, the outcome of their subjectivity and emotions. On the other hand, the economic status of their activity puts them in a strange hybrid position with respect to the industry. Although in an economic sense musicians are only service operators for record companies, agents and tour promoters, the particular nature of the service they perform demands that this service should be related to a quite different target group from the one which actually claims the service and pays for it. In terms of earning a living, musical performance is an economic relationship between the musician and the music industry, but in terms of the real nature of music it is a relationship between the musician and his audience. Thus, what the musician sells to the industry is not merely his musical ability, but this ability in relation to the particular audience for whom his music is intended. This allows the musician to occupy a position in which he represents his audience to the industry. This relationship reflects his personal conceptions, ideals and values as those of his fans, indeed as those of young people in general. He sees himself as the spokesman for *this* group of young people. The key to the ideology of rock lies in these thought patterns. The artistic and social concepts adopted by rock musicians are used in a way which always leads back to this.

It was Howard Horne and Simon Frith who drew attention to the role of the British art schools in the development of the artistic criteria and standards which underlay the development of rock music: 'Since the mid-1960s at least, every fine art student has been a potential rock musician. The history of British rock ... has been the history of the realisation of that potential: artists not just in music and song, but in terms of their multi-media organisation of image/performance/style.'[9] It is true that nearly all those British rock musicians who have had an influence on style have come from these artistic educational institutions, have completed design courses or have received the Diploma in Art and Design (DipAD), introduced in 1961. John Lennon was registered at the Liverpool College of Art from 1957 to 1959; Pete Townshend studied at London's Ealing Art College at the same time as Ron Wood, later a member of the Rolling Stones and Freddie Mercury of Queen; Ray Davies of The Kinks was from London's Hornsey Art College; Jeff Beck, guitarist with The Yardbirds, and Eric Clapton were both educated at London's Wimbledon College of Art; and even David Bowie and Adam Ant were art school graduates, from St Martin's School of Art and Hornsey Art College respectively. In this way there was always an impetus coming from British art schools which shaped musicians' artistic ideas, their view of the world and their conception of music. For instance, the jackets made out of Union Jacks with such a lack of respect, turning a whole series of sixties musicians into walking national flags, are an obvious adaptation of Jasper John's painted flag pictures from the world of American pop art, pictures which were part of the art schools' course material at the time. Behind Pete Townshend's spectacular orgies of destruction which at one time cost him his Rickenbaker guitar, amplifier and speakers every evening, lay a concept of art which was represented and taught at Ealing College of Art by the Austrian pop artist Gustav Metzke: art as the auto-destruction of objects. Here is one example of the way he did this: he would pour acid over pictures in order to produce art objects from the process of their decay; thus freed from the dimension of the 'manufactured' they do not remain attached to the flat reality of their appearance. In the sixties American pop art in particular was a constant source of inspiration for British rock musicians. Pete Townshend commented to *Melody Maker* in 1967: 'We play pop art with standard group equipment.'[10]

But apart from such direct influences from the fine arts, including the creation of album covers by famous pop artists – such as Peter Blake, who designed the cover for the *Sgt Pepper* LP, or Andy Warhol, whom the Rolling Stones have to thank for the cover of their LP *Sticky Fingers* – the art school experience, above all, provided rock musicians with the basis of their consciousness of themselves as musicians in artistic and ideological terms. The result was that, in contrast to the traditional pop song, the contradictory relationship of art and commerce, of artistic claims and popular culture, was reflected in rock music and became the driving force for its development. Later rock musicians were confronted with these problems at an early stage in the art schools. After all, the special position of these institutions within the British educational system forced the students to ask themselves right at the beginning, with one eye on later job prospects, how the claims of art and the necessity of earning a living could be reconciled.

British art schools are educational institutions relatively generously supported by grants which are supposed to maintain the ideal of the 'fine arts', something for which there has long been no room in the capitalist reality. When it comes down to it, however, the fine arts are not used by anyone and eke out an existence on the fringe of society. Even specialisation in the more practical sphere of design can hardly guarantee the prospect of a job. Industry prefers to rely on the pragmatism of its marketing strategists rather than to make space for the art school graduate's enthusiasm for improving the world. In fact, this situation allowed these semi-academic educational institutions to offer a singular cultural freedom, within which, far from capitalist theories of utility, a colourful student bohemian world gathered. Keith Richards of the Rolling Stones, who spent a few terms at Sidcup Art School in his home town of Dartford, but never graduated, later explained: 'I mean in England, if you're lucky you get into art school. It's somewhere they put you if they can't put you anywhere else.'[11] And, as Dave Marsh commented: 'In consequence, art schools tended to attract a great many students who were bright, lacked academic aptitude or discipline but hadn't the patience to learn a trade.'[12]

The atmosphere in the art schools was dominated just as much by intellectual snobbery as by the threat of coming up against a continuing crisis of existence. Their position as outsiders necessarily distanced them from the capitalist social system and its economic power centres, maintained the consciousness of the artist's social responsibility, but at the same time tempted students to adopt a limitless individualism. Art's claim to social and political effectiveness appeared here as an uncompromising avant-gardism. This view even intruded into the curriculum, where alongside fine arts courses, devoted to the traditional concept of art and to an individualistic modernism, there were also design courses, which investigated the artistic possibilities of modern mass communication through industrial design, fashion design and photography. The ideology of art which grew out of this was nicely described by Simon Frith and Howard Horne:

Art school ideology rests on the doctrine that art has something to say which produces unrest and movement. According to this definition, art could not be a passive instrument of capitalism's social and economic interests: it had to win back its central, influential position at the heart of cultural production – the mode of expression of students (and of rock) in the sixties borrowed heavily from Romantic philosophy with its emphasis on autonomy and creativity and from avant-garde manifestos of the early 20th century ... Art school ideology casts the self-love of the aesthete and the avant-gardist's sensitivity to the power of form into one style. In this ideology art, in its relation to the individual, is a matter of individuality, of a turning inward, of an obsession. In its relation to politics art attempts ... to reclaim proletarian street credibility (solidarity with those who vegetate on the fringe of the job market) as well as the bourgeois myth of the Romantic artist.[13]

The problem of how boundless individualism in artistic expression and social effectiveness could be linked to one another was thus bound to be forced onto centre stage. Creativity was a key term in the resolution of this problem. It legitimised the individualism of a bohemian artist's world, bound art to personality, individuality and lifestyle, but at the same time made it possible to see in art the liberation of man by reminding him of his own inner potential. Being creative meant removing the barriers which imprison man from within, meant self-realisation and freedom. Art appeared as the catalyst of this process as long as it succeeded in producing communication. And so, the second important plane of art school ideology postulated an ideal of communication, seeing in such an ideal the most immediate link between people. And again, the key to the realisation of the ideal of communication was to be seen in the individuality and personality of the artist. The more honest and sensitive, the more 'authentic' the artist's behaviour towards himself, the more immediate the communication with his audience. Thus the dominant image of the artist at British art schools was nothing more than a new version of the nineteenth-century Romantic philosophy of art. If so many art school students were attracted to rock music (which itself found its most receptive audiences in these art schools) it was because rock music offered them the opportunity of realising this image of the artist, of developing creativity and at the same time of earning a living. In addition, with its immediacy of rhythm and sound, rock music came nearest to the desired ideal of communication and was a source of cultural ideas. But above all, on the basis of modern mass communication, rock offered an opportunity of unifying art, music, design, fashion and youth in a single great experience. This aspect is the basis of rock's anti-commercial claim. Pete Townshend was being quite honest when he said in 1965: 'What we are trying to do in our music [is] protest against "show biz" stuff, clear the hit parade of stodge.'[14]

The individualistic artistic consciousness which the British art schools gave to rock music was not consistent with the commercial standardisation of music into a mass product based on the demands of the music market. Rock music had to be honest and a direct expression of the personality and individuality of the musician. In Simon Frith's apt description: 'the archetypal rock image is the guitar hero – head back, face clenched, his feelings visibly flowing through his fingertips'.[15] Behind the criticism of commerce, which was seen as the opposite of creativity and communication, lay the Romantic appeal to the autonomy of the artist, an ideal of honesty, upright behaviour and directness. The American rock critic Jon Landau put this quite characteristically: 'Within the confines of the media, these musicians articulated attitudes, styles and feelings that were genuine reflections of their own experience and of the social situation which had helped to produce that experience.'[16] Rock musicians' self-perception was dominated by the idea that music was the direct result of their particular individual subjectivity and emotions, a creative baring of man's inner psychic forces, of their belief that liberating these forces also freed man from the distortions and frustrations which the constraints of everyday life left behind them. Jimi Hendrix expressed this belief in these words: 'We make cosmic music, or ego-free music.'[17]

This conception had much to do with the fact that, during the late sixties, rock music was increasingly seen as a sound environment, open to new sound experiences – which sometimes led it far from its musical and cultural origins and included stimuli from non-European musical cultures as well as experimentation with electronics and recording techniques which went beyond the limitations of the song form. In the search for new possibilities of releasing creativity and penetrating to the innermost levels of consciousness and the depths of the unconscious, all previous musical boundaries which separated pop music from other fields of musical culture were overcome. In place of the motoric character of the *beat*, always driving onwards, music was now under the sign of *vibration*, the harmonious total sound of body, feeling consciousness and music. Within this, sound was considered a kind of materialisation of consciousness. The expansion of the sound environments which were traversed using music was seen as an expansion of consciousness, out of which were to arise new ways of perceiving the world and of acting within it. The important thing was to create out of music, light, physical and temporal feelings a total experience in which art and life were to be distilled into one unity. A widely held belief at the time was that the more creative the music, the more immediate the communication with the audience and therefore the fewer the compromises with commerce.

The artistic claims which this belief validated were aimed at the social effectiveness of music which began to separate 'progressive' rock from ordinary, 'commercial' pop music. Rock itself became an ideological category, for the postulated contrast between 'commercial' and 'progressive' music was above all a matter of musicians' self-perception. In fact, that rock music which saw itself as 'progressive' was under no less an obligation to the capitalist system of music production and distribution than its 'commercial' counterpart. Both adjectives functioned as value judgements which actually revealed more about the people who used them than about the music they were applied to. In 1968 CBS' Columbia record label put this to good use by constructing a promotional campaign using the slogan 'revolutionaries of rock' on the basis of the suggestive nature of the adjective 'progressive'. As Richard Neville reported:

Columbia Records' 'revolutionaries' program ... is being extended through April by field demand. The program's astounding success has forced the label to continue the campaign, which has been one of the most successful in Columbia's history and is even exceeding the success of Columbia's 'Rock Machine' promotion of last year. The 'revolutionaries' campaign is an all-out merchandising program on Columbia's rock album product and has served as the launching pad for a number of outstanding contemporary artists who had debuted on Columbia in the past three months.[18]

These included among others Janis Joplin, Santana, Blood, Sweat & Tears, Chicago and Leonard Cohen. But the crowd puller on this label was Bob Dylan, who had been under contract to Columbia since 1962. He was also the most important impetus towards a concept of rock which mediated itself through political contexts and therefore appeared claiming to be 'progressive'.

Dylan began in 1961 as a folk-singer in the tradition of the legendary American singer and worker-poet Woody Guthrie. In 1962, his connections with Susan Rotolo, full-time secretary of the Congress of Racial Equality (CORE), brought him into contact with the American civil rights movement, which was involved with the struggle against racial segregation in buses, schools, waiting rooms and restaurants and for the actual achievement of the rights laid down in the American constitution, regardless of skin colour and social origin. This movement quickly became a melting pot for all those people who wanted to settle the score with American capitalism after the conservative fifties. In April 1962 Bob Dylan wrote 'Blowin' in the Wind',[19] a song which became the battle-hymn of the American civil rights movement and which turned him into a singer of political protest songs. In August 1963 he stood next to Martin Luther King at the head of a column of 20,000 people, who were demanding an end to racial discrimination with a 'great march to Washington'. Dylan became a symbol of the protest against American capitalism. The battle lines of this conflict cut clear across all social groups and classes, but were drawn particularly between the generations. The conflict between the generations only broadened when the Johnson administration began to sacrifice the country's young men on the altar of a senseless and inhuman war in Vietnam. Bob Dylan, and with him Joan Baez, Phil Ochs and Tom Paxton, became the mouthpiece for this generation of American teenagers. Anthony Scaduto, Dylan's biographer, commented:

To Dylan must go some of the responsibility for the many hundreds of thousands of freaks around the country, trying to make a life outside the established society ... determined not to be caught in the traps of what is called civilization. Dylan's influence can be felt in those who are attacking the system by refusing to cooperate with it, or are mounting direct assaults against it ... Marcuse, Hesse, Fanon, Sartre, Camus, Proudhon and others, provided the ideology. But Dylan provided the emotional drive that brought it all home.[20]

Dylan's songs brought together all the people who took part in teach-ins and sit-ins, the activists of the Free Speech Movement in the American universities, and the hundred thousand plus participants in the anti-Vietnam war demonstrations in one great community, and they offered a connection between all the different groups in this diverse spectrum of the 'new left'. His songs took their political effectiveness from their power to foster this sense of community. What could be more natural, from this perspective, than to look for the political potential of the music of The Beatles, The Rolling Stones, The Who and the other British groups who, from 1964 onwards, were taking America by storm and uniting even more teenagers behind them. Might there not be a much greater explosive force in this music than could be achieved with sparse chords on an acoustic guitar? With this consideration in mind, in 1965 Bob Dylan went to the Newport Folk Festival, the annual place of pilgrimage of the folk music community, and, amidst the catcalls and booing of his traditional fans, linked his guitar to an amplifier and had the Paul Butterfield Blues Band accompany him with rock rhythms. The reaction of his followers led the folk musician Theodore Bikel to express himself directly afterwards in this laconic sentence from a letter to the magazine *Broadside*, the journal of the American folk movement: 'You don't whistle in church and you don't play rock'n'roll at a folk festival.'[21] But by doing this Dylan had shown a way forward which was not only followed by many former folk musicians but which placed rock music in contexts which led its development to follow increasingly political criteria.

Until this time, rock music as a form of commercial mass culture had encountered unanimous rejection from the political left. The arguments for this rejection had already been put forward in 1963 by the British *Daily Worker*, which, in the light of the beginnings of 'Beatlemania', concerned itself with the Beatles in a report from Liverpool. Its view was: 'The Beatles may be the pride of Merseyside, but it's too easy for talent scouts to exploit job-hunting youngsters, being fed dreams of instant fame and money.'[22] The fact that this music did in some way have its roots in the genuine everyday life of British working-class teenagers, instead of being created by professional songwriters, could not be argued away. But this did not change the attempt to see it as a particularly clever subterfuge of capitalist interests. Charles Parker probably formulated this most clearly when he wrote about British rock music: 'that pop is, in fact, now cherished by a ruling class as a peerless form of social control'.[23]

For a long time the political left considered rock music merely an unappetising expression of capitalism's ideological powers of temptation. What it found particularly galling was that a cultural phenomenon which had obviously become a mass social movement had allowed the sensuous pleasures of dancing and music to triumph so completely over a political consciousness seriously committed to the class struggle. This point of view now changed, released by Bob Dylan's spectacular conversion to rock music and in the light of the fact that in America this music affected the very generation of teenagers for whom the activists of the protest song movement saw themselves as spokesmen. If America's hopes were supposed to lie with its youth, as Bob Dylan formulated so emphatically in his song 'The Times They Are A-Changin''',[24] with a youth which was becoming increasingly radically politicised, then it was not a question of continuing to see youth's enthusiasm for rock in the same undifferentiated way as commercially inspired ideological imprisonment by capitalism. Protest songs brought with them the experience of the power of music to build a sense of community. And in the end this power proved stronger than the manipulative influence of the media, through which music had reached the mass of American teenagers and through which it had become a material power which manifested itself in the ever larger protest marches. Thus rock music was no longer under accusation for its dependence on the capitalist media and the naive political speechlessness of its lyrics. The political effectiveness of rock was supposed to be on a different plane, less easily grasped and therefore less easily controlled. Jann Wenner, who in 1967 founded the magazine *Rolling Stone*, the mouthpiece of 'progressive' rock music, expressed this view: 'Rock'n'roll music is the energy center for all sorts of changes evolving rapidly around us: social, political, cultural, however you want to describe them. The fact is, for many of us who've grown up since World War II, rock and roll provided the first revolutionary insight into who we are and where we are at in this country.'[25]

Rock music now looked like a time bomb, ticking loudly amidst the mechanisms of authority. It was seen as the source of energy which would make the motor of social change run faster and charge the batteries of social fantasy. The aesthetic radicalism with which rock bands sought to hold their ground against the norms of the traditional hit-parade pop which had dominated in the music business, was now seen as a sign of protest. In 1968, Robert Sam Ansons wrote in an essay for the news magazine *Time* that rock music is: 'not just a particular form of pop, but ... one long symphony of protest ... the proclamation of a new set of values ... the anthem of revolution'.[26]

The supposed protest character of rock's musical appearance relieved it of the necessity of taking a clear political position in its lyrics. The power of this music was in its effect on the senses.

John Sinclair, a former jazz critic who was one of the journalistic spokesmen of the protagonists of 'progressive' rock and also manager of the Detroit rock band MC 5 described this in the following words:

Rock is the most revolutionary power in the world – it is able to hurl people back to their senses and it makes people feel good. And this is exactly what revolution is made up of. On this planet we have to bring about a situation where everyone can feel good all the time. And we won't rest until we have achieved this. Rock is a weapon in the cultural revolution.[27]

Such positions, which gave rock a political ambience made up of protest, revolution and progressive claims for improving the world, concealed a potential for conflict which the American civil rights movement and particularly the Vietnam war allowed to mature. It was the students particularly who saw themselves faced with a situation which provoked them to political radicalism. The image of society with which they were presented in the universities clashed so intensely with the brutal reality of the Vietnam war, as portrayed every evening on millions of television screens, that a radical criticism of capitalism developed. It was consternation which led the students to act and encouraged them to see themselves as a social force both called to change society and in a position to do so. In their revolutionary model, revolutionary class consciousness was replaced by a generation consciousness to which rock music lent an apparent reality. Nowhere were these claims on rock music more clearly reflected than in a manifesto with which a group of students in San Francisco welcomed the Rolling Stones during their first American tour in 1967.

Greetings and welcome Rolling Stones, our comrades in the desperate battle against the maniacs who hold power. The revolutionary youth of the world hears your music and is inspired to even more deadly acts. We fight in guerilla bands against the invading imperialists in Asia and South America, we riot at rock'n'-roll concerts everywhere …

They call us dropouts and delinquents and draftdodgers and punks and hopheads and heap tons of shit on our heads. In Viet Nam they drop bombs on us and in America they try to make us make war on our own comrades but the bastards hear us playing you on our little transistor radios and know that they will not escape the blood and fire of the anarchist revolution.

We will play your music in rock'n'-roll marching bands as we tear down the jails and free the prisoners, as we tear down the State schools and free the students, as we tear down the military bases and arm the poor ... and create a new society from the ashes of our fires.

Comrades, you will return to this country when it is free from the tyranny of the State and you will play your splendid music in factories run by the workers, in the domes of emptied city halls, on the rubble of police stations, under the hanging corpses of priests, under a million red flags waving over a million anarchist communities ... ROLLING STONES – THE YOUTH OF CALIFORNIA HEARS YOUR MESSAGE! LONG LIVE THE REVOLUTION!!! [28]

Rock music was now placed in a context in which it no longer defined itself merely in musical terms, but also in political terms, in however illusory a manner these were expressed. If until then, for both musicians and fans, rock had been differentiated from the commercial 'plastic pop' of the 'stars' above all by its emotional directness and the honesty and sincerity of the feelings within it, it was now felt to be the carrier and expression of a generation consciousness, which the political activism of the students was supposed to have mobilised. Against this background the rock experience was supposed to be above all an experience of community and togetherness, wrenching teenagers out of their isolation in the family, in school, at work or in the universities, and reflecting their own frustrations back to them as the frustrations of their whole generation. Beneath the powerful rhythms and the amplified sounds they were welded together into a social force which was in a position to explode society. Or in Greil Marcus' words:

We fight our way through the massed and leveled collective safe taste of Top 40, just looking for a little something we can call our own. But when we find it and jam the radio to hear it again it isn't just ours – it is a link to thousands of others who are sharing it with us. As a matter of a single song this might mean very little; as culture, as a way of life, you can't beat it. [29]

Of course, the fact that rock music presented a realm of experience which allowed teenagers to feel themselves to be a community in spite of all social differences was just as much of an illusion as the political aspirations with which it was linked. But despite this, an element of community was to begin to play a decisive role in the consciousness of musicians. It put music under the postulate of a common experience and provided it with a political claim, and without these rock music – like rock'n'roll before it – would quickly have become an off-the-peg mass market product along the lines of hit-parade pop. But above all, this common experience and political claim contained the conceptual key which was to place musicians' artistic ambitions in a context which did not exclude commercial success but which also did not measure artistic achievements in terms of the highest royalties.

The concept of 'progressive' rock music concealed the problem of reducing commercial success and the musicians' artistic demands to a common denominator. The fact that rock musicians felt an obligation to an ideal of communication and creativity and that music was to them primarily a matter of the realisation of their own personality rather than merely a case of following a commercial calculation, did not mean that they were renouncing a mass audience or even that they were questioning mass success. In spite of their anti-commercial intentions, even for them mass effectiveness remained the basis for and gauge of artistic success. Manfred Mann once made this very clear: 'Pop music is probably the only art form that is totally dependent for its success on the general public. The more people buy a record, the more successful it is – not only commercially but artistically.'[30]

But if a relationship with a mass audience was not to be justified by crude market criteria, criteria were needed which could mediate between artistic demands and commercial success. This need was fulfilled by the theory of a common experience conveyed by music, a theory which had developed in the environment of the politically motivated involvement with rock music in the late sixties. So commercial success no longer implied conforming to the music market but rather the artistic realisation of what bound the rock community together. Admittedly, this was an ideological criterion which contained an inherent circular argument defending it against all criticism. Rock music was now seen as the expression of a community which rock itself had first established as it became commercially successful. That type of rock music which only followed the personal ideas of the musicians, without entering into any commercial compromises, and which was therefore 'authentic', counted as a mirror for the common experiences of all teenagers as long as it was able to chalk up commercial successes. The paradox of representing community with a type of music which is supported by the musician's individuality and the creative realisation of his personality dispelled an unshakeable belief in the common interests of musicians and fans which was the very basis of the ideology of rock.

Thus, rock music now found itself in a developed, argumentative context of reflection which was built up on the concepts of creativity, communication and a sense of community and which, to musicians, had become a framework for the definition of their own activity, of their role in society and their relationship with their audience. In the politicised climate of the sixties this naturally concentrated firstly on their political self-perception. It was this which determined the claim of their music to social effectiveness and which gave their artistic conceptions a concrete link with real life.

What this claim looked like and how it was politically formulated the Beatles documented in their song 'Revolution',[31] which also provoked a comprehensive debate on this issue. The statement behind the song presented a clear and unmistakable rejection of student political activism. Behind this lay a view of the world which projected society onto the individual's situation and which saw in the individual and in his deformities the origin of all problems. As long as people do not change, all changes to society are pointless. What is important is for man to revolutionise his consciousness and then 'it'll all be alright', according to this song's extremely vague credo. The lyrics were written from a standpoint which was indifferent to a dispute either over the role of music as a political instrument of social change or over the autonomy of the artist. For rock music the result of this was that it had to express the frustrations and manifestations of alienation in everyday life under capitalism in order to contrast them with the possibilities of a creative life. The sensory power of rock was to be the force which was really in a position to break through the encrusted realities of life. As John Lennon explained: 'The idea is not to comfort people, not to make them feel better, but ... to consistently put before them the degradations and humiliations they go through to get what they call a living wage.'[32] Of course this conjures up the idea that it is people's own conception of value which allows them to become prisoners of a system which cripples their lives with frustration and alienation. Pink Floyd's Roger Waters expressed this idea very clearly:

> Many people are robbed of their whole lives because they are trapped in the system. They are used to produce Volkswagens. People are paid for their work, buy televisions and fridges and believe that this compensates for the fact that they spend their whole lives putting cars together. And they live in this rut for 48 weeks out of every 52.[33]

To free them from this trap would first require the expansion of their consciousness, their field of experience and their sensitivity, would require them to add new dimensions to their lives, because this would be the only way to explode a system that lived off their deformities. It is not society, not the 'system' which shapes the people it needs to support it, people create a system which suits their needs. This is nothing more than the logical consequence of an individualism which looks at the world from the individual's point of view. Seen thus, every political act would have to appear as the inherent reaction of the system to problems which might indeed be placed in new contexts but which would not be solved. As Mick Jagger of the Rolling Stones clearly explained: 'I'm not rebelling against anything at all. I don't want to belong to this system, but that has nothing to do with rebellion.'[34] It is difficult to contradict this. Escaping the insidiousness of capitalism by renouncing televisions and fridges in order to free one's consciousness from the blessings of the giants of the electrical industry and the media groups really has nothing to do with rebellion and even less to do with revolution.

There was a prompt answer to the Beatles' 'Revolution', which had addressed the Left directly. It came from John Hoyland, who published an open letter to John Lennon in the Marxist newspaper *Black Dwarf*, the mouthpiece of the British student movement. The letter ran:

> What we're up against is not nasty people, not neurosis, not spiritual undernourishment. What we're confronted with is a repressive, vicious, authoritarian system. A system which is inhuman and immoral ... It must be destroyed, ruthlessly. This is not cruelty or madness. It is one of the most passionate forms of love ... Love which does not pit itself against suffering, oppression and humiliation is sloppy and irrelevant.[35]

Lennon reacted with a 'very open letter', published three months later in *Black Dwarf* in which, alongside his obvious annoyance at the personal attack on him as the originator of 'Revolution', he once again clarified his position. He wrote to John Hoyland:

I don't worry about what you, the left, the middle, the right or any fucking club boys think. I'm not that bourgeois ... I'm not only up against the establishment but you too. I'll tell you what's wrong with the world: people – so do you want to destroy them? Until you/we change our heads – there's no chance. Tell me of one successful revolution. Who fucked up communism, christianity, capitalism, buddism, etc. Sick heads, and nothing else.[36]

The storm of indignation which 'Revolution' provoked on its release as a single at the end of August 1968 had in fact already independently persuaded Lennon to make a significant change to the lyrics. This was done when the song was rerecorded for the double album *The Beatles*,[37] which because of the missing cover picture, also became known as the *White Album*. Here he added an 'in' to the original 'Don't you know that you can count me out', so that this line ran 'Don't you know that you can count me out/in'. This change was opportunistic, for with it he left it up to the listener to choose whichever version he preferred. However, this addition was missing once again from the author- ised version of the lyrics when they were printed. Lennon made the following comment on this in an interview: 'I put in both because I wasn't sure.'[38]

But quite apart from this, the standpoint that Lennon took in the debate about this song reflects more clearly even than the text itself the individualistic view of the world as seen from the perspective of the rock musician. The way this standpoint learnt to adjust to reality was through the prism of an individualistic artist's consciousness and this allowed it to see the problems of the world as a result of the problems of the individual. Looked at more closely, this point of view proved to be horrifyingly naive. During one of John Lennon's and Yoko Ono's spectacular peace demonstrations, their 'bed-ins' – demonstrations in bed for peace and love which attracted enormous publicity – they were asked provocatively by an interviewer whether they thought they would have been able to stop even Hitler and Fascism with music and love. This was the same 'bed-in', in May 1969 in the Queen Elizabeth Hotel in Montreal, when John Lennon's 'Give Peace a

Chance'[39] was recorded in their hotel room with the friends
and reporters who were assembled round the bed. Yoko Ono
gave the following answer: 'If I was a Jewish girl in Hitler's
day, I would approach him and become his girlfriend. After
ten days in bed, he would come to my way of thinking. This
world needs communication. And making love is a great way of
communicating.'[40] This speaks for itself. But it explains the
enormous over-estimation of the social possibilities of music
which underpinned both the development of rock and the
concepts according to which music was being performed. Communication, a myth of quite magical power, was supposed to
make people open up from the inside, to make them free and lead
them back to their own creativity, and this was supposed to be
the road to a real change in society. The common nature of the
rock experience and the sensory directness of this music made
it the most suitable means for achieving this.

The Rolling Stones also got involved in this conflict with
their 'Street Fighting Man', whose lyrics they sent to the newspaper *Black Dwarf* for publication as a contribution to the
discussion. In fact they questioned the activism of demonstrations and street fights no less than the Beatles. They countered
this activism with a position which declared rock music, 'singing
in a rock'n'roll band', to be an alternative.[41] This position
was somewhat different inasmuch as 'Street Fighting Man'
did not put forward the rather general demand of the Beatles'
'Revolution' but only validated the point of view that the time
was not ripe for changing the world by fighting in the streets. But
the result was the same – rock music was the real instrument
of revolution. Even this point of view did not remain unchallenged. At the time Jon Landau made the comment: 'The Stones
may not be sure where their heads are, but their hearts are out
in the streets.'[42] The music of the Rolling Stones, with its
'power, directness and repetition' as Jon Landau described it in
his debate about this song,[43] had its own language. And as long
as the Stones remained true to this they still produced, in spite
of everything, those revolutionary energies which the activists
of the political Left hoped rock music would provide. On this
point the Stones even met the critics of their songs.

But what is much more informative in this case is the story
of how this song came to be written, as described quite credibly

by Tony Sanchez, Keith Richards' personal assistant. In his description:

He [Jagger] leaped at the chance of joining the revolution when tens of thousands of angry young people stormed into Grosvenor Square to demonstrate their hatred of American imperialism and the Vietnam War outside the huge modern American Embassy. At first he was not noticed, and he linked arms with a young man on one side and a young woman on the other as the mob tried to smash their way through police lines and into the embassy. He felt a part of what was happening as though he were really contributing. But then he was recognized; fans demanded autographs; newspapermen scuffled with one another to interview him, to fire off their flashguns in his face. He fled, realizing bitterly that his fame and wealth precluded him from the revolution ... He poured this realization into a new song, 'Street Fighting Man'.[44]

Nothing makes the deep contradictions in the ideology of rock more clear than this story. The eccentric individualism of the 'rock artist', who justified himself through his expression of the common experiences of teenagers, was far removed from the social realities which he claimed to express and to change. If rock musicians are successful, with their wealth they take their place at the upper end of the capitalist social hierarchy, giving them a perspective which genuinely does not recognise other boundaries than those of their own consciousness. The Beatles' Paul McCartney once said to an interviewer with disarming frankness: 'Why can't we be Communists? We're the world's number one capitalists.'[45]

The value criteria and measures which musicians had developed for judging their music – communication, creativity and a common experience through music – were born of an extreme individualism, with which they hoped in ideological terms to avoid the constraints of the capitalist music business. As long as musicians succeeded in asserting themselves against the commercial pressures of the industry and being successful in spite of this, they felt they had achieved an element of self-realisation, which, as they saw it, undermined the logic of capitalism and countered the cultural production line steered by capitalist interests with something of a personal nature. Or as Steve Rawlings of the Danse Society put it in *New Musical Express* in 1984: 'The fact that bands can do exactly what they want and appeal to a mass audience is more subversion than a minor little revolution going on in your backyard. If you can creep into that big, shitty business and sell a million on your own terms, that's what's important.'[46]

For musicians rock music is the sphere of the free and creative development of personality and it was this which defined the purpose of their music, initially independently of playing style and style conception. They buried a deep personal purpose in the sounds of rock which was supposed to transform this music into a collective and common experience and make it express the personal experiences of each listener. From the eventful sixties rock music adopted an ideology which subjected it both to the premises of an individual and personal form of expression and to the postulate of a collective one. This contradiction was no less important in the shaping of rock than the cultural contexts of use in which it really exercised its function. This contradiction broke down at the end of the sixties when the strands of rock music separated into different stylistic directions, which either, like the art rock of Genesis, Gentle Giant or Yes, began to place the autonomy of the 'rock artist' above the demand for collectivity, or which, like the hard rock of Led Zeppelin, Uriah Heep and Black Sabbath, sacrificed the individualistic ideal of creativity to an unbroken common experience. But this music was always held to be the most honest, most direct and most sincere expression of their individuality as musicians, which was supposed to have an emancipatory power to bring people together and make them free – in the end a beautiful, but enormous illusion.

At the beginning of 1970 Ed Leimbacher summarised the development of rock music in the sixties in *Ramparts*, the American magazine of the New Left. Even today his words have lost none of their topicality:

We all know the Rock'n'Ritual: born of the virgin fifties, suffered under Chubby Checker, crucified by surf, died in Philadelphia, buried by the folk singers, rose again in the third year of the sixties and ascended to the pop music heaven, where it sits on the left hand of the generation conflict, to judge the politicians and the over-thirties. The reality is that rock is exactly as confused and muddled in this year of Our Lord 1970 as it has ever been. And in spite of this the music still manages to make itself look quite pretty. It is the hitherto subordinate 'revolutionary spirit' of rock – that schizophrenic dream made up of wishful thinking and self-delusion – which is having the most problems ... Just take a closer look at the Establishment. You will see that it is made of rubber – it adapts by spreading out, by stretching a little more and swallowing all the crazy excesses and deviations ...; and as soon as he gets a bit of the action, the angry young man calms down and pays lip-service to the revolution, a revolution of music, rage and characteristic nothingness.[47]

6

'We're Only in It for the Money': the rock business

'We're Only in It for the Money',[1] a record released in 1968
by Frank Zappa and the Mothers of Invention, was intended
as a biting satire of the Beatles' ambitious concept album *Sgt
Pepper's Lonely Hearts Club Band*. In a malicious and provocative manner this record contrasted the ambitious artistic claims
of the Beatles' production with the pure commercial reality of
rock. Even if it is not quite fair to describe the aesthetic and
political intentions of 'progressive' rock music as merely a
particularly clever veiling of real commercial motives, it cannot
be denied that in the end, even for the Beatles, money was a prime
concern. Within the overall relations of capitalism and under the
conditions of an industry structured along monopolistic lines the
relationship between goods and money is the foundation which
makes the production and distribution of rock music possible,
whether musicians admit this or not. In fact it is really ironic that
the ideology of rock should amount to anti-capitalism, even
though this is only illusory, since more than any other this music
is inextricably linked to the basic mechanisms of capitalism and
itself became an industry organised along capitalist lines. Every
successful rock band already represents a capitalist enterprise of
often considerable size with its own commercial activities in the
music industry. Just recall, for instance, the Beatles' Apple
organisation. Yet the whole thing was underpinned by a structure
controlled by just a few multinational media companies and
monopolistic to a degree rarely found in any other field of
business. Michael Lydon is therefore quite correct when he
writes: 'From the start, rock has been commercial in its very
essence ... it was never an art form that just happened to make
money, nor a commercial undertaking that sometimes became
art. Its art was synonymous with its business.'[2] But to conclude

114

from this that rock music was driven by only one motive, to achieve fame and fortune easily and quickly, is to mistake its real contradictory character. This conclusion is more likely to uncover the cynical gloating of those people who, from the start, deny the masses the ability to determine their own lives and who want to see in the mass success of music only a commercially led manipulation. As Simon Frith once commented very aptly: 'Teenagers know, as they always have, that they're being exploited: the thrill is that all this commercial effort is being made just for them!'[3]

Of course, it would be naive not to recognise at the same time that the commercial contexts of rock's production and distribution are in no way only external to it. The rock business is not carried on around the music without touching its essential nature. It is more that the rock business places rock music within an ideological environment and stamps it with a pattern of values which, independently of the intentions of musicians and fans, make it anything but a peripheral element of the reproduction of imperialist power structures. The ideology inherent in rock only apparently contradicts this, for it is precisely the individualism on which it is based which is the functional element linking it to the economic and ideological interests of capital. Therefore it makes no difference whether the demand behind it is aimed subjectively at an evasion of the existing conditions or whether it sees in them the best of all possible social structures. The more marked the musician's individualism, the more convincingly the capitalist order appears as the true basis of individual self-realisation and the more convincing the motive for purchasing his record as an expression of the consumer's same individualism. And this process sets in motion the circulation of money which merely makes those in power stronger still. The more unconsciously this whole process functions, the more effective it becomes. For then the mechanisms of power under capitalism seem to be obligations based on common sense, free from every suspicion of ideological interests or an exertion of influence for a particular purpose.

In this sense the idea that the rock business puts the manipulators, marketing strategists and ideologists to work falls far short of the truth. It is the contexts in which rock music finds itself, on the basis of the total relations of capitalism, which always function in the interests of capital, both economically and ideologically. They are structured in such a way that they can only function in this manner. Therefore they need no further manipulative intervention in order to force from them their stabilizing effects. These lie in the logic of the music business and simply appear to be inherent forces in the nature of things. Therefore it is also no surprise that the powerful people in the music industry do not as a rule see themselves in any way as cultural and ideological dictators, but also feel exposed to commercial pressures. Jerry Wexler, at that time Vice-President of Warner Brothers Records, one of the pillars of the media giant Warner Communications, once expressed himself along very similar lines at a conference of the *Recording Industry Association of America* at the end of the sixties:

A lot of us executives are walking around physically ill – needing to pretend that we are creating something artistically worthy – or maybe they do not realize that it is a sham ... Since we are all capitalist enterprises, we have to capture the lowest possible denominator ... What is wrong is the fact that we have to cater to the rancid, infantile, pubescent tastes of the public ... Each company must do its best to fill the pulsating needs of mediocrity in order to maximise its potential for success. We might as well be selling hubcaps.[4]

According to this it appears that the music industry's products are produced simply in response to the pressure of consumer needs. In fact the context is exactly reversed. The industry does not give people what *they* want, but what it, the industry, wants. And this curious reversal is brought about by the mysterious nature of money.

In fact it all comes down to investing money in the manufacture of a product in order to increase the value of the investment by selling it, an increase which ultimately shows a profit with a percentage increase in the money. And yet this has far more influence than can be seen from the turnover figures. Indeed the agencies of capital are, to use Frank Zappa's formula, really only in it for the money. And in order to follow this logic they are only allowed to identify with money and with nothing else. Therefore their relationship with what is influenced by their money is totally unimportant. At the very most they are completely indifferent to it. Dick Clark, one of the most powerful figures in the American music business as a result of his position as host of the television programme 'American Bandstand', once coined this phrase: 'I don't make culture. I sell it.'[5]

This is as apt as it is incorrect. Doubtless nothing could be more disastrous than to mix the logic of money with other criteria, to want to make not only a profit but also 'culture'. This would take away the power of capital, rob it of its flexibility and its ability to make each and every thing useful for its interests. But this is precisely the form that the production of culture *does* take under capitalism. Money is an abstract measure of value – the distribution of property which it represents, the circumstances in which it circulates, the mechanisms which lead to its increase, and the particular nature of the products which are made by using it are not obvious. In spite of this it always functions within concrete constraints which at the same time it reproduces. From the point of view of money as a measure of value it is immaterial whether it represents records or hub caps, artistically 'worthy' or 'worthless' music, 'progressive' or 'reactionary' content. But in its function as capital and therefore as the representative of particular social property relations and the class interests linked to them, its movement acquires a tendentious purpose, in which everything which comes into contact with it is made to serve the economic and ideological interests of capital. Anything which counters this is excluded from the start by the concept of 'no commercial potential'. David Pichaske is quite correct to write: 'The music biz is an ideological whore. It is dedicated to maximum profit, and it won't wring the neck of a goose that lays golden discs out of pure philosophical differences. But it happens that a smoothly functioning system generates more golden discs than a non-system, because it turns out the most product for the least effort.'[6]

But such a 'smoothly functioning system' includes ideas, norms, values and concepts, even when these are not consciously created. The overall context built up on the basis of capitalist property relations ensures that nothing can happen to it which runs counter to capital interests. Although the music industry seems only to be interested in money, while strictly following the logic of money it generates around rock music a cultural and ideological context which overlays it with more insidious and systematic meanings than would be possible by a direct exertion of influence. Its effect follows in a functional manner, through the structures which are set around behaviour, without going through consciousness. This is the way in which the ideology of the ruling class becomes dominant even when, as we have already shown, musicians and their fans have by no means submissively surrendered to it.

In order to investigate this dominant ideology a little further we need to look at least in general terms at the Moloch that is the 'music industry'. Taken as a whole this is a network of record companies, studios, agencies, the mass media – radio, television, film and press – local promoters, publishing houses, chains of record shops and specialist shops, a network which is difficult to disentangle. Yet at the centre of this network there are no more than five international media organisations – CBS (Columbia Broadcasting System), RCA (Radio Corporation of America) and Warner Communications based in the USA, Thorn-EMI (Electrical & Musical Industries) in Britain and PolyGram, a joint Dutch-West German firm. Together these five companies control around 70 per cent of the turnover of the capitalist world market in records and cassettes, estimated in 1977 at eight to nine billion dollars.[7] Within this overall figure their market share in a number of countries is far more than 70 per cent: also using 1977 figures, in Denmark 97 per cent, in Canada 94 per cent,[8] and in Britain 95 per cent.[9] This makes property relations in the music industry quite clear. For although in Britain, for example, there are more than 200 record companies, it is these five media organisations who control the music business here unchallenged because of their market share. Susanna Hoff of the Los Angeles female quartet The Bangles explained what this looked like from the musician's point of view: 'The recording industry is not set up for the artist to make money, it's set up so the company makes money and then somewhere down the line the agents make money and the promoters make money and then maybe the band get to see some of it.'[10] The industry's view of itself on this point can be deduced from its advertising copy. EMI, one of the oldest record companies in the world, with a history going back to 1898, describes itself as a company which: 'operates in every continent, through group companies in 33 overseas countries. Using hundreds of promotion men and over a thousand salesmen it has the power to stimulate demand both in quantity and quality and to meet the demand when sales accelerate'.[11]

In 1970 EMI employed 41,900 people to do this.[12] And although, with its numerous labels and a whole network of sales agreements with small and medium-sized firms, EMI counts as the largest record company in the world, only about 50 per cent of its $1,742 billion 1979 turnover figure could be directly attributed to sales of records or pre-recorded cassettes.[13] Alongside its musical interests, the EMI empire is involved in commercial television and in the film industry, having taken over the Associated British Picture Corporation and Thames Television in 1969. EMI owns cinemas, theatres, dance halls, clubs, discotheques, agencies and tour promoters, runs the biggest trading organisation in Britain for musical instruments and accessories, and in HMV owns a chain of record shops, including the biggest record shop in the world on London's Oxford Street – a multi-storey shop devoted completely to records, cassettes and CDs. EMI produces or sells analog and digital computers, television transmission technology, studio technology, amplifier systems, tape recorders, record players, televisions, cassette recorders, microelectronic components for the most varied of uses, dry batteries in all sizes and packages, medical equipment, radar systems, missile systems with electronic and laser guidance. As well as these EMI owns a number of music publishers who between them earn around 20 per cent of all music publishing income.[14] Of course printed music barely plays any role in rock music now but the exploitation of copyright in a song means financial gain practically without any production costs, especially since as a rule the songs have a longer life than the records. They still yield receipts from copyright when there are no more records on the market. Therefore all the big record companies are affiliated under fantastic names, which conceal their ownership from the outside world, to publishing departments who manage the copyrights of those musicians who are under contract to them. For an author, the transfer of copyright protection to a publisher, naturally together with a percentage of the income this brings him, is the only possible way of securing his rights in the jungle of the music business.

Behind the whole thing is an impenetrable web of interconnections of interests and people which Dave Harker once tried to disentangle using the example of one of the EMI directors, Bernard Delfont:

The Royal Variety Show takes place in a theatre owned by Associated Television (ATV), which is run by Lew Grade – who just happens to be Bernard Delfont's brother. The proceeds from the show go to a charity – presided over by Bernard Delfont. Delfont is also a director of EMI, the largest record manufacturer in the world. Recently, EMI absorbed one of England's two big cinema circuits – Associated British Pictures – of which Bernard Delfont is also a director. Bernard Delfont is also deputy chairman and joint managing director of the Grade Organisation, which is owned by EMI (of which Mr Delfont is a director). Bernard Delfont thus owns himself – twice. So, if you read the TV Times, buy Pye, Marble Arch, Regal, Columbia, Parlophone, HMV, Pathe, Music for Pleasure, or Odeon Records; if you watch ATV or Thames Television, go to the Talk of the Town, the London Palladium, Victoria Palace, Hippodrome, Her Majesty's, Globe, Lyric, Apollo, or Prince of Wales theatres; if you go to one of ABC's 270 cinemas or twelve bowling alleys or one of Ambassador's ten bowling alleys, then Bernard Delfont has an interest in what you're doing.[15]

Associated Television (ATV), mentioned above, with Lord Grade as the chairman of the board – whose Associated Communications Corporation (ACC) is incorporated into EMI, although EMI, through Thames Television, is one of the important competitors of ATV in the commercial television market – bought the music publisher Northern Songs in 1969. Northern Songs owned the rights to the Beatles' songs, which had in any case been released on EMI's Parlophone label. The maze is impenetrable. Access to music in Britain, in whatever form, even if it is only changing the batteries in a cassette recorder, without making profits for EMI is quite impossible. In spite of this, the gigantic EMI empire was swallowed up in 1979 by an even bigger company, Thorn Electrical Industries, an electronics firm.

This produced a characteristic merger of a type which, since the mid-sixties, has increasingly linked all five multinational media giants to the electronics industry and therefore to the military-industrial complex which lies at the heart of the political economy of imperialism. Even in 1970, Keith Richards of the Rolling Stones described in an interview the military involvement of their record company Decca, which in the meantime has become part of PolyGram:

We found out, and it wasn't for years that we did, that all the bread we made for Decca was going into making little black boxes that go into American Air Force bombers to bomb fucking North Vietnam. They took the bread we made for them and put it into the radar section of their business. When we found that out, it blew our minds.[16]

In this respect the comprehensive merger of the music and electronic industries which took place during the seventies was only a logical consequence of the activities of the big record companies which were moving in this direction. In fact the connection which brought record production and the development of military technology together under one roof may at first sight seem a little strange. The link between them is communications technology. This technology not only occupies a key position in both fields, but is also extremely cost-intensive and subject to a high loss of morale due to constant new developments, driven mostly by the spiral of the arms race. To use this technology later in entertainment electronics in order to control the 'software', i.e. the music, was therefore quite natural. Peter Williams, an Australian producer who worked very successfully for Cliff Richard, Joan Armatrading, The Hollies and Leo Sayer among others, made this point: 'Audio is a fairly obscure backwater of electronics. When people do go out to design a new chip they're not thinking how many recording studios can we sell it to. They're thinking how many missiles can we stick this in. Most electronic development is highly military.'[17]

On the other hand, the big firms in the music industry reached a production volume such that it was not the level of production but the control of the product which decided the battle with the competition. But this control comes through technology, so that even here there arose a need for direct access to communications technology. PolyGram found the ideal form of this technology in 1983 with the compact disc, a reproduction system which was based on the digital recording process introduced at the end of the seventies as a by-product of computer technology. The technical foundations for the system were developed jointly by the Dutch firm Philips, which is part of the PolyGram group through its Phonogram subsidiary, and Sony in Japan. So the whole system was in the hands of one company, and, since it is not compatible with existing systems and neither conventional records nor record players can be used with it, it represented total control over the product, at least until the competition caught up. David Wooley, sound engineer with the London company Trillion

Video, pointed out in this context that for a long time it has not been the audiences who have pressed for further improvements in the technical quality of music production: 'The pressure to improve quality generally comes from within the industry rather than from the end consumers.'[18] And this pressure is not least towards the link between the music and electronic industries, leading to an enormous increase in capital for the particularly risky music business, where large gains can only be made if high losses can also be absorbed.

The structure of Thorn-EMI, with a production profile that includes the whole communications and media sector in technology and applications, reflects that of the other four giants of the music industry in every respect. Their activities in the musical field are only a secondary branch of the whole organisation and are subject to its overall strategy. This not only created the optimum conditions for maximum gain, but also made possible an action in the media combine which considers music, film, television, video, sporting and cultural leisure activities, entertainment in its widest sense as one context and in this form makes it controllable. The development of the pop video is just one particularly concise example of this. But the level of concentration and centralisation which was linked to these developments also brought with it a decisive disadvantage which became very obvious in the early seventies.

The success of the Beatles and British beat music was initially seen by the industry simply as a matter of quantity and it acted accordingly. After all, the 230 songs of the Beatles alone had sold, as Larry Shore calculated,[19] over 200 million records between 1962 and 1967. The fact that this music brought with it decisive qualitative changes, which made the sales concept of simply flooding the market with records impossible, was something that the large firms in the music industry only noticed when they suffered a few serious disasters with this strategy and saw a whole series of small and middle-sized firms springing up next to them, such as Atlantic, Island, Polydor, Bell and Charisma, which were very successful with rock music. The reaction to this was a wave of mergers, from which the five multinational media organisations emerged in their present form. Steve Chapple and Reebee Garofalo gave the following description of this phenomenon:

In the middle and late sixties a large number of companies in the music industry bought up or merged with other companies involved with music, or were themselves bought out by large conglomerates from outside the industry. Some of these mergers represented a response to new rock music or, put another way, a response to the continuing success of the independent companies. But the merger movement in the music industry was also a 'natural' process of centralization in which successful companies joined to save expenses, to control prices and the market more effectively, and to amalgamate companies specializing in different types of music into one corporation that provided greater financing and simpler, central, distribution.[20]

By about 1970 the disappearance of the small and medium-sized firms had left an appreciable gap, which soon made itself felt. Organisations of the size which had developed were able to draw maximum profits from existing material, but their central-ised organisation with its financial and bureaucratic structures was far too large and clumsy to continue to undertake the necessary reconnaissance and talent-spotting. Serge R. Denisoff illustrated this phenomenon using the example of CBS Records: 'CBS Records ... must produce an enormous amount of product to keep its various bureaus, agencies and departments busy. Of every ten records released, only two or three will sell. Conse-quently, large companies must produce massive amounts of product to sustain their larger corporate bodies.'[21]

The only suitable plane for this is the international market-place, using music that can be sold throughout the world. But rock music does not arise in the markets marked out in the offices of the media organisations but in local and sub-cultural contexts, indeed precisely on that plane from which the music industry had slowly cut itself off in the late sixties in the interests of central-isation. The resulting vacuum led to the paralysis of rock in the superlatives of the music business. Pink Floyd, Emerson, Lake & Palmer, Yes, Genesis, Gentle Giant and Kansas began to devote themselves to a mania for size in equipment, which with stage structures like power stations and a technically flawless sound became the framework within which the musicians celebrated a mysticism far removed from reality. An 'art business' originated with rock operas, rock oratorios, rock masses and symphonies, rock suites and concerti. The costs of this 'art business' became ever greater, which gradually began to force working-class teenagers, who had less money to spend, out of rock music. Once the social connection had been lost, a trivialised sensation-seeking became a more than questionable bridge between performers and audience. The void was filled with horror and transvestite shows, with pornographic exhibitionism and comical perversions. Musical performance was reduced to the acrobatics of a formal high-performance perfectionism. People tried to synthesise rock music with every possible musical concept – jazz, country, folk, classical or Latin-American music – in order to bring a trend back into rock music which had commercial prospects. It was only the punk revolution from 1976 onwards which at last gradually broke up the centralised structures of the music business and once again allowed hundreds of small and mini-firms to spring up alongside the great media organisations, firms which concerned themselves with the local groundwork. The industry learnt its lesson from the debacle of the early seventies and has since then left a narrow but viable sector of the music market untouched where the small and medium-sized firms find a field of operation for the development of talent without losing their independence. Since these firms lack the necessary capital for lucrative long-term contracts, the large firms can always step in whenever 'commercial potential' becomes clear somewhere. Richard Lyttleton, international manager for EMI, saw it like this:

What the independents can do, often better than us, is produce extremely sound marketable material. I think there's room in the world for both of us. But, as has happened over the past five years, they won't be able to attain total independence. We'll see creative satellite companies being born, retaining their artistic integrity, but using the larger companies for distribution. I don't think anybody can distribute records from scratch, on a worldwide basis, more efficiently than the large multinationals can. We've been doing it for a long, long time, and we've built up heavy networks.[22]

It is true that it is not production but sales that is the real problem of the music business, because sales demand advertising, are very costly in terms of organisation, and depend largely on access to the retail trade. In spite of this, the small firms – known as 'independents' – who market their own products through businesses specialising in this type of product, even if they rarely run to pressings of more than one or two thousand, have become vitally important to the multinational media organisations. Geoff Davies of Probe Records, an independent label based in Liverpool, which has been one of the most active pilot firms of this type in Britain, explained this relationship: 'The large firms use the independents as a testbed. We provide them with a sort of demo-tape, which we pay for. We try things out and see what works. We look for the bands for them who – if they agree – they then only need to market.'[23]

Thus the rock business consists of two very different sectors which make up a functional unity: the highly centralised environment of the multinational media organisations on the one hand, and on the other the decentralised structure of the independents – not just record companies, but also small agencies and local promoters. The difference between them is the criteria according to which they work, but not their aim, which is to sell records or tickets respectively. For the one the rock business is just part of a huge commercial organisation and only of interest in terms of turnover figures, earnings calculations and profit rates, for the others it is first and foremost working in and with music – but the *music business* only arises out of the conjunction of both of these. This results in a cycle which George Melly described very vividly:

A local enthusiasm for some form of music gradually crystallizes around a particular group or artist. At this point an entrepreneur, sometimes a local enthusiast with an eye to the main chance, sometimes an outsider led towards the scene by apparently fortuitous accident, recognizes the commercial potential of the group or the artist and signs them up … If he is successful, his 'property' becomes first nationally and then internationally famous. In the wake, other groups or artists, many from the same local or musical background, some simply recognizing that a particular sound or image has become commercial, swim along feeding on the vast plankton of popular flavour. Then, inevitably, the interest and hysteria die away, and there is a variable time-lag before the same thing happens again.[24]

At this point it is necessary to make a decisive differentiation in order to bring the cultural and ideological mechanisms exercised by the music industry into view. In the strictly economic sense the product of this industry is in fact not music, as it might appear, but the record. Such a distinction may appear to be hairsplitting, since a record in its role as carrier can only be sold in combination with music, but it is particularly significant.

Only from this standpoint can the mechanisms of this industry be understood and only thus does it become clear that the creative process itself, both musical performance and involvement with music, remains outside its direct reach. This is a process carried out between musicians and their fans. The creativity of the musician and the technicians who support him can neither be controlled by the industry nor replaced by advertising and promotion. The 'production departments' of the record companies therefore do not look upon themselves as music producers. Their job is to manufacture records which will sell as many copies as possible, to which end, among other things, they enlist the service of musicians, technicians and producers. These departments do not consist of studios and artistic staff, rather they are bureaucratic set-ups with A&R (artist & repertoire) managers, who organise and manage the development of records as a commercial product. This is more of a contractual activity than an artistic one, although it naturally requires a detailed knowledge of the music market and the ability to make choices. If the record companies ever do have their own studios, these are usually rented to musicians and producers.

The confusion in this matter arises from the fact that two very different production processes are concealed behind the term 'production', the production of music and the manufacture of records. Economically these two are strictly separate, although their products, music on the one hand and records on the other, appear as a single unity whose division seems completely illogical. But, as it developed, the music industry itself has systematically pushed this division along by relinquishing economic responsibility for the unpredictable creative process in order to be able to concentrate that much more intensively on its own original product, the record. This does not exclude the possibility that A&R managers like George Martin for instance, who was employed by EMI until 1970 as manager of the Parlophone label, might also be working as music producers in the studios. Martin in fact worked mainly for the Beatles. The critical point is the economic division which means that the musicians or an independent producer carry the costs of the music production (even if this is paid for with an advance against the subsequent sales income of the record), while the record companies simply take over the finished master tape in return for a five to seven per cent share of earnings.

Behind this lies the instinctive insight that the path to profit maximisation cannot be found via a 'raising' of the musician's creativity but only via the mechanics of marketing him. As Richard Lyttleton of EMI commented: 'I think it's very difficult to rationalize an industry which basically is irrational.'[25] Of course, it is impossible to manipulate the creative process and in some way to programme hits. The British Phonographic Institute, the market research arm of the industry association of the British record companies, determined for 1977 for example that only one in nine singles and only one in sixteen LPs, eleven or six per cent respectively of record releases, made a profit. And this was in spite of the fact that at that time on average a record only had to sell 23,000 copies to cover its costs, and it was only after sales of around five million that it was called a hit.[26] Simon Frith once estimated that it only took seven per cent of all record releases to secure the economic foundation of the music industry,[27] because these brought in such high profits that they not only balanced the losses but, in spite of these, also secured above average profit rates below the line. The only problem with this is that it is absolutely impossible to forecast which records will belong to this seven per cent. Of course proportional losses can be reduced by creating a trend in the wake of a successful record, but the necessary profits cannot be achieved with copies of previous hit records. The only way to escape this extraordinarily high sales risk is therefore to indulge in a massive overproduction of records and an extension of the commercial field of operation in order to be able to compensate for the inevitable losses with equally high sales when a success does come along. In principle the calculation that this is based on is quite simple. The likelihood of high profits rises with the number of new releases, whatever this is, for, statistically speaking, this brings a greater share in that part of the year's releases which will be sold at a profit. In other words, the competition between the record companies is a quantitative one and only appears to be about the quality of music. It all comes down to market share – the higher the market share the higher the share of the year's hits.

Seen from this angle, the incessantly repeated statement of the industry that it has nothing to do with the quality of music, it only gives people what they want, seems to be well-founded. If this statement is nevertheless untrue, it is because the numbers game of hit lists, turnover figures, production figures and pressing quantities conceals a decisive point at which these purely quantitative criteria turn into qualitative ones behind the backs of the people involved, which lead the whole process in the interests of the industry.

If the A&R managers really knew 'what people want', the proportional losses of the record companies would be considerably lower and their profits even higher. But they do not know. Nevertheless they have to decide to which music they should best link their product, the record, and this decision is far from being an arbitrary one. Simon Frith gives the number of rock bands in Britain in 1978 as around 50,000, of which fewer than 1,000 ever get the chance of a recording contract.[28] So which criteria affect this choice? Peter Jamieson, EMI's managing director, gave the following answer to this question: 'The art in our business is to find out what people want to buy. The buyer decides and we simply try to do justice to his decisions.'[29] This is doubtless an honest view and even sounds logical. After all, how can you sell people things that they do not want? But this statement is only the outward appearance of quite different circumstances. The decisions are in fact made according to what is *marketable*, and not according to 'what people want'. Superficially, these appear to be the same. Nevertheless they mean two very different things. The aim of the process of marketing is to sell as many as possible of the black discs, whatever music they carry. The industry calculates sales in terms of numbers and not in musical categories. The marketing of records is a process which exclusively follows the product criteria of the record companies. Of course the record is only an independent product according to the economic criteria of the industry, in fact it is only viable in connection with music. As a result, the process of marketing records is necessarily reflected in the musical process, which, like every mirror, provides a mirror image. This seems a little confusing but is quite simply untangled if we look a little more closely at what is called 'marketing', instead of concealing the process with such general terms.

The starting-point for the marketing of any product is the

definition of its market, for a 'market' only exists as a fact in economic categories. In capitalist language *marketing* has now become a technical term. Which needs represent a marketable demand and therefore form a 'market' is decided and defined by the industry according to its criteria, i.e. profit. 'What people want' is only of interest to it if this desire is linked to an ability to pay and is likely to provide the highest possible sales for its product. For example, around 1980 the sharp rise in youth unemployment in the late seventies, particularly among working-class teenagers, led to a clear market shift away from the former towards teenagers from the lower middle-classes. The musical needs of working-class teenagers ceased to be marketable because of their decreasing disposable income and willingness to buy, in spite of the fact that, in purely quantitative terms, this social group offered far more potential record buyers. This shift had far-reaching consequences, for the musical needs of lower middle-class teenagers not only have a quite different structure, but in this social group television also plays a dominant role in involvement with music. This led directly to the development of the pop video. Thus it is not the teenagers who decide which music is pressed on record, but the industry, which decides on the basis of which music sells most records. Of course before this the industry has already investigated musical needs and classified them in order to discover whether, according to its criteria, they represent a demand for the sale of records which is coupled with the ability to pay. If we simply look at the process in relation to the music, then it seems to be the exact opposite, as though records were sold because teenagers wanted this music and no other. John Beerling, BBC programme controller, once explained: 'You know how things are marketed these days. You bring in an import, hold it back for a while and then sell enough to get it in the charts. It doesn't always mean it's universally popular.'[30]

Over the actual needs structures which are present and the music linked to them a second level of needs is laid down, which the industry's marketing experts define as their market and which proves to have a completely different structure. In the mass media, this second level acquires reality and is made quite realistic. Depending on the level from which we consider the development of music, we see a different image. On one level it appears to be embedded in cultural and sub-cultural contexts of use in which it takes place as a complex juxtaposition to a very diverse multiplicity of playing styles and stylistic concepts. On this level records and the mass media are only a means of using music, a means whose quantitative dimensions are irrelevant in this context. After all, teenage rock fans do not ask how many records a group has sold before they enthuse about it. On the other level, however, music is only the means to the end of selling records. On this level its development appears to be a linear series of uniform trends, organised according to quantitative criteria, which follow one another in 'waves'. This is why what is represented as rock music on the radio, on television, and by high record sales is something quite different from what is actually developing on the spot. Richard Middleton is undoubtedly correct when he writes in relation to the first level: 'But it ought by now to be generally accepted that commercialists do not create, they cash in. They intensify or fix a taste; they accentuate a trend. They cannot start either. They are not leaders; they are parasites.'[31]

Even if we do not contradict this, commercial people with their marketing strategies still bring about that second level which is laid over the real development process of rock music like a quantitative framework, and which is reflected and also strengthened by the mass media. It is at this point, according to commercial criteria, that music begins to live a life of its own and becomes independent as a trend. But since these two levels do not exist independently of one another interference occurs, as in that process in physical oscillation which, when two mutually phase-shifted sinewaves are superimposed, leads to their attenuation or amplification. Music which functions on both levels acquires more weight through the media and necessarily increases its social and artistic status. Alan Durant described this phenomenon in relation to the weekly charts and the playlists of the radio stations on which they are based: 'institutions of chart and radio playlist on the basis of sales have the effect that even sales to one very specific social grouping can come to be represented as popularity, "general" currency and a national entertainment repertoire, by virtue simply of attaining a threshold for gaining airtime on "national" radio'.[32] Thus the whole process starts out on a road which – as can easily be proved – leads to the sale of more and more records in a shorter and shorter space of time. While in the fifties a hit might expect to sell about one million records a year, in the seventies the number would be more like five million, and in 1983/4 Michael Jackson's *Thriller*[33] sold more than 32 million copies in only 18 months.[34]

But marketing is only one aspect of the commercialisation process. The other and more important one is *promotion*, the presentation of the product through advertising, image-building, and through the media of radio, television and the press. Harry Ager, Vice-President, Marketing, for PolyGram, once put it like this: 'If pitching is 70 per cent of baseball, promotion is 70 per cent of the record business.'[35] For a long time the over-production of records had led to a situation in which it was impossible for record buyers actually to make their choice from all of the new releases. If around one hundred thousand songs appear on record in the USA and Britain every year, then a daily uninterrupted twelve-hour listening marathon would still not be enough even to listen to this whole crazy amount of music inside the 365 days available. Paul Hirsch once calculated that of all the singles released, just 23.7 per cent are played more than once on radio, and 61.6 per cent are never played at all which, in view of the importance of radio in the music business, means these sell very few copies.[36] Thus for the record companies everything depends on bringing as many as possible of their record releases to the attention of the vast range of potential buyers. Just heaping a large number of new releases onto the market is not enough to optimise the firm's percentage share of the yearly hits. Walter R. Yetnikoff, President of the CBS Recording Group explained the process:

Things are considerably different than a few years ago, when the philosophy was to throw a lot of products against the wall and see what sticks. That approach is too expensive today. Now, every album that goes out has a complete marketing plan – with full details on advertising, airplays, discounts for the trade, personal appearances by the artist, sales targets and national and regional breakdowns.[37]

In the meantime enormous sums of money are spent. Roy Carr did some research using the example of WEA International, the overseas representative of Warner Communications: 'WEA, to quote just one of the big firms, considers that it needs to invest at least $250,000 in order to give a new release a fair starting chance. And even a superseller like the Bee Gees' *Spirits Having Flown* needs a promotional spend of $1 million in order to realise maximum sales.'[38] Of course, this goes far beyond the actual production costs. This is naturally not based on the naive idea that high expenditure on advertising will convince people of the necessity of buying this particular record. It is much more a matter of competition on the plane of product presentation, where the number of competitors declines with increasing expenditure and therefore the company's market share grows. It is quite impossible to persuade someone to buy a record, let alone to force them to do so. But the more a particular record is brought to the attention of the buying public, the less likely it becomes that it will not be bought simply because it is unknown. Thus an extensive system of product presentation has grown up in the music industry which gives the record a secondary and incorporeal existence in the media combine of radio, television, film, the music press and fan magazines, and, since 1981, video, posters and poster advertising. An image of the record is projected into the consciousness of its potential buyers, a process which achieves far more than merely pushing the competition out. The music too is integrated in this image and is not played on the radio or television merely for its own sake. The aim is to build up a context around the record, using the media, which makes the potential buyer feel that it is important. He will not buy the record just because of this, but this process makes sure that, from the immense selection available, only those new releases come to his attention which are made to seem important by vast expenditure. In this process there are no moral or other limits to the imagination of the promoters, the end literally justifies the means. The fact that the expenditure is admittedly worth it and that its result is completely calculable was confirmed by Geoff Travis (boss and owner of Rough Trade Records, a distinctive independent New Wave label with a middling commercial scope) with the following facts: 'If we succeed in getting a group and their song onto the BBC television programme "Top of the Pops", the sales figures will go up by around £50,000 in the following fortnight.'[39]

As Paul Hirsch determined, since a record only has a life of around 60 to 120 days as far as the music industry is concerned,[40] and sales over longer periods are an exception, the image conception is primarily concentrated on the personality of the musician or the collective 'personality' of the band, for their commercial viability is normally an order of magnitude higher. Charlie Gillett pointed out that: 'for most record companies what's important is to produce and sell an *act*, an image, and not just a record – in the long run it's easier to run a star with assured sales than to have to work on a series of one-offs'.[41] If the band has a stable image, this can be carried over onto each of their records which considerably reduces costs. But this stable image can be even sharper than a group image, and therefore more effective, if it is linked to a single musician, usually the band's lead singer. The result of this is an unparalleled star cult, and the concentration of capital in the music industry has given this factor increasing weight. Using larger and larger sums of money each record company tries to chase the others from the battlefield, out of the consciousness of the potential buyer.

But the ideological mechanisms which are set in motion are far more important than the media spectacular with all its comic side effects. The whole apparatus of promotion is constructed so that it creates a field of reference which draws in the listener as an active participant, thereby influencing him in a very subtle way. He himself must find the record presented to him so important that he recognises its existence and possibly even buys it. The repeated playing of the record on the radio, press comments, interviews with the musicians, television appearances and the rest of the circus tend to lead to the conclusion that this record must be important, and this is the buyer's own conclusion. He is not persuaded to feel like this, nor directly forced to, rather the rules of the whole system rely on his free, voluntary and active participation. But by doing this, without being conscious of it, he is placed in a social role in which he behaves primarily as a record buyer and not – as he himself believes – as a recipient of music. It was not the music which made this record more important to him than the many other nameless ones, but the frame of reference in which the music industry placed it. Only later does he look at the record from the musical point of view and possibly even buy it. Instead of trying to exercise a direct influence on his behaviour, to direct him and dictate to him – an attempt which would in any case end in failure – the music industry continually flexibly arranges things around him so that his 'free' decisions always benefit it. The industry does not control his decisions but does control the results. However he behaves, things are arranged so that the result is always the same – profit. And as a part of this process he is tied into a context which makes him feel that the music industry is realising his interests and not vice versa. The mechanisms of the music business reconstruct social reality in his mind in such a way that it seems to correspond to his interests. At the same time, these mechanisms reflect social circumstances back to him from such a perspective that they become an expression of a style of behaviour that conforms to the system. Jon Landau developed this point very vividly using the example of the star cult:

Its only demand on the intellect is that we should accept what is, in fact, a flagrant lie: good versus evil, impossible romances between the mighty and the humble, the visible triumphs of zeal, hard work and steadfastness over dishonesty and laziness, or whatever. Of course, these assertions are nothing more than the myths and lies of culture. And the star cult, with whose help these lies are lived out on our behalf, is the greatest of all lies. For through this cult we are taught to identify with the supermen who act out these fantastic images and through this to make these images credible, attractive, motivating and erotic. We are taught that the unreal existence which they represent is possible, not that we ourselves are not qualified for it.[42]

Riches and fame through one's own efforts – this is the ceaselessly repeated credo of the star, which turns social class barriers into individual barriers to achievement.

The mechanisms of the rock business speak a language that everyone understands, but in a voice that no one can hear and identify. They have no identifiable subject and this is what makes their effect so insidious. They give to the music which comes into contact with them a meaning which the listeners ultimately adopt as their own.

7

'Anarchy in the UK': the punk rebellion

It was on 6th November 1975 at St Martin's School of Art in London that a band called the Sex Pistols first took to the stage. At first glance there was nothing special about this; the British art schools have always been some of the most receptive venues for live rock. And live rock had always been significantly different, at least in the cities, from what the mass media called rock music. While the latter was composed of 'supergroups' aiming for 'higher things' with their bombastic artistic and technical pomposity, teenagers in the clubs and pubs of city working-class districts were once again enjoying more and more the simple patterns of rock's original forms in the rhythm & blues tradition. What they wanted was bands as young as possible showing simplicity and real pleasure in playing. It is therefore not surprising that the art schools, the intellectual centres of the British rock development, opened their doors to this growing trend which had started in 1973 and sought to outstrip each other in the discovery of unknown groups.

In spite of all this the events on that 6th November were quite memorable. For after just a few minutes the performance threatened to dissolve into complete chaos. Instead of the expected simplicity and enthusiasm of the basic sounds of rock there was a wild noise coming from the stage mixed with graphic insults of the audience, which the scarcely eighteen-year-old musicians, their pale faces fixed in cynical mask-like expressions, accompanied with a careful dramaturgy of aggression and force. There was no attempt to conceal the dilettantism behind this performance, it was all challengingly displayed. In every respect the whole thing fulfilled the attributes of an 'anti-music'. It was the concept of the band's manager, Malcolm McLaren, for whom this represented the carefully prepared conversion of

135

an avant-garde art project. McLaren professed the art philosophy of the 'International Situationists', an (anti-)art concept which grew up in France in the fifties in relation to Paris Dadaism and which experienced a renaissance in British art schools in the sixties, while McLaren himself was studying at St Martin's School of Art. But on the evening of this 6th November the students probably saw the spectacle taking place before them as a business-minded ridiculing of their snobbish attitude of considering themselves a forum for young and unknown bands. After the fifth 'song' the School's social secretary felt obliged to turn off the band's power. The Sex Pistols had hardly spent ten minutes on the stage.

Less than a year later, on the 20th and 21st September 1976, the first British punk rock festival took place in the famous 100 Club in London's Oxford Street. It was opened by the Sex Pistols and included The Clash, Siouxsie and the Banshees, The Damned and a whole series of other groups who did not become so well-known later. Hours beforehand, during the rush hour on this largest and most famous shopping street in the British metropolis, hundreds of teenagers in very strange costume had already formed a queue several blocks long in front of the doors of the club. They stood there dressed up in the discarded fashion of previous decades, in pieces of uniform and ladies' underwear cut into rags and held together with safety-pins, with their hair dyed green, red or purple, hung about with razor blades, bicycle chains and toilet chains, wearing iron-studded dog collars around their necks, out-sized safety-pins through their cheeks and multi-coloured make-up on their faces, pestering the passers-by and spreading an atmosphere of aggression, surrounded by the photographers of the popular press.

The elitist anti-art programme of McLaren – who, with the fashion designer Vivienne Westwood, otherwise ran a boutique characteristically called 'Sex' at the less refined end of London's fashionable Kings Road – had become a teenage sub-culture which gradually drew in the whole country, a sub-culture symbolised by a form of rock music whose aggressive force surpassed everything that had been heard before. What counted for music in this sub-culture seemed to be defined through the uncompromising negation of those aesthetic criteria which had in the meantime made rock music an accepted part of contemporary cultural activity. The polished sound structures of a rock 'art' concerned with 'content' were now opposed by a challenging dilettantism which only had to sound loud, aggressive and chaotic to be accepted as rock music. No more technical apparatus, which in the meantime had become just as incomprehensible to musicians as to their fans, no more stars fingering runs on guitar or keyboards at breakneck speed with contorted faces, no more singers picked out to great effect by spotlight in the undulating stage fog, no more grand forms whose meaning was merely in their length: just simple, brutal rhythmic patterns with three guitars and drums, to whose accompaniment the musicians screamed out their view of their situation in selected obscene street slang – this was the embodiment of the new music cult. Once again rock had the inimitable self-made music flair of the early sixties, just more aggressive, louder, shriller, more hectic and full of cynicism with none of the naive innocence of the Beatles' 'Love Me Do'. And it was accompanied by the violent barging of a 'dance' style called the *pogo*, an indescribable tangling together, shoving, jostling, pushing and jumping. And behind the whole thing only the incessant repetition of one message: NO FUTURE.

To some people punk rock was the direct musical expression of unemployed teenagers' political protest against a society that had turned them into superfluous outsiders, while to others it was a particularly cunning capitalist subterfuge to overcome the decline in the record market because of the recession. In either case it provoked vehement arguments about the social and political nature of rock music. Once again the crux of the matter was, as it had been in the sixties, whether rock music is by its very nature anti-commercial, anti-capitalist and progressive in terms of its political content or whether it merely represents an entertainment product, tailored to suit teenagers' needs and divert the social potential for protest into the safe and yet profitable realm of a rebellious music cult. In 1976 Derek Jarman was already writing about the 'clique of Kings Road fashionable anarchists who call themselves punk':

The music business has conspired with them to create another working class myth as the dole queues grow longer to fuel the flames. But in reality the instigators of punk are the same old petit-bourgeois art students, who a few months ago were David Bowie and Bryan Ferry look-alikes – who've read a little art history and adopted Dadaist typography and bad manners, and are now in the business of reproducing a fake street credibility.[1]

In contrast, to Ulrich Hetscher punk was 'the manifestation and articulation of a rebellion', a teenage protest in musical form:

However we choose to judge the punks with their (self-) destructiveness, their egocentricity, their sexism etc ...: they brought rock music out of the large concert halls with their expensive tickets and out of the high-technology studios and back into the small pubs and onto the streets. A large part of the rock music produced in the early seventies was too artificial and the gulf between the musicians and the interests and needs of the audience too large to let teenagers put rock on their banner as the musical expression of their protest and their dissatisfaction.[2]

It is certainly true that the punk rebellion was to become a unique example of the contradictory relationship of social, cultural, aesthetic and commercial factors to which rock music owes its existence.

Even punk rock as a musical concept did not arise 'on the streets', but was – as its constantly suppressed early history makes clear – the product of a veteran of the student movement with artistic ambitions, Malcolm McLaren. In fact the impulse for the Sex Pistols project even came from America. Between 1973 and 1975 McLaren had been in America managing the New York Dolls, a group which was part of New York's decadent transvestite scene. There he came into contact with the eccentric anti-art experiments of the New Wave avant-garde of the New York underground. Linked to the pop art of the early sixties, artists from very varied directions were here trying to create a punk art. The term 'punk' – meaning something like muck, trash, rubbish, even whore – described this attempt. What was generally worthless, banal and trivial was to be the starting-point for an artistic practice which takes its materials from the sup-pressed waste products of bourgeois everyday life, whether the obscene sexual fantasies of pornography, the secret horror images behind the normality of bourgeois respectability, the commercial stereotypes of television culture pushing its way into the furthest corners of ordinary life, or simply the rubbish moun-tains of a questionable civilisation. Using the most shocking presentation possible of what was worthless, the New York punk artists tried to question a value system whose other side they thus displayed. The requirement behind this was to re-create a relevant cultural position for art in everyday life. This 'scene' was composed of art students, scholarship holders, young film-makers, video artists, photographers and journalists, i.e. the intellectual bohemian world of Greenwich Village and Man-hattan's Lower East Side, the artists' district. The first musical evidence of the new avant-garde appeared in 1974 with the release of the single 'Piss Factory'[3] by Patti Smith, a journalist who wrote and recited poems and who had gone over to playing rock-like sound pictures as background music to performances of her unwieldy verses. Along with Patti Smith, it was above all The Ramones, Blondie, Television and the early Talking Heads who transformed the concept of punk art into rock. As publicity increased the whole movement was labelled New Wave in analogy with the Nouvelle Vague of the French cinema. Later this was to become yet another pigeon-hole for the commercialisation of rock, once the music which belonged to this field had become viable even in the USA because of the spectacular success of British punk rock. In any case one principal difference remained between American New Wave and British punk rock which the journalist Mat Snow summarised later:

Unlike British punk, American New Wave never really conveyed a sense of history in the making, of bands being harbingers of social change. Nor did the commercial success of Patti Smith, Talking Heads and Blondie influence pop's mainstream and record industry to the degree that did punk in Britain. Artistic diversity and freedom was the New Wave's common cause, which quickly became incorporated into the marketing wisdom of the majors.[4]

And in this sense even the Sex Pistols were at first nothing more than an art project with which McLaren tried to translate the early New York New Wave/avant-garde into a Situationist performance art and to develop it further according to his own ideas. What was in the forefront of his mind while he was doing this was the conception and achievement of a novel type of artist, a type which he believed he himself realised. For he considered management not just as a commercial service activity but also an art form, creating a sort of collective work of art within a multi-media organisation. To the manager-artist the media are the instruments he plays, a skill which McLaren, as we shall see, had genuinely mastered. Thereby he opened up prospects which, after him, particularly Paul Morley and Trevor Horn with Frankie Goes to Hollywood were extremely successful in continuing. In a multi-media art of this kind the musicians themselves are merely the material for the art production, whereas the artistic result consists of the creation of an extensive media image. When the Sex Pistols broke up in 1978 after a chaotic American tour, McLaren had no intention of doing anything further with punk rock and turned instead to more or less advanced video projects. The press release from his management company Glitterbest on this occasion is typical of the nature of his musical commitment: 'The management is sick of managing a successful rock'n'roll band. The band is sick of being a successful rock'n'roll band. Burning down concert halls and destroying record companies is more creative than being successful.'[5] But quite independently of the intentions of the initiators, the destructive and anarchic concept of punk in Britain was to set off an avalanche, as a result of which arose both a musical counter-movement against the highly monopolistic production conditions of rock and a sub-culture of unemployed teenagers. With its systematic dismantling of cultural values, punk fitted smoothly into the general process of the decline of values which until then had smouldered beneath the surface but which now appeared openly with the deepening crisis of capitalism.

Britain went into the second half of the seventies facing an increasingly black future. Unemployment reached critical levels never known before. Fewer and fewer teenagers had the opportunity to find an apprenticeship or a job after they left school. In 1974 less than half of all school leavers received full vocational training. In 1977 the figures just for unemployed teenagers under eighteen were given as 29.6 per cent for girls and 28.6 per cent for boys.[6] Unemployment benefit of £18 a week and the occasional chance of a temporary job brought these teenagers very close to the Government's definition of the poverty line. At the same time, continuing unemployment led to the alienation of an increasingly large proportion of teenagers, especially working-class teenagers, for the longer they remained unemployed the less chance they had of ever being re-integrated into the work-force. The rate of inflation was consistently at 10 per cent or more. Wage strikes rocked the country. In 1976 the first serious race riots broke out in London's Notting Hill, in which black immigrant teenagers who were the most affected by these factors – the unemployment rate for this group was more than 80 per cent – carried on a civil-war like battle with mounted policemen all day. The decline in tax receipts linked to the lack of income of increasing numbers of the population ruined the municipal authorities and their services, from refuse collection to road building. Whole districts of the cities began to show the signs of decline. And at the same time the effects of a mistaken sixties city redevelopment policy made themselves felt. The expensive new blocks of flats from this period could no longer be maintained and stone deserts were created out of decaying new buildings. The crisis of capitalism now had a face.

While the country came apart at the seams, its political structures were paralysed in a right-wing conservatism which also became Government policy with the election of Margaret Thatcher as Prime Minister in 1979. A political course of confrontation was set which directed itself against the trade unions, against peace movements and against foreigners, in short against everything which was to the left of the extreme right and which did not represent capital-intensive interests. The war in Northern Ireland intensified, and IRA bomb attacks stirred up the defeatist mood. The mass media, and the press in particular, increased the latent chauvinism present in public opinion. Their headlines hammered the word 'crisis' into the public consciousness in larger and larger letters. A call for 'law and order' swept across the country.

Against this background the Sex Pistols appeared as an embodiment of the general situation. They provided the crisis with a cultural symbol which pushed this society's pathological nature to monstrous heights, gave the decline a vivid and immediate form by translating it into chaos and anarchy. Their first single 'Anarchy in the UK'[7] is quite symptomatic of this.

This anarchist credo was literally spat out by Sex Pistols lead singer Johnny Rotten in a barely articulated scream. The whole thing was accompanied by a frenzied noise made up of the monotonous screeching sound of guitars played in parallel and drums being flogged mercilessly. Undisguised anger hammered the short phrases of a minimalist two-chord aesthetic into the heads of their listeners. This was the sensuous force of rock speaking, more uncompromising than ever before and with no consideration for the musical values of the rock elite celebrated by the media. The increasingly elitist attitudes of Gentle Giant, Yes, Pink Floyd, Roxy Music or David Bowie, and their morbid intellectual and artistic claims, had removed rock music further and further from the social realities of the everyday teenager. Although at first it was this very effect which had formed the attraction of these groups and musicians, their attitude quickly led them to lose their foundation in the rock audience, the more so as the real situation of the audience brought quite different problems to light than those which they received in such an intellectual game with rock's various forms of expression. It is not surprising that the anarchy which the Sex Pistols demonstrated with the radical reversal of all rock music's conceptions of value offered the increasing number of unemployed school leavers in particular an opportunity for identification. Yet this in no way represented a politically articulated protest against their situation, but rather expressed an indifferent hopelessness, resulting from the failure of political opportunities for action with the student movement at the end of the sixties and the apparent lack of prospects for political action. Over this point there was doubtless agreement between the initiators and the fast growing teenage punk following. Sex Pistols' lead singer Johnny Rotten had this to say: 'We mean musical anarchy ... politics is simply too stupid. All liars up there. Musical anarchy means chucking away all the boring, bourgeois, organised stuff. As soon as the game gets too organised – we'll simply take off.'[8]

And this was exactly what they did when they broke up in 1978 at the commercial high point of the punk wave. For unemployed teenagers in Britain they were above all the comprehensive symbol of a social situation which had in any case lost every element of normality so that even 'normal' rock categories were no longer suitable. They were not in the least concerned with a direct musical translation of their situation, with the recognisable image of their real life conditions or even the mediation of these circumstances in a political form. So we must agree with Simon Frith in every respect when he questions the circumstantial equation of punk rock with the social consequences of youth unemployment – as the often quoted term 'dole queue rock',[9] coined by Peter Marsh suggests:

So the notion of dole queue rock needs redefining, at least. For the vast majority of the young unemployed, pop music is an ever-present background to social activity, but has no particular ideological significance. And, in this respect, punk is just another form of pop. It is not heard as an expression of their conditions. Their problem is work, punk's concern is leisure.[10]

The relationship between punk rock and the social consequences of youth unemployment was on a quite different level.

Spreading unemployment among school leavers created a teenage sub-culture which gave the difficult experience of unemployment a cultural form. Punk rock was part of this, one element among others, and was therefore not the direct 'expression' of this experience. This was a novelty in so far as all previous sub-cultures had developed from the problems of teenage class experiences. But unemployment, and particularly long-term unemployment, creates its own social reality which pushes any links with all-embracing class contexts into the background and ultimately makes them meaningless. The experience of unemployment is structured by different factors: social isolation, the decay of any time structure that might regulate each individual's life, and boredom. This does not in any way overlook the forms of a new poverty, linked to the loss of income, in all the capitalist industrial countries. But as is obvious from youth unemployment, which of course does not only affect teenagers from the lowest social classes and whose material hardships can then be compensated for by parents, the factors listed above are those that have the most serious effects which cannot be removed even through financial improvements. The sub-culture which arose around punk rock was moulded decisively by these factors. The bizarre costumes of the punk fans take their significance from this context, as a concrete form of the cultural contexts which mediated the problems of unemployment.

Subjectively, the most important of these factors was undoubtedly boredom, for this is the one factor experienced most directly. In fact as a general rule boredom should not be underestimated as an element of the cultural contexts within which involvement with rock music takes place. Peter Weigelt captured this barely describable situation very vividly:

Boredom is when there's nothing going on but you still have the feeling that something must be happening. On the other hand, a lot can be happening without you getting very excited by it. At one point the world around you is not attractive enough to make you warm to it. At another point you feel that these exciting surroundings are not at all able to include your own need to change your current situation.[11]

Thus boredom has less to do with a real lack of activities on offer than with a subjective lack of enthusiasm for the available activities. In the circumstances of unemployment this becomes even more potent if unemployment becomes a hopeless permanent situation. What makes sense any more when each day no longer has a goal and is no longer regulated by clear periods of time which set a boundary even to boredom, but instead passes formlessly? The result of this is a subjective devaluation of everything which ends in pure nihilism. And it is this that is the key to the punk sub-culture. The prerequisite for the cultural activities which developed here is to experience the world as a heap of worthless junk. It is only this prerequisite which shows the logic of the strategy developed by the punks of the cultural use of everyday objects, of obsolete fashions, of banal objects from the rubbish heap of civilisation and of a dismantled rock music. This inner logic consists of the production of a permanent crisis of meaning.

The punks combined everything that they could obtain in such a way that things lost their meaning and displayed this lack of meaning sharply. Dick Hebdige describes this in great detail:

Like Duchamp's 'ready mades' – manufactured objects which qualified as art because he chose to call them such – the most unremarkable and inappropriate items – a pin, a plastic clothes peg, a television component, a razor blade, a tampon – could be brought within the province of punk (un)fashion. Anything within or without reason could be turned into part of what Vivienne Westwood called 'confrontation dressing' so long as the rupture between 'natural' and constructed context was clearly visible (i.e. the rule would seem to be: if the cap doesn't fit, wear it). Objects borrowed from the most sordid of contexts found a place in the punk's ensembles: lavatory chains were draped in graceful arcs across chests encased in plastic bin-liners. Safety pins were taken out of their domestic 'utility' context and worn as gruesome ornaments through the cheek, ear or lip. 'Cheap' trashy fabrics (PVC, plastic, lurex, etc.) in vulgar designs (e.g. mock leopard skin) and 'nasty' colours, long discarded by the quality end of the fashion industry as obsolete kitsch, were salvaged by the punks and turned into garments (fly boy drainpipes, 'common' miniskirts) which offered self-conscious commentaries on the notions of modernity and taste. Conventional ideas of prettiness were jettisoned along with the traditional feminine lure of cosmetics ... Hair was obviously dyed (hay yellow, jet black, or bright orange with tufts of green or bleached-in question marks), and T-shirts and trousers told the story of their own construction with multiple zips and outside seams clearly displayed ... The perverse and the abnormal were valued intrinsically. In particular, the illicit iconography of sexual fetishism was used to predictable effect. Rapist masks and rubber wear, leather bodices and fishnet stockings, implausibly pointed stiletto-heeled shoes, the whole paraphernalia of bondage – the belts, straps and chains – were exhumed from the boudoir, closet and the pornographic film and placed on the street where they retained their forbidden connotations.[12]

This was simultaneously a reversal of the principle of advertising. While in advertising things were combined in order to give them an additional meaning designed to provide an impetus to purchase – for example the combination of washing powder with whiter than white washing and the happy smile of the housewife – the punks combined these things in order to take away their original 'natural' meaning and to make them artefacts of futility. The shocking thing about this style was that it refused every sensible classification into existing categories.

But at the same time this aggressive cult of the ugly which the punks carried quite purposefully from the working-class suburbs into the elegant inner-city district of the City concealed the rather wretched attempt to overcome an experience which Richard Hell described in these words: 'to belong to a generation classified null by society'.[13] Unemployment always means social isolation, being shut out from other people's normal everyday life, which for the punks led to a marked consciousness of the division between 'us' and 'them', expressed in a form of self-presentation which made the contrast quite visible. They were literally walking rubbish sculptures, deliberately exposed to public view in such a way that confrontation had to follow and the sores in the healthy world of consumer capitalism were cynically displayed. Dick Hebdige commented on this: 'the punks dissembled, dying to recreate themselves in caricature, to "dress up" their Destiny in its true colours, to substitute the diet for hunger, to slide the ragamuffin look (unkempt but meticulously coutured) between poverty and elegance'.[14]

So these teenagers acted out their own fate in a way calculated to produce a certain effect. Each of them interacted with public opinion in his own way and posed in front of the media mirror. It was only in the media image, in the press and on television, that the comical arrangement of selected ugliness had any significance: i.e. to transform alienation from society into a reabsorption, if a negative one, through the reactions which it provoked. Thus Rudi Thiessen is quite correct when he writes about the punk sub-culture: 'Those who get excited about the lack of taste forget to ask what must have happened when vulnerability cannot effectively be expressed in any other way.'[15] The punks gave unemployment a cultural and aesthetic form by functioning as presenters and designers of their own everyday life. To be a punk meant draping oneself in a collection of rags and shocking objects and being on display like this every evening. The hopelessness of this activity speaks for itself.

Within this sub-culture, developed by unemployed teenagers in conflict with their everyday life, the musical anarchy of the Sex Pistols was transformed into a style of dress in which a context of cultural activities materialised. In this context the music was included as an element of confrontation, as a leisure environment and as a means of expression. Music was integrated into the cultural activities of these teenagers and used in the same way as any other object in the punk ensemble, except that music made a multi-dimensional involvement possible and made it the basis of the whole sub-culture. It functioned both as leisure environment and the background for the 'scene' in clubs, cellar bars and pubs, and was simultaneously an aesthetic medium of expression and a stylistic element in the punk confrontation ensemble, as well as the ideological form which mediated these teenagers' consciousness of themselves as unemployed and their consciousness of their social status. This necessarily linked musical performance to different criteria than those upon which rock music had previously been based. But what were far more important than the conflict with stylistic and conceptual questions of music were the social and cultural activities which supported such a conflict – the role of music as an alternative to unemployment (whatever this might bring with it) and its accessibility within those cultural contexts which matched the opportunities of unemployed teenagers. If punk rock is interpreted as the result of a search for more genuine musical forms of expression, closer to reality, it is fundamentally misunderstood. We should not challenge Simon Frith's view that: 'The "realism" of punk can be more easily explained as the result of the "lack of realism" of mainstream rock and pop.'[16]

What was at issue here was the re-opening of rock music to those opportunities for cultural use which had originally been part of its nature, but which were no longer accessible to these teenagers. But this cannot simply be put down to the one-dimensional formula of an aesthetic of content which considers the realism of these songs, their closeness to ordinary life and even their protest content as the only criteria. Of course there are punk songs which are influenced by a politically formulated attitude of protest, like The Clash's 'Garageland'[17] or 'White Riot'.[18] But on the whole the song, structured through the verbal message, plays only a subordinate role in punk rock. It is nowhere more clear than in punk rock that rock music is supported by a multi-dimensional matrix of cultural activities, from which a musically closed image as the form of the social content included within it cannot be separated. Punk rock does not owe its structure to a new social realism but to the cultural activities of its fans – as background and framework for their gatherings every evening, as live dance music, as compensation for boredom, as an element of confrontation in the cultural context they have developed, as an opportunity to do something once music was no longer linked to particular technical or musical constraints. Simon Frith condensed this into the following formula: 'This music is about making the best of a bad situation; it is not about changing it.'[19] With this in mind it is pure romanticism to explain punk rock as the musical means of expression for the social protest of the young unemployed. They did indeed place rock music in a specific cultural context of use, but this context was determined not by their political consciousness but by the structures of the everyday life they lived. Within this context music, although bound to other requirements than those already mentioned, again followed the characteristic dynamics of a commercially organised mass music.

It is also true of punk rock that it is not a spontaneous 'grass roots' music, supported by the community of musicians and fans, even though these were precisely the terms on which musicians justified their claim to access to the industry's production opportunities. This view found a programmatic expression in the fan magazine *Sniffin' Glue* – published by Mark Perry, a musician with the group Alternative TV – one of those cheaply produced and photocopied broadsheets 'by fans for fans'. This extract is typical:

> Music is a perfect medium for shoving two fingers up at the establishment. Once it becomes respectable it loses all its potency. That's what occurred during the seventies. All the aggression had faded and rock stars seemed more interested in becoming tax exiles or partying it up with royalty than looking after their fans who, after all, had put them on the top. What they needed was a firm boot up the arse. And that's what they got. No more farting about, just raw, honest rockin', brought back on the intimate level of the band and their audience. Back to the roots, expressed in a contemporary manner.[20]

In spite of this the punk bands, no less than any others, fulfilled their prescribed role as musicians whose status was quite different from that of their fans, simply because they were employed. Just how big this difference was was often more than clear in their statements. For example, Hugh Cornell of The Stranglers once said in an interview: 'The depression has affected us as much as anybody else just by seeing the expressions on people's faces, and anyone being generally pissed off.'[21] Seeing these things is admittedly quite different from being affected by them oneself. What changed within the contexts developed by the punks was the way the musicians saw themselves and therefore the ideology of rock. It was no longer their individuality as musicians but their common ground with their audience which was over-nourished. With this shift, instead of being linked to an ideal of creativity, music once again became more strongly linked to the actual cultural use of rock. However, the basic structures of the relationship between musicians and audience, organised along commercial lines, were untouched by this. There was no question of a rebellion against the commercial mechanisms of the music industry. The rebellion was merely aimed at the concept of rock established within those mechanisms.

When the first British punk rock festival took place in September 1976, it was organised with the same aim as all such events have, namely to ensure the attention of record company representatives, media people and journalists in order to pave the way for lucrative record contracts. So it is not surprising to discover that the organiser was none other than the clever Malcolm McLaren. And even the industry was not slow to include this music in their sales categories. In August 1976, *Melody Maker*, the trade newspaper of the British music industry, had already commented on the front page: 'Out of the gloriously raucous, uninhibited melee of British punk rock will emerge the musicians to inspire a fourth generation of rockers.'[22] And events ran their course as they always do, so that just a few months later the Sex Pistols' lead singer Johnny Rotten was already complaining: 'We are still the only band that doesn't have a press conference every two weeks, paying for the elite chaps to go boozing, bowing and scraping, and flying every reporter from the music press who comes running over to New York in a private jet.'[23] Admittedly the Sex Pistols no longer needed to do all this since they were the first to achieve a record contract with the music industry. Barely three weeks after the British punk rock festival in the 100 Club – organised especially for the various bosses of the rock business – they signed with EMI for a £50,000 guarantee. Nick Mobbs, EMI's A&R manager, made the following comment:

Here at last is a band which young people can identify with; a group which parents will certainly not tolerate. But it's not only parents who will benefit from being shaken up a little, but also the music business. That's the reason why a lot of A&R people wouldn't put this group under contract – they took it all too personally. But what other band at a comparable point in its career has produced so much excitement both on the stage and in the audience? As far as I'm concerned, the Sex Pistols are a reaction against the 'nice little band' syndrome and against the general stagnation of the music industry. They had to come, for all our sakes.[24]

Their single 'Anarchy in the UK' was released on 26th November 1976. Inside just a few months punk had established itself as a new category in the music business.

In fact this was concealed by the unique occurrence of a rock group, in the case of the Sex Pistols, proving to be unmarketable, in spite of the fact that their record sold quite well. Just fourteen days after it was released it reached number 38 in the British charts. But their manager Malcolm McLaren had been able to

give them such a well-aimed negative image against the background of his concept of a Situationist performance art based on
shock technique, that the beginning of the normal promotion
campaign for the single provoked a storm of indignation in
British public opinion. A television chat show appearance,
extensively peppered with volleys of offensive language, was
what provoked this. It was not the radical aesthetics of their
music and certainly not its basic anti-commercial stance, but
rather the image of the Sex Pistols, conceived by McLaren and
impossible to integrate into the usual marketing strategies of the
industry, which had the spectacular consequence that one of the
largest record companies in the world stopped selling a record and
paid the group the legal guarantee of £50,000 to order to break
the contract. EMI's business manager Leslie Hill later explained
this decision in a statement which offers a deep insight into the
logic of the rock business:

Supposing, for example, they were doing a tour. Now supposing we'd
done what we usually do with them on tour, which is to have a press
party or a party at the end of the do, or some sort of reception. You
imagine what would have happened. There would have been a riot ...,
there would have been people outside protesting, there would have been
photographers everywhere, there would have been press people
everywhere. That's not an environment in which we can operate in a
normal fashion. Now, the thing came out of it was – cos I was saying
to them: look, you do understand that if you, if you pursue this line of
publicity then it makes it difficult for us to promote your records,
because we can't do the normal things. I mean, how do we for example
promote your records overseas, because the only thing we have –
newscuttings – are all about the filth and the fury from the *Daily Mirror*.
That's very difficult to hang the promotion of records on. You know,
you can't send them all round the world and say: look at this wonderful
group we've got.[25]

It will have to remain McLaren's secret how he managed to repeat
the same ploy with the American firm A & M Records, this
time with a guarantee of £75,000. The Sex Pistols signed their
contract in the company's London office on 9th March 1977 and a
week later, on 16th March 1977, they were standing outside the
door again with a cheque for £75,000. McLaren's comments on
this to the London *Evening Standard* are not without malice:
'I keep walking in and out of offices being given cheques. When
I'm older and people ask me what I used to do for a living I

shall have to say: "I went in and out of doors getting paid for it."[26]

Of course McLaren did actually succeed in unmasking the music business with a carefully constructed publicity campaign, by making public what it is that the record companies are really interested in, namely not music at all. If the marketing of their product, the record, is made impossible, the record companies are prepared to pay considerable sums of money to stop the contradiction between their view of the product and that of their teenage purchasers – who still believe that they are paying for music – becoming all too obvious. However, it would be a mistake to suspect a politically motivated attack on the capitalist mechanisms of the music business. McLaren had realised his idea of a multi-media total work of art. To him the production was most important, the result only mattered in so far as it suited his economic interests. After this he placed the Sex Pistols under contract to his long-standing friend Richard Branson, who owned Virgin Records, one of the largest of the independent record companies (and one which had become an important factor in the British music business at the beginning of the seventies with Mike Oldfield and Tangerine Dream). Ultimately the two of them demonstrated that even a negative image can be successfully marketed. Branson placed a full-page advertisement every week in the music press which consisted of an embarrassing list of those shops who refused to sell Sex Pistols records and those disc jockeys who refused to play their records on the radio. McLaren made sure that the list never grew shorter. The success of this strategy was overwhelming.

There is no doubt, then, that punk rock also developed within the same music industry contexts as had always been characteristic of rock music. However, punk was linked to a change in the structures of the music business as a result of which a new musical infrastructure arose, made up of small independent firms, labels owned by musicians themselves, local concert agents and promoters – all of which is often used as the argument for the supposed anti-commercial character of punk. But in fact this only made the commercial mechanisms of the music business more efficient because it compensated for the disadvantages of its centralisation. John Peel, one of the most committed and most popular British radio disc jockeys, with his own programme on the BBC – the only one, by the way, who did not ban the Sex Pistols from his programme in spite of his director's strong 'recommendation' to do so – assessed this factor very realistically:

to me the most important thing that came out of the punk years was the demystification of the whole process of making records. Prior to that, there were two things. One, it was assumed – correctly – that you had to come to London and place yourself in the hands of some sharp shit entrepreneur to get ahead in the world of showbiz ... Two, the only bands in the mid-70s who got signed up were bands who contained at least one member of a previously successful band. It was extraordinarily difficult for a band of unknown people to make a record ... I can remember Bryan Ferry sitting in our office in 1972 and trying to persuade Walters and myself of the virtues of this band of his, and I'm sitting here thinking, 'yeah, but there's nobody famous in it'![27]

In other words, the 'independents' significantly increased the opportunities for entry into the rock business rather than creating an alternative to that business.

It only remains to stress that ultimately the punk rebellion conceals nothing more than a transformation of the aesthetic criteria according to which rock music defines itself. But this reveals with a previously unseen clarity how every one-dimensional attempt to explain the reality of this form of music misses the point. If we return to the starting-point, the radical aesthetic change linked to punk rock cannot be attributed either to the innovationary forces of the music industry or to teenagers' need for musical expression. It is due far more to the contradictory context of social, cultural, aesthetic, musical, technological and economic factors, within which context both have their role to play. Rock music cannot be reduced to a single-level basic model which was maintained more or less successfully throughout its development. Thus even punk rock did not return rock music to its 'real' origins, and equally punk rock does not provide the proof for the thesis that rock ultimately represents only a particularly cleverly manufactured entertainment product for the commercial exploitation of teenagers' leisure. In Alan Durant's opinion:

At points of complexity such as these, the reductiveness in much orthodox 'sociological' thinking on rock music, which seeks to explain it as either capitalist exploitation or sub-cultural dissent, is exposed.

What represents revolt to one audience, can at the same time be the planned creativity of an industry and the market for a different audience, whilst the two disparate frameworks frequently share identical 'texts' and agencies.[28]

Rock music exists on different planes, in different relationships and has links to different contexts, within which it appears with different functions and linked to different meanings and values.

8

'Wild Boys': the aesthetic of the synthetic

The after-effects of punk rock were characterised by a multiplicity of overlapping developments, by different musical concepts and by a variety of stylistic forms of expression. The punk-inspired opening up of the music business to the activities of small independent firms, local promoters and alternative directions in music, resulted in a creative explosion which pushed the succession of styles, fashions and trends to breakneck speed. The strands of pop music development which had previously been carefully kept separate now ran together in the most remarkable crossovers to make a mixture of disparate musical forms. Disco music, funk and reggae found themselves in an unconventional synthesis with punk, hard rock and heavy metal, as in the punk-funk fusion of Bush Tetras, in the heavy metal-funk of Level 42 or in the symbiosis of rock and reggae produced by The Clash and a series of British punk bands. Dub, rap and the sound creations of overstyled electronic dandies, labelled the New Romantics, provided the background for a wave of dance crazes in the discotheques. Peter Tosh, Big Youth and Inner Circle were offering reggae in a pop-influenced disco mix. Rockabilly, ska, soul, rhythm & blues, rock'n'roll and the unmistakable Liverpool Merseybeat guitar sound of the early sixties were experiencing a revival which broadened out into a discriminating reappraisal of the whole musical heritage of rock history.

Post punk, with groups like PIL, Pop Group or Gang of Four, as well as the American No Wave bands like DNA or Teenage Jesus, introduced itself with a mixture of aggressive noise, musical minimalism and stereotyped repetition with clear references to the 'minimalist music' of the classical avant-garde in Philip Glass, Terry Riley and Steve Reich. Linked to an insistent disco-funk rhythm and the chains of sound of synthesisers and sequencers this became the synthetic pop of Human League, Depeche Mode, Duran Duran and Bronski Beat. And with this the once carefully guarded boundary between rock and pop collapsed. In contrast, the New Wave, the direct descendants of the punk attack, revived the rebellious spirit of early rock music, dressed in a thoroughly electronic sound, mixed with the urbane images of the experience of technical industrial landscapes, the reflexes of an alienated everyday life and the explosive nature of the growing social potential for conflict. Meanwhile on the other side of the Atlantic, Bruce Springsteen was celebrating un-expected success with a rebirth of classic rock'n'roll. While on the one hand David Bowie, Boy George O'Dowd of Culture Club and Jimi Somerville of Bronski Beat dissolved the gender-specific code of stereotyped manhood in an oscillating image of homo-sexuality, on the other hand a women's movement arose in rock, which sought to formulate a female identity in music under the slogans 'Rock against Sexism' or 'Women's Liberation'. In Britain, with the successful establishment of the 'Rock against Racism' campaign, political contexts in particular began once more to act as catalysts for the different rock playing styles. Former activists of the punk movement like The Jam, The Clash, Boomtown Rats and the Tom Robinson Band left behind their anarchic anti-capitalism in favour of a clearly leftist political profile, which then gave rise to the plebeian cult of the Redskins and the political commitment of Billy Bragg. At the other end of the political spectrum a radical right-wing version of rock arose for the first time with the extremely reactionary Oi Music.

From now on every concept of a continuing course of develop-ment of in some measure clearly differentiated playing styles, however formulated, seemed to vanish into thin air. An acceler-ated expansion of aesthetic codes, of musical and cultural styles, removed earlier boundaries and poured out in a diversity of multiple directions, each of which also continued to change throughout their course. Iain Chambers' diagnosis was: 'Musical and cultural styles ripped out of other contexts, stripped of their initial referents, circulate in such a manner that they represent nothing other than their own transitory presence.'[1] A boundless 'pluralism of pleasure' (Chambers) was the only law which still held good for this development which was continually collapsing into fragments, forming symbiotic relationships and collapsing again. This situation marks quite unmistakably a phase of radical change where neither the end of the phase nor even the outlines of future horizons were already discernible.

New media and new technologies have achieved validity, and have on the one hand placed music in changed contexts, while on the other hand their technical reproducability has reached its limit. Hi-fi cassette recorders and the triumph of the Walkman undermined the supremacy of the record, and home taping of borrowed rather than purchased records became the industry's nightmare. Cassette technology had reached a point in its development at which the low price of the equipment (which made it universally accessible) almost outweighed the deficiencies in quality in comparison with records. According to a representative market research project undertaken by the German company BASF, 1.15 billion cassettes were sold worldwide in 1978.[2] The record had lost its exclusivity in the distribution of music.

In fact the late seventies and early eighties saw a decline in the development of the record industry after a long period of uninterrupted growth throughout the sixties and seventies. In 1980 sales of records had fallen to the 1972 level. EMI, which in 1970 had made 12.7 per cent of its annual total profit from record sales, in 1979 could only produce 0.4 per cent of the company's annual profit from the music division.[3] The British Phonographic Institute, one of the most renowned market research institutes in this field, declared in 1981 that in 1980 the British music industry had lost more than £1 million per day (!) in turnover because of home taping.[4] Whether this figure is exaggerated or not, with recently improved quality standards cassette technology doubtless represented an alternative medium for the distribution of music that was very difficult to control commercially. This fact was not at all affected by the common practice of releasing pre-recorded cassettes in parallel with records. Of course, we should not overlook the fact that the losses in the record business which the multi-national media organisations in particular were complaining about meant a profit for the same companies' hi-fi equipment divisions and cassette factories.

But it was two quite different factors which affected the falling turnover figures of the record companies more directly. The first of these was an increase in the price of records due both to the shortage of oil, the raw material for vinyl, and to the arrival of new technology in music production, particularly the change to digital recording. The second was the simultaneous and progressive worsening of the social situation of working-class teenagers in particular, together with the seemingly unstoppable spread of mass unemployment. In 1981 a UNESCO report on the situation of young people in the capitalist industrial nations in the eighties forecast:

The key words in the experience of young people in the coming decade are going to be: 'scarcity', 'unemployment', 'underemployment', 'ill-employment', 'anxiety', 'defensiveness', 'pragmatism', and even 'subsistence' and 'survival' itself. If the 1960s challenged certain categories of youth in certain parts of the world with a crisis of culture, ideas and institutions, the 1980s will confront a new generation with a concrete, structural crisis of chronic economic uncertainty and even deprivation.[5]

In most of the capitalist industrial nations this forecast was to be realised in far more drastic terms than was obvious at the beginning of the decade. The music industry's gold seam threatened to run out as, not the interest in rock, but the demand for records and the ability to pay for them declined among its key teenage markets. The logic of the system, simply oriented to production quotas, turnover figures and profit, forced investment in new technology and new media in order to open up new markets which would once again promise continuing growth. Music production's conversion from analog to digital technology, and therefore its adaptation to the use of computer systems, brought with it market advantages, limited only by innovation, which were linked with novel sound materials and sound effects. This strategy continued in the digital compact disc (CD), successfully introduced by PolyGram at enormous cost. The 1985 figures released by the British Phonographic Institute prove that this development was a success in every respect. According to these figures, sales of singles in Britain still showed a 0.9 per cent decline over the previous year, sales of LPs once again showed a growth of 7.5 per cent, whereas the growth rate for sales of CDs was 300 per cent.[6]

However, the extensive development of the cable television network in combination with the satellite transmission of television programmes should have been of far greater significance to the music industry, for this increased not only television's commercial reach but also its programme capacity. Music Television (MTV) emerged and with it the pop video. Via satellite, programmes could now be fed directly from the control centres of the multi-national media organisations into the commercial cable network all over the world. This development gave the television market a structure similar to that of the record market and thereby opened up totally new prospects for the marketing of music. Instead of sending a band on worldwide tour at enormous cost to promote their record, a video produced to go with the record could be sent out through the cable networks to achieve the same effect. In this way the record companies began to exercise almost total control over the image of bands and musicians. Thus, within a very short space of time, the development of music found itself in a new media context, one which was not to remain without effect on its immanent aesthetic strategies and rules of formation, which removed existing musical categories and replaced them with new ones as well as linking musical performance to altered technical, economic and institutional requirements. This resulted in an extensive shift of direction and marketing towards those teenagers from the *petit bourgeois* middle classes who still had more money to spend and who, in contrast to working-class teenagers, could most effectively be reached via television.

This development made one thing very clear, namely the extent to which, in the context of mass culture, even music functions as one element of the whole, a whole which influences each of its elements in its role as overall context. What was previously still produced in separate production spheres, each with its own conventions, its own history and its own traditions and which only worked as mass culture in the overall structure, was now drawn together directly in the pop video. Of course, in the fifties film and television had already played a role in the spread of rock'n'roll. We only need to recall the Elvis Presley or Bill Haley films or the television show *American Bandstand*, which became an institution of American musical life. So links between these fields are not really very new, just as both media had always been integrated in teenagers' cultural everyday life alongside music and here, at least, alternately had an effect on each other, even when they operated separately. In contrast to this the pop video unified the most popular media of mass culture – music, television and film. In 1982 John Howkins considered this in an analysis of the structural effects of the new information technologies on the music business published in the yearbook of the British Phonographic Institute:

Many industries, hitherto very separate in their traditions, industrial practices and finances are converging around this video nexus. The TV industry, the film industry, the music industry, telecommunications, publishing and computers, which at present operate under different government departments, regulations and conventions, are now finding themselves sub-industries of a whole new area of activity.[7]

This is a process which is no longer comprehensible merely from the logic of music development alone, even though to a great extent it was driven by the large companies in the music business and, particularly in this sphere, demonstrates important consequences which made the pop video one of the most momentous of the new media, at least in terms of popular art. In the pop video, strands of musical development join together which – even if at first they have clearly been made to function thus in the commercial interest – break down the existing rules of artistic discourse, deprive the inherited musical and visual stereotypes of mass culture of their traditional meanings and, in a combination of images, styles, signs, symbols, myths, rhythms and sounds which swallow everything, allow the possibility of an audio-visual media art to appear within the context of everyday life. The realisation of this is admittedly still far off and within the iron bonds of commerce is probably not to be expected in the near future.

The creation of the pop video, the coupling of music and image in a visualised song, was directly linked to the American cable television project MTV: Music Television. Of course the pop video had its antecedents in film, whose history stretches back into the thirties, just as both the video cassette and the video disc had already been used in music distribution. It was at the height of the swing era in the thirties that the practice arose of filming performances of the most popular songs as shorts for cinemas' supporting programmes. In the fifties these became jukebox-films, circular loops of film in music machines which showed the rock'n'rollers of the time in action. One further development was video disc machines, introduced in America in the late seventies. Even after this film versions of individual songs were occasionally produced, usually for television, such as the Beatles' songs 'Penny Lane' and 'Strawberry Fields Forever' or the 1975 Jon Roseman production for the Queen song 'Bohemian Rhapsody' which was closer in style to the current pop video. Since home video recorders have been available – they appeared on the market in 1977 – pre-recorded video cassettes with recordings of rock groups in concert have been sold. But the pop video, also called a video clip or simply, and tellingly, a promo, differs from all the above not only through its inclusion in functional contexts determined purely by commercial factors, but above all through its peculiar laws of creation, which naturally had their effects on music and its development.

MTV, introduced on 1st August 1981, was the first 24-hour cable television station broadcasting nothing but music. MTV was owned by the Warner Amex Satellite Entertainment Company (WASEC), a joint enterprise of Warner Communications and the banking consortium American Express founded in 1979. The cable station, consisting of little more than an office and a small studio in Manhattan, transmits its programme in stereo sound via the RCA-owned communications satellite COMSAT, meaning that yet another giant of the American music business is in on the act. MTV goes into over 2,700 cable networks with about 24 million subscribers in 48 states in America, as well as into the Canadian cable networks and also daily, for an hour at a time, into the commercial music channel Music Box, run on similar lines by Thorn-EMI, Virgin Records and Yorkshire Television, which since 1983 has been feeding its programmes into the cable networks of the whole of Western Europe and Scandinavia from London via satellite. MTV, like its Western European counterpart, is one of the cable networks' standard channels which can be received free of charge apart from a monthly basic fee for the cable connection. Thus the programmes are financed exclusively by advertising scattered extensively between the pop videos, presented by a 'video jockey'. The programme is based on the video clips made available by record companies so that, with the exception of the interspersed contributions from the presenter in the New York studio, the MTV programme costs practically nothing. However, the investment and running costs of the station are enormous since satellite transmission of the programme is extremely expensive. Although WASEC runs two 'pay-TV' channels, The Movie Channel and Nickleodeon – linked to Warner Communications' film interests and which can only be received on payment of an additional fee per programme – and although it has a large income from advertising on all three channels, achieving a turnover of around 3 billion dollars per year, the company's initial losses still ran into the millions. In 1983 Kevin D'Arcy reported in the magazine *Broadcast*:

The American Express and Warner combine – Warner/Amex – is reckoned to be losing 40 million dollars a year and has so far cost some 800 million dollars. But even here the odds are favourable on their making a profit breakthrough within five years. Their Movie Channel had an increase in audience of around 30% in the last year, Nickleodeon put on 60%, while Music TV, the 24-hour pop channel, has 40% more viewers.[8]

This highlights the real level of interest behind the MTV project, for investment at this level and with these sorts of losses is always calculated very exactly. The company paid 20 million dollars for the initial market research. The whole project is only indirectly concerned with television and television entertainment. Apart from the forecast long-term effects, which must always have attendant risks and which on their own would have been unlikely to tempt even such a capital-intensive supporter as the combination of Warner Communications and American Express to such a large investment, it is the side-effects of MTV which constitute the real business for both companies. According to Andrew Goodwin's analysis: 'Warner's interest here is a classic example of consolidation, since MTV has been shown to have significant effects on record sales. American Express have a similar interest in cable, since interactive cable systems can have enormous implications for home banking and shopping.'[9]

The fact that it is precisely in this area that companies who are normally only too happy to offer information are guarded about their figures and that they would rather put themselves forward as self-sacrificing pioneers of progress in communications in the common interest, speaks for itself. Indirect profits, which give an insight into the way the web of interests of a few major organisations penetrates everyday life in capitalist societies, and which would be disclosed by the construction of a self-regulating system, are not to be found in any of the statistics. Instead, Robert Pittman, former programme director of MTV, had this to say about the way the company saw itself:

We're now seeing the TV become a component of the stereo system. It's ridiculous to think that you have two forms of entertainment – your stereo and your TV – which have nothing to do with one another. What we're doing is marrying those two forms so they work together in unison. We're the first channel on cable that pioneers this ... MTV is the first attempt to make TV a new form, other than video games and data channels.[10]

In reality, MTV is purely an advertising channel with two simultaneous functions, apart from the usual product advertising which is integrated into the programme. The video clips advertise records and the attraction of the music advertises the cable connection. However, even a capital-intensive company like WASEC had ultimately overreached itself with the MTV project, offering an insight into the gigantic costs of media entertainment. At the end of 1985 WASEC was forced to sell the MTV-Network, renamed after the addition of a second pop video channel – VH-1 – in January 1985. It was bought by Viacom International, an international television programme service, for a mere billion dollars.

Its origins make the pop video a form of advertising. It is precisely this which distinguishes it from all previous fusions of film and music or television and music, which like the rock films of the past or the television pop music programmes attempted to transmit visually the experience of music. By contrast, the pop video overlays music with the language of images belonging to advertising and it follows its own aesthetic, which necessarily penetrates the music. The British journalist Don Watson commented: 'Never has the world of pop culture been so close to the world of advertising, the world of lifestyle sales.'[11]

It is no coincidence that video producers are dominated by former advertising film-makers and that they have shaped the imagery of the videos with their professional standards. The outward characteristics of this are swift computer-controlled image sequences, slow motion, hard cut-out images, frequent changes of format and perspective, unusual camera angles and the whole advertising film repertoire of visual and technical effects. The song that is presented in this manner becomes part of a function which subjects it to the aesthetic rules of advertising. Paul Morley summed up this development:

The video champions the idea that the pop single is something purely to be sold, it destroys the lingering belief that a single can be composed and packaged because a few people feel a violent need for that song to be thrust abrasively into the world. The video claims that the pop song is a canned object, not any kind of event.[12]

The consequences of this are most clearly observable in the trend of the British 'boy groups' – Duran Duran, Frankie Goes to Hollywood, Bronski Beat or Wham – which owes its existence entirely to the commercial effectiveness of the video. Musically a techno-sound, set to rhythm computers and fabricated using all the possibilities of the recording studio, made up of breathy and excessively repetitive patterns, these productions only come to life on video.

A prototype of these productions was the November 1984 Duran Duran release 'Wild Boys',[13] which Russel Mulcahy made into an exemplary video. The aesthetic peculiarities and artistic possibilities as well as the problems of the pop video are more clearly visible in this video than in practically any other example. The song itself is a classic example of the high energy dance music of the eighties, labelled synthi-pop, given a rather aggressive undertone by the distorted heavy metal sound of the guitar which dominates the song and the howling lilt of the title phrase in the refrain. This is in contrast to the soulless mechanical rigidity of the basic rhythm. The lyrics, sung in a forced high-pitched voice, practically whining, consist of a loose series of linguistic images rich in metaphors with no recognisable story-line.

The video of this song shows a surrealistic and apocalyptic world full of confusing symbolism. Nightmarish, dark, unconnected images rush by frantically in no particular order, bathed in a pale blueish light or in the flickering glow of flames. The images change every few seconds, often merely leaving behind the fleeting trace of an impression, only to freeze again into painfully captivating detailed scenes. The camera perspective continually moves between all the imaginable angles, making any spatial orientation, any relation of up and down, right and left, practically impossible. Instead a ceaseless, directionless movement runs through the sequence of images. The scenery is dominated by battle, attack, aggression and stylised force. The members of Duran Duran are included in these ghostly events, but at the same time stand outside them – they appear on video on a screen which is continually brought into the action. The collection of symbols is devoid of any logic: men knock tables over, bathed in flickering shadows, tongues of flame blaze from their mouths, a figure enveloped in a floating cape approaches dangerously slowly; a robot-like man/machine head turns, spewing flames, to a video screen which shows Duran Duran playing 'Wild Boys'; half-naked savages, dressed in leather shorts, with painted upper bodies and punk hair styles perform archaic dances; on the screen a time bomb begins to tick; flames leap up; laboratory equipment becomes visible; a lift platform sinks into a metal stucture; bodies whirl through the air like bullets; a windmill appears with Duran Duran's lead singer tied to one of the sails, rotating through the air; another of the group, locked in a cage, is working hard at the most modern computers, while a third is undergoing a form of brain-washing using photographs of himself; the savages and their barbaric dance games dominate the scene again; out of nowhere appears a mediaeval flying machine with a man in it; one of the savages tries to catch it with a lasso, but it races straight into the windmill, releasing the lead singer from his rotation torture; he then immediately finds himself in shimmering green water, threatened by a monster; the band's guitarist hangs from the metal structure, barely holding on to the supports, playing his guitar; the pictures follow one another faster and faster – and then suddenly Duran Duran, having escaped from the nightmare, are in an old American car, being showered with confetti, with pictures of the dancing savages interspersed, like memories.

The music, mostly made up of rhythmicised layers of pitch repetition, drives the sequence of pictures and structures the visual course of movement yet without justifying or even affecting this apocalyptic nightmare with its mechanical synchronisation. The music is somehow rather empty, a mere pattern of movement. It is also scarcely possible to establish any clear references to the lyrics, and those references that are possible are formal and aimed at isolated terms like fire, war, blood, wild boys. But even then there are no clear classifications. Who are the wild boys in the video, the dancing savages, Duran Duran, both? And equally other visual symbols like the windmill, the laboratory equipment, the mediaeval flying machine and the luxurious old American car do not correspond meaningfully to anything in the lyrics or music. But for all this the images are by no means meaningless. Looked at more closely, each scene is a carefully constructed quotation from the repertoire of action sequences from adventure and science fiction films and therefore refers to the viewer's previous media experiences, since he has probably seen the relevant scenes in hundreds of different versions in the cinema or on television and therefore has the visual stereotypes to hand. But in the video these are denuded of their logical connection and of any continuing development and are fragmented. The scenes are repeated, and after a few seconds once again show the same movements and gestures. But the results and the consequences are missing. At the same time these scenes are linked to obviously unconnected images – the flying machine reminiscent of Leonardo da Vinci's visions, the windmill, alchemistic laboratory equipment, the most modern computer technology, outsized video screens, cages, futuristic metal structures, the mythical creature in the water, the old American car, the savages, modelled on comic strip characters and given punk accessories. What is at work here is the aesthetic law of advertising.

Advertising is based on a simple and effective principle, the combination of two apparently disparate sign systems through a series of formal techniques. It attempts to give a product a particular meaning for its potential buyers by combining an aesthetically prepared symbol of it, perhaps a photographic representation, with another, more emotionally effective symbol. For example a bottle of orange juice appears in close-up on a picture showing an artistic south seas sunset. The photograph of the bottle in itself means little more than that it is a particular brand of orange juice. But the picture of the sunset is full of affective meaning, representing holidays and the experience of nature. There is no logical connection between the photograph of the bottle and the photograph of the sunset, the connection is established formally. The pictures are put together in such a way that the result is a harmonious unity in terms of colour combination and proportion, which allows the picture to appear quite natural when it in fact presents an equally arbitrary and illogical composition. But through this technique the orange juice has acquired the refreshing and relaxing effect of a summer holiday and the force and exotic appeal of nature. This does not alter the taste one jot, but the product makes an impression. Precisely because of this it is often very similar products which appear in this senseless competition over image in advertising. This is an aesthetic of the synthetic, in which context-less sign systems, images, materials, objects and symbols are combined using formal techniques – colour composition, image construction, film editing and music – to produce a new, fictitious aesthetic reality, which apparently allows the values and meanings with which it is always invested to grow together organically.

The pop video follows the same principle and uses the same techniques, except that the product that it is advertising, the record, is absent. So although it operates within the functional context of advertising, at the same time it also reverses it, since it liberates the highly developed techniques of this industry from their concrete relationship with the product. The record, whose purchase it is promoting, remains invisible. It is represented by the song, but this too is unable to take over the role of product since it also has to function as the sound backdrop for the visual events. Thus it is possible to use the aesthetic equipment of advertising in a playful and more creative way. It is precisely this which has made the video so attractive to people leaving advertising, since it lacks the constricted limits of traditional product advertising – the necessary presence of the product and the necessary limitation simply to one alternative symbolic plane as a system of reference, for it is only by doing this that the product being advertised can be given a clear, unambiguous and impressive profile. And even image-building for musicians and bands which is naturally associated with the video brings with it nothing like the pressures of the usual advertising spot. As the Duran Duran video illustrates (and there are countless other examples of this) the musicians can be included in the events in different roles quite independently of the agreed image concept. Thus the pop video opens up a completely new area of application for the formal techniques of advertising. The imagination can be given free rein to relate media images and symbols, verbal, musical and visual stereotypes to one another structured simply by formal connections – the rhythm of the music with the rhythm of the scenes, using panning and perspective to link unassociated objects, image sequences as brackets in developments that leap time and space, and so on. In the meantime a practically limitless reservoir of these sorts of possibilities has been built up.

The 'Wild Boys' video is a perfect example. In this, men throwing tables over, flames and mysteriously twitching shadows are linked into an associated event with flashing image sequences; circling camera movements allow archaic savages, machine constructions of the modern age and a time bomb ticking mercilessly to appear in the picture alternately as if these formed an organic whole; futuristic structures, man-cages reminiscent of the Dark Ages and ultra-modern computer equipment are set in relation to one another by the horizontals and verticals of their lattice structure; isolated single words in the lyrics become the key terms for whole sequences of images; the rhythmic patterns of the music synchronise unconnected series of pictures; a short guitar solo, developing and rising out of the music, serves to allow the flying machine which suddenly sweeps into view to appear as a completely natural part of events – it is practically impossible even to begin to describe the cleverly spun web of formal relationships and references in exhaustive detail.

The original meaning of the symbols, objects and stereotypes in this conglomeration refers to one another in such multi-dimensional and multi-layered synthesised forms with a clearly fictional character, erase one another, are often barely perceptible in the swift sequence of scenes, mix together and thus produce a field of associations which attracts like a magnet the visual memories of the viewer, fragments of his consciousness, his imagination and his powers of fantasy. The accusation that is often all too hastily levelled at video, that it adds yet another, visual, interpretation to the songs which in the end standardises the way these songs are perceived and even extinguishes the scope for individual associations, is just not true. It is more true to say that this is just a continuation and extension of what has already been laid down in the aesthetics of rock music. Just as there is little ground for saying that this aesthetic is merely the verbal and musical translation of a pre-formulated 'message', when in fact it is open to very different uses and to being invested with very different meanings, there is equally little ground for seeing video as the simple addition of a further, visual, plane of 'expression'. Instead video makes clear, much more so than previously, that the concept of a step-by-step translation of logical 'messages' via text, music, performance and now pictures too into the heads of the recipients is an empty one. On the contrary, the aesthetic of the synthetic, which is the basis of the pop video, through the formally created integration of verbal, musical and visual stereotypes leads to the dissolution of fixed patterns of meaning. The playful nonsense, its absurd or banal constructions, the frequent repetition of scenes, the exhibitionist use of cliches and stereotypes, instead of altering the imagination of the teenage viewer – who has grown up with these standards as the recipient of relevant films and music and who always has them to hand – rather enhances it. This can be seen as a continuing creative processing of previous media experiences. The video is also not an object of contemplation, not a 'work of art' in the traditional sense. Video responds more to television habits, which have been continuously changing, and to acquired media experiences, just as in its time rock music reacted to the way people became involved with music, an involvement altered by the portable radio and the single. In this context the attraction of video doubtless has a lot to do with the fact that, through teenagers, television has become a far more organic part of everyday life. It is no longer an emphasised family evening ritual of fixed staring at the screen, but is used in a similar way to radio – admittedly on a more prolonged basis than before, but also more selectively – as a casually accepted background which is part of meeting friends or of public leisure environments such as discotheques and is made an element of the most diverse leisure activities.[14] Thus the pop video has enormous power if, like the Duran Duran video, it can make both music and songs more open to the meanings which teenagers themselves have developed and if it can anchor them even more deeply, in a more complex, multi-dimensional and comprehensive way, in their everyday life through the attractive combination of discovery and experience.

But if there is still a decisive contrast between this and the cultural contexts of use in which rock music exists, a contrast which has also influenced the musical nature of that strand of development which is linked to the pop video in a manner that cannot be ignored, the root cause is the massive economic functionalisation of video. This has less to do with the logical reference to the visual rhetoric of advertising, which is quite capable of developing with the creative potential of aesthetic productive powers concentrated here, than with the firm linking of the pop video into the exclusively commercially determined context of the multi-national media organisations. Because of the continuing cost of the technology, video is just not as universally accessible as playing music is. Of course, it is also true that the recipients of video are not the consumer slaves of the industry, but rather build up an active involvement with this type of media product, determined by their everyday experiences, which can undermine the commercially established contexts. But it is the industry that has exclusive control over video and over the patterns of value pre-formed in it. Mark Hustwitt made the following comments on this: 'All the major routes by which promos reach the British pop music audience exist within specific economic relations which preceded the current boom in promo making, and which have direct effects on the promos seen and how they are viewed. The media carrying promos also have cultural and aesthetic effects upon the promos they use.'[15]

Because of its commercial function the pop video is geared towards fascinating, confirming and overwhelming. Even if it liberates the aesthetic techniques of advertising from their product-related constraints and opens up for them a new field of application, even in this new field it still functions as a visual impulse for the economic interests of capital in the music and media industry. Videos are not produced to expand the aesthetic opportunities and cultural potential of music, but to promote records. Therefore the pop video does not just form mental motivation structures and desires, but it also influences stereotypes of perception and judgement, tempts its viewers through its synaesthetic sensuous attractiveness to a basically affirmative, confirming and assenting attitude towards the content of what is perceived in video reception. But with this it conditions a particular way of looking at the world and structures an image of the world with which, precisely because this is not apparent on the surface of the sequence of scenes, it can have an effect deep in the ordinary consciousness. Julien Temple, the director of countless pop videos and of two very accurately observed music films, is quite correct to write: 'MTV is a way to the eyes, the brain and hopefully the balls of the world.'[16]

The pop video links experience and discovery, reality and illusion into one unity which, in spite of its flexible meanings, underlays it with ideological standards and standard ways of looking at the world. They infiltrate the music which it packages more effectively, more concretely and more directly than can happen via the ideological appeal function of the 'star' system. In video, because of its aesthetic effectiveness and promotional style, aesthetic values and ideals are embodied, patterns of value are laid down, social norms stabilised, which are principally founded on affirmation and assent. Of course, this is not obvious and as a rule cannot be deduced from the sequence of images – as the Duran Duran video confirms – but functions through the connotations acquired as a result of the contexts which it advertises so attractively and fascinatingly.

And it is this that makes the video into a quite ambivalent example of mass culture, in which the boundaries of monopolistic ownership of the media of social and cultural communication, the transformation of culture into a product in order to realise maximum profits, become more obvious than ever before. Although opportunities for creating cultural everyday contexts which are still not very obvious are inherent in video's most developed forms, its effects on music development are highly problematic because of the contexts in which it is placed. It is difficult to contradict Paul Morley's view that:

The video dumps us back into the most sinister part of the pop music game ... The arrival, or at least the pop industry's misuse, of the video is a major reason, or indication, why pop music is ceasing to move at all and beginning to suffocate ... The video becomes the flash symbol of what could be the final reduction of pop into the most artificial of confections, the most normal of conditionings.[17]

This is even more true since the vast majority of videos do not in any way exhibit the complexity seen in the Duran Duran video but rather offer montages, pieced together from existing material for as little money and in as short a time as possible. In these cases the important thing is simply to be present on the screen in some way. For these, existing film archives are cleared without further ado, in order to combine a few more or less suitable sequences from the existing film material with pictures of the band recorded somewhere, if indeed the videos are not just offering a quick recording of a live appearance. It should not be overlooked that the majority of pop videos carry the marks of an equally thoughtless and superficial style suffering from a chronic lack of both time and money, a style which overlays the songs with a crude mish-mash of images made up of the most hackneyed advertising film cliches.

Above all, the entry of the video into record promotion clearly shifted the weighting in the social process of debate about the cultural values and meanings of rock in favour of the music industry. The cultural context relationships which the industry built up around the songs became significantly tighter with the advent of video, and the industry's control over music and musicians significantly more comprehensive. Annie Lennox of Eurythmics explained her views on this process to *New Musical Express*:

I mean when other people in general get access to what we do; like somebody got into Eurythmics at a very early stage and they video'd the very first performance we did. It was supposed to be a thing for MTV; before we knew it, because we didn't have as much control of the situation as we should have done, it was being made into something sellable. And we hated it, cos we didn't feel that it represented us at all, and we wanted to buy it off them. But we couldn't, cos there was a contractual thing that we had no access to our own work.[18]

Thus musicians are integrated into a production process which they cannot control and often cannot understand, a process which makes them an element of an industrially manufactured media product without allowing them any influence over it any more. On video they can be placed in aesthetic contexts, transported into ideological and cultural contexts, quite independently of the degree to which these correspond to their own artistic intentions. Holly Johnson, lead singer of Frankie Goes to Hollywood, once expressed this feeling very succinctly: 'I am no longer a singer, I have become a work of art.'[19] There is not much more to add to this.

Seen in this way, video is one of those marketing strategies with which the industry has always actively sought to force the development of music in the direction of what it finds most effectively controllable. The record companies' objective has always been to remove music from its class-specific contexts of use through the fascination with formal and technical effects, in order to chain its development to criteria which correspond to their, financial, control. The sales crisis which started in the late seventies made these efforts more strenuous and now and again even provoked quite unconcealed comments on the nature of their aims. John Burrow, the producer of the British TV rock programme *Riverside* presented his programme in the *Radio Times* (the magazine listing BBC programmes), on the occasion of its introduction on BBC 2 in 1982 with the following words: 'I think many young people are tired of hearing about the dole queues and are now discovering that with time on their hands they can be creative, perhaps become involved in music or fashion.'[20]

It is almost impossible to be more cynical, and this at a time when the shocking experience of mass unemployment had already long since changed into debilitating resignation. Thus it is no coincidence that it is mainly those forms of music which are linked to the commercial penetration of video which, with their sterile technical perfectionism, their degree of formalisation and their quickly threadbare fashionable effects inhabit a social vacuum, within which they are only barely able to adopt the real everyday experiences of teenagers and to pass on the values and meanings which they have developed. Greil Marcus character-ised this as follows: 'Rock'n'Roll ... is now simply "mainstream music" – pervasive and aggressively empty, the sound of the current sound, referring to nothing but its own success, its own meaningless triumph.'[21]

This is by no means the often forecast end of rock music, but rather its transformation back into those contexts which once again are exclusively dominated by the media and the industry and which are generally labelled pop music. The fact that today this stands in the foreground to such an extent is to do with the commercial effectiveness of video and the fact that the tech-nology of its production and the channels of its distribution are still far removed from the highly centralised structures of multi-national media organisations. But this does not mean that in the wake of punk the diverse multi-layered character of rock has given way to the synthetic pop of the British 'boy groups' or the polished disco-funk brew of Michael Jackson or Prince. It is just that this spectrum is not even beginning to be reflected in the pop video because it is only used very selectively in view of the costs associated with it. In Britain in 1984 no more than 800 songs were turned into videos, and in America no more than 1,500.[22] In spite of this there can be no doubt that video production is aiming at a radical change in the existing cultural system of values, at a change in everyday culture with corresponding results for the development of music, especially since, with the growing spread of video techniques, this medium too moves into functioning sub-cultural contexts and, like music, becomes the object of cultural class debate. The first signs of this are already present, but where they will lead is still unclear.

9

Postscript: 'The Times They Are A-Changing'

At the end of this overview of the contexts in which rock music has formed and developed into a multiplicity of styles it only remains to draw some sort of conclusion.

My starting-point was the premise that rock music produces new experiences in art, that, within the framework of a high-grade, technology-dependent mass culture, a totally altered relationship between art producer and recipient has asserted itself; that everyday life and creativity, art and media have been brought together in a new context. I have attempted to trace these developments in rock music, considering them from different standpoints and in relation to different aspects. But is that all there is to be found? Is there not also a cultural and political potential concealed in these processes, one which points beyond the horizon of our current plight, one which allows us to recognise political prospects which await us in spite of the constructed experiences and disillusionment over their fulfilment which have taken place?

There is no doubt that the illusions which once assigned to rock music the power to undermine social relations, to explode them and to build a more human, a 'better' world in their place have long since faded away. Such a world would in any case have been one of unrestrained masculinity; one which would not even have offered ideals for the other half of humanity, women. The role of women in rock culture was always modelled on the cliches of pubescent male adolescents. And anyway, the revolutionary aura which once surrounded youth has today given way to the cynical image of the 'yuppies'. The supposedly subversive potential of rebellious teenagers, fighting for progress, guitar in hand, has been reduced to a romantic notion which ekes out a rather miserable and dusty experience on the desks of overly theoretical sociologists. The sober capitalist strategists in the music and media industry, calculators in hand, have developed an essentially more realistic picture of the state of this world. The increased buying power of a hypertrophied youth, which made teenage dreams, values and pleasures the focus of the commercial universe, could not withstand the strategists' unerring balance figures. Since then the sponsors – soft drinks producers, breweries and consumer goods manufacturers – have reigned supreme. And to them this childish game with music is at best just another sales aid to allow them to open up markets where they stand to gain more than just teenagers' pocket money. Even the record companies prefer to concentrate on the exploitation of music copyright – already crumbling due to samplers and home taping – rather than rely on record-buying teenagers, a proportionally dwindling group in the demographic structure of the population. It is pointless to speculate whether this means the end of rock music, whether this book is just providing an elegant funeral oration. The validity of the attempt to research the aesthetics and sociology of this music is not exhausted by the often abrupt changes in the music market. Something more fundamental than that is at issue: insights into the contradictory and complex character of cultural mass processes, insights which are only to be gained from those objects which have played their part in these processes, which have formed and influenced them. And it is irrelevant to this issue whether the rapid change of fashion and trends has once again allowed new ones to take their place, whether the talk in magazines and the trade press has long been dominated by the endless chain of new names. What remains constant in all this are the working masses, of whatever age, whose culture is mediated as the mass-lived experience of daily life through the media and its products. The really decisive question is whether today such cultural mass processes still contain the prospect of social change.

And yet was it not the case that in the course of its development rock music – in spite of all the restrictions imposed by a subsequent political analysis – exhibited instances of convergence with the progressive and democratic mass movements, which first nourished those illusions I have already mentioned? Is it not true that 'Sun City', the initiative of 'United Artists Against Apartheid' in the USA, or 'Red Wedge' in Britain – to mention just two examples chosen at random – are events where political mass movements and mass culture in the form of rock music touch one another? And how does it then come about that this field of political debate – excluding the individual efforts of musicians – has been left almost completely to capitalism, while the organised Left has retreated defiantly to a shadowy existence of marginal activities, which in any case reach only a dwindling circle of like-minded people? And how has it happened that in those countries where the power of capital is limited, where socialism has become the dominant political form and where cultural development is possible free from the dictates of the soft-drinks producers and the brewery owners, a spirit of cultural provincialism reigns in the forms of rock and pop music that have mass effectiveness, a provincialism which at best has failed in the face of the challenges of a modern mass culture? Does the organised labour movement have a cultural concept at its disposal that is at its best in these times, that meets the cultural challenges of communications and information technology with political answers and that – even if this cannot be realised overnight in the face of the existing relations of power and control – in this way still represents social progress? Probably not, since otherwise these concluding reflections might have been based on a more optimistic description of the situation.

Yet these are questions which are provoked by the view of the aesthetics and sociology of rock developed in the preceding chapters. That these questions are only taken up here in the last few pages of this book is itself an eloquent comment on the situation. Although the debate over popular music forms has in the meantime achieved a measure of academic standing and although there is no shortage of articles in scientific journals and books from renowned publishers on this theme, popular music itself and the theoretical debate over it has still not been taken seriously in political terms. What political conclusions could be drawn from the views collected in seminar rooms, dissertations and books is, and remains, an open question, one which is beyond the scope of this study. Yet there is no need to be a sectarian or dogmatic follower of one or other movement in the spectrum of the political Left in order to recognise the enormous political status that mass culture has acquired today, whether mediated through music, film or television. It has long been the case that television programmes and records are sent out on preview to the investors, before people get down to business behind closed doors all over the world. In the depoliticised language of the business community this is called 'market preparation', a term which the Left has replaced with the less popular, but nevertheless more accurate, concept of 'cultural imperialism'. And precisely this concept has resulted in the accusation that rock music itself has never been anything other than a particularly clever capitalist ruse designed to direct working-class teenagers away from their real interests and towards an ineffective media consumption instead. A counter-argument to such one-sided exaggeration has led to the equally one-sided daydream that the political aims of capitalism cannot be more effectively avoided than through leisure and a music based on popularity and mass effectiveness.

In this fundamental argument over the pros and cons of mass culture, in which the ideologues of the Left have, it seems, long written off contemporary forms of pop music, we should remember Bertolt Brecht's opinion, formulated a good fifty years ago. As a result of his 'Threepenny trial' (the legal proceedings he initiated over the censorship of the film version of the *Threepenny Opera* which he wrote with Kurt Weill) he addressed himself to the Left: 'There can be no hope of success in devising a particular "culture" to which you want to persuade reality. Such a deduction only takes away the possibility of understanding how reality functions and thus finding out which are the revolutionary and which the reactionary intentions in what already exists.'[1] And it is in this sense that I conclude, therefore, by asking once more, from a political point of view, what has actually been created with rock music, what fundamental cultural developmental tendencies and contradictions are concealed in it.

And in asking these questions we should hold fast to one thing above all. With this music a form of cultural praxis has developed in teenagers' everyday lives which, in spite of – or perhaps *because* of – its commercial organisation, is more dynamic and essentially far more democratic than is revealed by mere examination of the capitalist relations of its production and distribution. Even if, as an industrial product, it remains bound to these relations, as a cultural praxis, it has its origins in the lifestyle of working-class teenagers and in the problematic of their class experience. And essentially this has not altered even in the face of the changes in the musical landscape since the beginning of the eighties. Rather, it has acquired an additional dimension through technological development, home taping and home recording. For the first time the basis of the capitalist exploitation of music is clearly visible – i.e. the successful maintenance of private ownership of products which are by their very nature a social communication form; in other words, the legal construction of copyright. Mass culture, in whatever artistic form, is a deeply contradictory phenomenon. As a cultural everyday praxis of the masses, it remains influenced by their real living conditions and the experiences that spring from them, even though it is mediated through capitalist institutions. In rock music this contradiction has been sharpened, simultaneously making it more clearly visible. Thus, a conception which considers rock music only in relation to the economically and politically dominant capitalist social institutions, fails to recognise its essential nature. In this context, rock is genuinely no more than a means to achieve the commercial exploitation of teenagers' leisure, a means that in its effects conforms to the system. And this is true quite independently of musicians' intentions, is a context that is not divisible, not even with reference to the differing marketing strategies of multi-national media conglomerates on the one hand and the independent labels on the other, no matter how different the musical results may be. Such a distinction is based on a fallacy which has led time and again to unsustainable miscalculations. The social and political relevance of music is not determined by its commercial potential, whether positive or negative. As music, a commercially successful song or a highly marketed musical trend is not necessarily any closer to capitalist ideological interests than one which is less successful according to capitalist criteria. Strictly speaking, the latter is still based on a silent, if unintentional, agreement with the commercial criteria of the music industry, but in a negative rather than a positive sense. But music does not escape the dominant economic and ideological relations just because it is less successful in sales terms.

At the same time these relations also produce class conflicts, because it is still true that seriously different social and political interests arise from the possession or non-possession of the means of production, whatever these may be. In this context music, inasmuch as it reaches the masses, is always part of those functional contexts determined by working-class lifestyle. Their involvement with music is not external to their everyday lifestyle nor removed from their real social experiences and cultural traditions, just because the music is supplied to them by capitalism through record companies and media organisations. Thus music, like all the various forms of mass culture, becomes the object of a cultural struggle, influenced by social conflict, about the cultural values, meaning and significance that circulate through it. With their productions, bands and musicians continually supply this struggle with a field of reference and, the more closely both sides of this cultural conflict crystallise in their songs, the more successful they become. Music which does not conform to the system, which does not function in the markets and within the marketing strategies defined by capitalism, does not become part of mass culture. It is excluded from the mechanisms of mass production and distribution on the basis that it has 'no commercial potential'. But on the other hand music which is not simultaneously linked to the real social interests, cultural needs and experience of the masses, which does not take these up and pass them on, has equally little prospect of success. To ascribe to music the power to paralyse the social realities of the ordinary life of the masses and to establish 'false' needs is pure idealism, since life is always lived in highly profane and obviously material relations. Thus rock music is neither the expression of a culture *for* the mass of working-class teenagers nor *their* musical instrument of articulation. The latter view, which in essence amounts to a folkloric explanation of the social and political relevance of music, completely misses the point of the conditions of cultural mass processes mediated through the media. Yet media and mass culture and the popular arts integrated into these two do not play such an important role in contemporary cultural processes merely because they correspond to capitalist economic and ideological interests. The attraction of technical media for cultural styles of behaviour in everyday life and leisure has its origin equally and more importantly in the cultural potentialities which exist in the mass media. These signify a concentration and centralisation of music production which in this form reaches far beyond the limited developments of local cultural activity.

And they permit an all-embracing and differentiated development of particularly those aspects of culture which are capable of integration in the daily processes of living. There is no other cultural development for the working class within the constraints of their daily lives.

With its concentration on media and mass culture for the achievement of its ideological and economic interests, capitalism uses nothing other than the legitimacy of cultural development processes which, in spite of all autonomy, still remain a form of reproduction of material production. And it achieves this so successfully, remaining unchallenged in this field, because it rarely comes across any alternatives which need to be taken seriously. A point in passing: nowhere has there been a more painful learning process than in the socialist countries, where there was a belief in the autonomous laws of culture, based on an idealistic overvaluation, in order to escape the 'evil' of a modern mass culture mediated through the media. This turned out to be impossible to achieve either with enormous grants to basically traditional cultural performances, or with, as is common knowledge, state force, restrictions and prohibitions. The culture of the working class, the producers of society's wealth, who have learnt how to handle the most technically advanced production methods, is hostile neither to technology nor to the media, and cannot be developed under this premise. Indeed it is characteristic of this class that it develops the cultural potential of the most advanced forces of production and communications systems of the time. Although these are created by capitalism as the means of exploitation of this class, their cultural values and possibilities are only opened up by the masses as they integrate them into their daily lives and imbue them with their own values. Only then is there a basis for the commercial exploitation of these forces by the culture industry. And there is no inevitability about it. There are enough instances where, quite independently of the economic value of an investment, the cultural use of a technical development failed because it had no cultural value for the masses. Remember the inglorious fate of quadrophonic sound or the impossibility of achieving general acceptance of the video disc in place of the video recorder, in spite of the fact that the former was significantly more profitable.

But, by intervening between the musician and his audience,

the media are already continually projecting a need interpreted according to their (technical, economic and political) criteria onto the musician as a reference point for his music, just as they seek to bring the listener into a relationship with the music determined by the same criteria. In this lies the true foundation of their political and ideological effectiveness. But this is not fulfilled, as is often suspected, by the ideal means of the transfer of ideas, by agitation and persuasion, directly from the mind of one individual via verbal or non-verbal communication into the mind of another individual. Instead, it is realised by a highly real action matrix, of which cultural behaviour is a part and which makes such behaviour a component of a complex lifestyle – perhaps through its link to the act of buying, through its fixation at any given time with particular media (bear in mind the displacement of the dominant coordinates of music reception from radio to television by MTV) and by its interweaving with other activities. From such an action matrix arises the social construction of an individual identity which then results in a particular way of looking at the world, in other words a particular ideology, one far more effective than could ever have been produced by mere persuasion.

Thus, in terms of their cultural effect the media are simultaneously powerful instruments in the production of ideology as well as being, in terms of their existence as *mass* media, dependent on the masses due to their technical and economic qualities. In this context music is the result of the *combination*, however full of conflict and contradiction, of the working class and the music industry. In the case of rock music this found expression in an aesthetic which both opened up new dimensions in its class-specific use by working-class teenagers, as well as permitting a musical development based on the most technically advanced possibilities of music production. And this is linked to a far-reaching dissolution of the character of music as an object of contemplation, typical of the bourgeois concert hall tradition. Music becomes an essentially open field of reference for the most varied cultural activities. And in this process to a great extent it loses its textual quality and instead acquires a *media* character and itself becomes a mass medium – here taking the concept of 'medium' in its original, scientific, meaning: an agent, a material substance in which a physical or chemical process takes place. And just as the quality of the material substance is decisive for the nature of the processes which take place within it, so the nature of the medium music is of decisive importance for the cultural processes which are realised through it. Of course this does not mean that music appears here as a basically inter-changeable sound background for social and cultural processes which have little to do with it as music, as sound material structured in a particular way. It is merely that the peculiarities of its structure should be understood not as the embodiment of a text, but in a media function. And with this a system of social and cultural interactions arises around music, supported by its particular fans, which *produces* meanings, values, significance and pleasure instead of functioning as a mere instrument of consumption and reception, accepting music as a kind of sweet supplied from outside, filled with messages, offers of significance and incitements to pleasure, and merely realising these 'con-tents'. Any music- or art-centred approach will fail to uncover this change in emphasis from the production of meanings and values, of 'contents', to the plane of cultural systems of inter-action which go far beyond music. For in this case the most important thing seems to be the musical form, its differentiation, its quality of expression and representation, within which is sunk some kind of programme of behaviour, thought and feeling which, within certain tolerances, 'directs' the act of listening. Yet such a view misses the social conflicts through which rock songs, with their connection to the highly developed production and distribution apparatus of the mass media on the one hand and the class-specific cultural contexts of use of their teenage fans on the other, must circulate.

The aesthetic nature of rock music is of far-reaching impor-tance for any political involvement with it. It is not only that behind this music lie very contradictory and socially conflicting cultural processes, but the music itself is also not to be taken as a textual embodiment of ideology, an ideological text, however deeply it is linked to contexts which determine the apparatus of the production of ideology. For a democratic and politically progressive concept of culture this must have the consequence of not laying the emphasis of political activity in a traditionalist manner on an 'alternative text production', here taken to mean that art-centred manner of thinking and viewing the world, which mostly reduces this to a question of the ideologically 'correct' lyrics. What are more important are those social and cultural systems of interaction and their (political) organisation to which music is linked as a specific medium, even one of the production of ideology. Anything else is, at best, ineffective. But for this an 'alternative *politics* of culture' is required, and this can hardly be developed in books, but only in revolutionary praxis. Even if at the moment there seems no prospect that such a project could count on a political mass movement in the foreseeable future, times change. Historically, more than one opportunity has been lost because the necessary concepts and models for action which were current and which might have been used to deal with the political realities of mass culture were missing at the critical moment. Thus, the consideration of this point remains a task still to be undertaken, even if currently there are more questions to formulate than answers to give.

Notes

1 'ROLL OVER BEETHOVEN': NEW EXPERIENCES IN ART

1 Michael Lydon, *Rock Folk. Portraits from the Rock'n'Roll Pantheon* (Dutton) New York 1971, p. 171.
2 Richard Buckle, in *The Sunday Times*, December 1963; quoted from Iain Chambers, *Urban Rhythms. Pop Music and Popular Culture* (Macmillan) Hampshire 1985, p. 63.
3 Carl Belz, *The Story of Rock* (Oxford University Press) New York 1972, p. 3.
4 Chuck Berry, 'Roll Over Beethoven', Chess 1626 (USA 1956); © 1956 by Arc Music Corporation, New York.
5 Quoted from *Black Music & Jazz Review*, November 1978, p. 14.
6 Quoted from Hunter Davies, *The Beatles* (revised edition, Dell Publishing) New York 1978, p. 283.
7 Simon & Garfunkel, 'The Boxer', CBS Columbia 4-44785 (USA 1969).
8 Quoted from Spencer Leigh, *Paul Simon. Now and Then* (Raven Books) Liverpool 1973, p. 54f.
9 *The Blackboard Jungle*, Director: Richard Brooks, Warner Columbia, USA 1955.
10 *Rock Around the Clock*, Director: Fred F. Sears, Warner Columbia, USA 1956.
11 *Don't Knock the Rock*, Director: Fred F. Sears, Warner Columbia, USA 1957.
12 Ian Whitcomb, *After the Ball. Pop Music from Rag to Rock* (Allen Lane) London 1972, p. 29.
13 Kurt Blaukopf, *Neue musikalische Verhaltensweisen der Jugend* (*Musikpädagogik. Forschung und Lehre*, ed. S. Abel-Struth, V) (Schott) Mainz 1974, p. 11.
14 David Riesman et al., *The Lonely Crowd. A Study of the Changing American Character* (revised edition, Yale) New Haven 1961, xlv.
15 Simon Frith, *Sound Effects. Youth, Leisure and the Politics of Rock'n'Roll* (Pantheon) New York 1981, p. 201.
16 Iain Chambers, *Urban Rhythms*, p. 5.

17 Quoted from Jon Pareles and Patricia Romanowski, *The Rolling Stone Encyclopedia of Rock & Roll* (Rolling Stone Press; Summit Books) New York 1983, p. 322.

18 Quoted from Ralph Denyer, 'Chris Tsangarides Interview. The Producer Series', *Studio Sound*, July 1985, p. 88.

19 The Eagles, *Desperado*, Asylum 1 C 062-94386 (USA 1973).

20 Quoted from Mike Wale, *Vox Pop. Profiles from the Pop Process* (Harrap) London 1971, p. 67.

21 Frankie Goes to Hollywood, 'Relax', ZTT 12 ZTAS 1 (GB 1983).

22 Quoted from *New Musical Express*, 22/29 December 1984, p. 53.

23 Pink Floyd, *The Dark Side of the Moon*, Harvest 11163 (GB 1973).

24 Michael Naumann and Boris Penth, 'I've always been looking for something I could never find', in *Living in a Rock'n'Roll Fantasy* (Asthetik und Kommunikation), eds. Naumann and Penth, West Berlin 1979, p. 38.

25 Chris Cutler, *File Under Popular. Theoretical and Critical Writings on Music* (November Books) London 1985, p. 145.

26 Elvis Presley, 'Hound Dog', RCA Victor 47-6604 (USA 1956).

27 Willie Mae Thornton, 'Hound Dog', Peacock 1612 (USA 1953).

28 Bill Haley, 'Shake, Rattle and Roll', Decca 29204 (USA 1954); Joe Turner, 'Shake, Rattle and Roll', Atlantic 45-1026 (USA 1954).

29 Peter McCabe and Robert D. Schonfield, *Apple to the Core. The Unmaking of the Beatles* (Sphere) London 1971, p. 79.

30 Simon Frith, *Sound Effects*, p. 18.

31 Chris Cutler, *File Under Popular*, p. 100.

32 Jon Landau, *It's too Late to Stop Now. A Rock'n'Roll Journal* (Straight Arrow Books) San Francisco 1972, p. 15.

33 Quoted from Nicholas Schaffner, *The Beatles Forever* (Pinnacle Books) New York 1978, p. 30. Lennon is referring here to the two books he wrote: John Lennon, *Spaniard in the Works* (Cape) London 1965; John Lennon, *In His Own Write* (Cape) London 1968.

34 Quoted from *John Lennon erinnert sich* (Release) Hamburg, pp. 37–8.

35 Paul Willis, *Profane Culture* (Routledge & Kegan Paul) London, Boston, Henley 1978, p. 6.

36 Henri Lefebvre, *Critique de la vie quotidienne* (L'Arche Editeur) Paris 1958 and 1961.

37 Iain Chambers, *Urban Rhythms*, p. 6.

38 Iain Chambers, 'Popular Culture, Popular Knowledge', *OneTwo-ThreeFour. A Rock'n'Roll Quarterly*, 2, Summer 1985, p. 18.

2 'ROCK AROUND THE CLOCK': EMERGENCE

1 David Pichaske, *A Generation in Motion. Popular Music and Culture in the Sixties* (Schirmer) New York 1979, p. 3.

2 Bernard Malamud, *A New Life* (Chatto & Windus) London 1980, p. 229.

3 Quoted from William L. O'Neill, *Coming Apart. An Informal History of America in the 1960's* (Times Books) Chicago 1977, p. 4.

4 Lloyd Grossman, *A Social History of Rock Music. From the Greasers to Glitter Rock* (David McKay) New York 1976, p. 62.

5 Quoted from David Pichaske, *A Generation in Motion*, p. 46.

6 Arthur Coleman, *The Adolescent Society* (Free Press Glencoe) Chicago 1961, p. 3.

7 Bernard Morse, *The Sexual Revolution* (Fawcett Publications) Derby, Conn., 1962.

8 Chuck Berry, 'School Day', Chess 1653 (USA 1957); © 1957 by Arc Music Corporation, New York.

9 Greil Marcus, *Mystery Train. Images of America in Rock'n'Roll* (Omnibus) London 1977, p. 166.

10 Patti Page, 'Tennessee Waltz', Mercury 5534 X 45 (USA 1950).

11 Fats Domino, *The Fat Man*, Imperial 5058 (USA 1950).

12 Champion Jack Dupree, *Junker Blues*, Atlantic 40526 (USA 1940).

13 Cf. *Anschläge. Zeitschrift des Archivs für Populäre Musik*, Bremen, I, 1978/2, p. 113.

14 Chuck Berry, 'Maybellene', Chess 1604 (USA 1955).

15 John Grissim, *Country Music. White Man's Blues* (Paperback Library) New York 1970.

16 Rudi Thiessen, *It's only rock'n'roll but I like it. Zu Kult und Mythos einer Protestbewegung* (Medusa) West Berlin 1981, pp. 22–3.

17 Bill C. Malone, *Country Music USA* (University of Texas Press) Austin, Tex., 1968, pp. 229–30.

18 Elvis Presley, 'That's All Right (Mama)' / 'Blue Moon of Kentucky', Sun 209 (USA 1954).

19 Paul Willis, *Profane Culture*, p. 71.

20 Quoted from Peter Guralnick, 'Elvis Presley', in *The Rolling Stone Illustrated History of Rock & Roll*, ed. J. Miller (Random House; Rolling Stone Press) New York 1980, pp. 19–20.

21 Mathias R. Schmidt, *Bob Dylan und die sechziger Jahre. Aufbruch und Abkehr* (Fischer) Frankfurt (Main) 1983, p. 156.

22 Greil Marcus, *Mystery Train*, pp. 142–3.

23 David Pichaske, *A Generation in Motion*, p. 44.

24 Bill Haley And His Comets, 'Rock Around the Clock', Decca 29124 (USA 1954); © 1953 by Myers Music Incorporation, New York.

25 Sonny Dae And His Knights, 'Rock Around the Clock', Arcade 123 (USA 1953).

26 Michael Naumann and Boris Penth, 'I've always been looking for something I could never find', p. 17 (emphasis in original).

27 Chuck Berry, 'Sweet Little Sixteen', Chess 1683 (USA 1958); © 1958 by Arc Music Corporation, New York.

3 'LOVE ME DO': THE AESTHETICS OF SENSUOUSNESS

[1] Elvis Presley, 'Love Me Tender', RCA Victor 47-6643 (USA 1956).

[2] David Pichaske, *A Generation in Motion*, p. 41; the comment about 'Aura Lee' refers to a song by the Norman Luboff Choir, a particularly sentimental number (The Norman Luboff Choir, 'Aura Lee', Columbia 5-2424 (USA 1951)).

[3] Anthony Scaduto, *Bob Dylan. An Intimate Biography* (Grosset & Dunlap) New York 1972.

[4] The Beatles, 'Love Me Do' / 'P.S. I Love You', Parlophone R 4949 (GB 1962).

[5] Carl Perkins, 'Sure to Fall', Sun 5 (USA 1956).

[6] Bruce Channel, 'Hey Baby', Smash 1731 (USA 1962).

[7] George Melly, *Revolt into Style* (Penguin) Harmondsworth 1973, p. 26.

[8] Dave Harker, *One For the Money. Politics and Popular Song* (Hutchinson) London, Melbourne, Sydney, Auckland, Johannesburg 1980, p. 86.

[9] Cf. ibid.; cf. also Jürgen Seuss, Gerold Dommermuth and Hans Maier, *Beat in Liverpool* (Europäische Verlagsanstalt) Frankfurt (Main) 1965, p. 20.

[10] Bill Harry, *Mersey Beat. The Beginnings of the Beatles* (Omnibus) London, New York, Cologne, Sydney 1977, p. 15.

[11] Bram Dijkstra, 'Nichtrepressive rhythmische Strukturen in einigen Formen der afroamerikanischen und westindischen Musik', in *Die Zeichen. Neue Aspekte der musikalischen Asthetik II*, ed. Hans Werner Henze (Fischer) Frankfurt (Main) 1981, p. 75.

[12] Dick Hebdige, *Subculture. The Meaning of Style* (Methuen) London, New York 1979, pp. 49–50.

[13] William Haley, *The Responsibilities of Broadcasting* (BBC Publications) London 1948, p. 11.

[14] Quoted from Dave Harker, *One For the Money*, p. 67.

[15] Jeff Nuttal, *Bomb Culture* (Paladin) London 1969, p. 21.

[16] Ian Whitcomb, *After the Ball*, p. 178; cf. also Dave Harker, *One For the Money*, p. 67.

[17] Hunter Davies, *The Beatles*, p. 166.

[18] Derek Johnson, *Beat Music* (Hansen) Copenhagen, (Chester) London 1969, p. 6.

[19] Mark Abrams, *The Teenage Consumer* (London Press Exchange) London 1959, p. 13.

[20] Dick Hebdige, 'Towards a Cartography of Taste, 1935–1962', in *Popular Culture: Past and Present*, eds. B. Waites, T. Bennett and G. Martin (Open University; Croom Helm) London 1982, p. 203.

[21] Ian Whitcomb, *After the Ball*, p. 226.

[22] Iain Chambers, *Urban Rhythms*, p. 4.

[23] Quoted from Arthur Gamble, *The Conservative Nation* (Routledge & Kegan Paul) London, Boston, Henley 1974, p. 78.

[24] Ian Birchall, 'The Decline and Fall of British Rhythm & Blues', *The Age of Rock. Sounds of the American Cultural Revolution*, ed. J. Eisen (Vintage) New York 1969, p. 97.

[25] Dick Hebdige, *Subculture*, p. 74.

[26] Dick Hebdige, *Subculture*, p. 50.

[27] P. Johnson, 'The Menace of Beatleism', *New Statesman*, 28 February 1964, p. 17.

[28] Quoted from Iain Chambers, *Urban Rhythms*, p. 38.

[29] Quoted from Iain Chambers, *Urban Rhythms*, p. 60.

[30] Bob Woller, 'Well Now – Dig This!', *Mersey Beat. Merseyside's Own Entertainment Paper*, I, no. 5, 31 August–14 September 1961, p. 2.

[31] Richard Mabey, *The Pop Process* (Hutchinson) London 1969, p. 48.

[32] Simon Frith, 'Popular Music 1950–1980', in *Making Music*, ed. G. Martin (Muller) London 1983, p. 32.

[33] Rudi Thiessen, *It's only rock'n'roll but I like it*, p. 13.

[34] Quoted from a tape transcript of a conversation the author conducted in Liverpool on 23 November 1984.

[35] The Beatles, 'Roll Over Beethoven', EMI Electrola 1C 062-04 181 (GB 1963).

[36] Roland Barthes, *Mythologies*, translated by Annette Lavers (Granada) London 1973, pp. 123–4.

[37] Simon Frith, 'Popular Music 1950–1980', p. 35.

[38] Quoted from Raoul Hoffmann, *Zwischen Galaxis & Underground. Die neue Popmusik* (Deutscher Taschenbuch Verlag) Munich 1971, p. 39.

4 'MY GENERATION': ROCK MUSIC AND SUBCULTURES

[1] Simon Frith, *The Sociology of Rock* (Constable) London 1978, p. 198.

[2] Graham Murdock and Robin McCron, 'Music Classes – Über klassenspezifische Rockbedürfnisse', in Rolf Lindner, *Punk Rock oder: Der vermarktete Aufruhr* (Fischer) Frankfurt (Main) 1977, p. 24.

[3] Charlie Gillett, *The Sound of the City. The Rise of Rock and Roll* (revised edition, Souvenir) London 1983, p. 265.

[4] Lawrence Grossberg, 'Another Boring Day in Paradise: Rock and Roll and the Empowerment of Everyday Life', in *Popular Music 4. Performers and Audiences*, eds. R. Middleton and D. Horn (Cambridge University Press) Cambridge, London, New York, New Rochelle, Melbourne, Sydney 1984, p. 225.

[5] The Who, 'My Generation', Brunswick 05944 (GB 1965); © 1965 by Fabulous Music Ltd, London.

[6] Quoted from Dave Marsh, *Before I Get Old. The Story of the Who* (Plexus) London 1983, p. 131.

7 John Clarke, 'Style', in *Resistance through Rituals. Youth Subcultures in Post-war Britain*, eds. S. Hall and T. Jefferson (Hutchinson) London 1976, p. 187.

8 Boris Penth and Günter Franzen, *Last Exit. Punk: Leben im toten Herz der Städte* (Rowohlt) Reinbek b. Hamburg 1982, p. 41.

9 Paul Corrigan and Simon Frith, 'The Politics of Youth Culture', in *Resistance through Rituals*, eds. Hall and Jefferson, p. 273.

10 Ibid.

11 Iain Chambers, 'Popular Culture, Popular Knowledge', p. 15.

12 John Muncie, *Pop Culture, Pop Music and Post-war Youth: Subcultures* (Popular Culture, Block 5, Unit 19, Politics, Ideology and Popular Culture 1) (Open University Press) Walton Hall, Milton Keynes 1982, p. 59.

13 Graham Murdock and Robin McCron, 'Consciousness of Class and Consciousness of Generation', in *Resistance through Rituals*, eds. Hall and Jefferson, p. 203.

14 John Clarke, Stuart Hall, Tony Jefferson and Brian Roberts, 'Subcultures, Cultures and Class', in *Resistance through Rituals*, eds. Hall and Jefferson, p. 47.

15 Mark Pinto-Duschinsky, 'Bread and Circuses. The Conservatives in Office, 1951–64', in *The Age of Affluence*, eds. V. Bogdanor and R. Skidelsky (Macmillan) London, New York 1970, p. 56.

16 Quoted from Mark Pinto-Duschinsky, 'Bread and Circuses', p. 57.

17 Charles Radcliffe, *Mods*; quoted from Dave Laing, *The Sound of Our Time* (Sheed & Ward) London 1969, p. 150.

18 Rolling Stones, '(I can't get no) Satisfaction', Decca F12220 (GB 1965); © 1965 by Essex Music International Ltd, London.

19 Iain Chambers, *Urban Rhythms*, p. 57.

20 John Clarke, 'Style', p. 151.

21 Iain Chambers, *Urban Rhythms*, p. 62. In November 1963 the Beatles appeared before the Royal Family in the Royal Variety Show, the most important event in the British show business calendar, and they received a similar honour later in the year when the film *A Hard Day's Night* (Director: Richard Lester) was given a Royal Premiere.

22 Gary Herman, *The Who* (Studio Vista) London 1971, p. 54.

23 Simon Frith, *Sound Effects*, pp. 219–20.

24 Lawrence Grossberg, 'Another Boring Day in Paradise', p. 244.

25 John Clarke and Tony Jefferson, 'The Politics of Popular Culture. Culture and Sub-culture', Stencilled Occasional Papers, Sub and Popular Culture Series, SP no. 14 (University of Birmingham, Centre for Contemporary Cultural Studies) Birmingham 1973, p. 9.

5 'REVOLUTION': THE IDEOLOGY OF ROCK

[1] Quoted from 'The Rolling Stone Interview: Pete Townshend', *Rolling Stone*, 28 September 1968, p. 14.

[2] The Beatles, *Sgt Pepper's Lonely Hearts Club Band*, Parlophone PCS 7027 (GB 1967).

[3] The Beatles, 'Hey Jude / Revolution', Apple R5722 (GB 1968).

[4] The Rolling Stones, *Beggars Banquet*, Decca 6.22157 (GB 1968).

[5] Pink Floyd, *A Saucerful of Secrets*, EMI Columbia 6258 (GB 1968).

[6] Simon Frith, 'Popular Music 1950–1980', p. 36.

[7] Quoted from Paul Willis, *Profane Culture*, p. 154.

[8] Quoted from Helmut Salzinger, *Rock Power oder Wie musikalisch ist die Revolution? Ein Essay über Pop-Musik und Gegenkultur* (Fischer) Frankfurt (Main) 1972, p. 124.

[9] Simon Frith and Howard Horne, 'Welcome to Bohemia!', Warwick Working Papers in Sociology (University of Warwick) Coventry 1984, p. 13.

[10] Quoted from 'The Pop Think-In: Pete Townshend', *Melody Maker*, 14 January 1967, p. 9.

[11] Quoted from 'The Rolling Stone Interview: Keith Richards', *Rolling Stone*, 19 August 1971, p. 24.

[12] Dave Marsh, *Before I Get Old*, p. 47.

[13] Simon Frith and Howard Horne, 'Doing the Art School Bob. Oder: Ein kleiner Ausflug an die wahren Quellen', in *Rock Session 6. Magazin der populären Musik*, eds. K. Humann and C.-L. Reichert (Rowohlt) Reinbek b. Hamburg 1983, p. 286.

[14] Quoted from Nick Jones, 'Well, What Is Pop Art?', *Melody Maker*, 3 July 1965, p. 11.

[15] Simon Frith, *Sound Effects*, p. 161.

[16] Jon Landau, *It's Too Late to Stop Now*, p. 130.

[17] Quoted from Raoul Hoffmann, *Zwischen Galaxis & Underground*, p. 128.

[18] Richard Neville, *Playpower* (Paladin) London 1970, p. 75.

[19] Bob Dylan, 'Blowin' in the Wind', on *The Freewheelin' Bob Dylan*, CBS Columbia CS 8786 (USA 1963).

[20] Anthony Scaduto, *Bob Dylan*, p. 360.

[21] Quoted from *Broadside*, no. 61, August 1965, p. 11.

[22] 'Working Class?', *Daily Worker*, 7 September 1963, p. 5.

[23] Quoted from Simon Frith, *The Sociology of Rock*, p. 193.

[24] Bob Dylan, 'The Times They Are A-Changin'', CBS Columbia CS 8905 (USA 1964).

[25] Quoted from David Pichaske, *A Generation in Motion*, xix.

[26] Robert S. Anson, *Gone Crazy and Back Again. The Rise and Fall of the Rolling Stones Generation* (Doubleday) New York 1981, p. 129.

27 John Sinclair, 'Popmusik ist Revolution', *Sounds*, I, 1968/12, p. 106.
28 Quoted from Ralph J. Gleason, 'Like a Rolling Stone', in *The Age of Rock*, ed. J. Eisen, pp. 72–3.
29 Greil Marcus, *Mystery Train*, p. 115.
30 Quoted from Tony Palmer, *Born Under a Bad Sign* (William Kimber) London 1970, p. 145.
31 The Beatles, 'Revolution', Apple R5722 (GB 1968); © 1968 by Northern Songs Ltd, London.
32 Quoted from Jon Wiener, *Come Together. John Lennon in His Time* (Random House) New York 1984, p. 8.
33 Quoted from Raoul Hoffmann, *Zwischen Galaxis & Underground*, p. 77.
34 Quoted from Raoul Hoffmann, *Zwischen Galaxis & Underground*, p. 152.
35 John Hoyland, 'An Open Letter to John Lennon', *Black Dwarf*, 27 October 1968.
36 John Lennon, 'A Very Open Letter to John Hoyland from John Lennon', *Black Dwarf*, 10 January 1969.
37 *The Beatles*, Apple PCS 7067/8 (GB 1968).
38 Quoted from Jon Wiener, *Come Together*, p. 61.
39 John Lennon & Plastic Ono Band, 'Give Peace a Chance', Apple 1813 (GB 1969).
40 Quoted from Jon Wiener, *Come Together*, p. 84.
41 See the Rolling Stones, 'Street Fighting Man', on *Beggars Banquet*, Decca 6.22157 (GB 1968); © 1968 by Abkco Music Incorporation, New York.
42 Jon Landau, 'Rock'n'Radical?', *Daily World*, 22 February 1969, p. 18.
43 Ibid.
44 Tony Sanchez, *Up and Down with The Rolling Stones* (Signet) New York 1980, pp. 127–8.
45 Quoted from Barry Miles, *Beatles in Their Own Words* (Omnibus) London 1978, p. 62.
46 Quoted from *New Musical Express*, 21 April 1984, p. 13.
47 Ed Leimbacher, 'The Crash of the Jefferson Airplane', *Ramparts Magazine*, January 1970, p. 14.

6 'WE'RE ONLY IN IT FOR THE MONEY': THE ROCK BUSINESS

1 Frank Zappa & The Mothers of Invention, 'We're Only In It For The Money', Verve V + V6 5045X (USA 1976).
2 Michael Lydon, 'Rock for Sale', *The Age of Rock 2. Sights and Sounds of the American Cultural Revolution*, ed. J. Eisen (Vintage Books) New York 1970, p. 53.
3 Simon Frith, *Sound Effects*, p. 260.
4 Quoted from *The Village Voice*, 29 February 1979, p. 26.

5 Quoted from David Pichaske, *A Generation in Motion*, p. 160.

6 Quoted from David Pichaske, *A Generation in Motion*, p. 158.

7 Quoted from Martti Soramäki and Jukka Haarma, *The International Music Industry* (OY, Yleisradio Ab., The Finnish Broadcasting Company, Planning and Research Department) Helsinki 1981, pp. 11 and 7.

8 Quoted from Roger Wallis and Krister Malm, *Big Sounds from Small Peoples. The Music Industry in Small Countries* (Constable) London 1984, p. 74.

9 Quoted from Phil Hardy, 'The British Record Industry', IASPM UK Working Paper 3 (IASPM British Branch Committee) London [1984], p. 9.

10 Quoted from *Melody Maker*, 15 February 1986, p. 14.

11 *EMI, World Record Markets* (Westerham Press) London 1971, p. 10.

12 Quoted from Simon Frith, *The Sociology of Rock*, p. 117.

13 Quoted from Martti Soramäki and Jukka Haarma, *The International Music Industry*, p. 11.

14 Taken from Simon Frith, *Sound Effects*, p. 140.

15 Dave Harker, *One For the Money*, p. 91.

16 Quoted from *The Rolling Stone Interviews, Vol. II*, ed. Ben Fong-Torres (Warner Books) New York 1973, p. 292.

17 Quoted from *Sound Engineer*, July 1985, p. 32.

18 Quoted from Richard Lamont, 'Mixing the Media', *Studio Sound*, July 1985, p. 64.

19 Larry Shore, 'The Crossroads of Business and Music. The Music Industry in the United States and Internationally', unpublished manuscript, p. 95.

20 Steve Chapple and Reebee Garofalo, *Rock'n'Roll Is Here To Pay. The History & Politics of the Music Industry* (Nelson-Hall) Chicago 1977, p. 82.

21 R. Serge Denisoff, *Solid Gold – The Popular Record Industry* (Transaction) New Brunswick, N.J., 1975, p. 97.

22 Quoted from Roger Wallis and Krister Malm, *Big Sounds from Small Peoples*, p. 92.

23 Quoted from a tape transcript of a conversation which the author conducted in Liverpool on 23 November 1984.

24 George Melly, *Revolt into Style*, p. 41.

25 Quoted from Roger Wallis and Krister Malm, *Big Sounds from Small Peoples*, p. 92.

26 Cf. Peter Scaping, ed., *BPI Yearbook 1979* (British Phonographic Institute) London 1979, p. 140.

27 Simon Frith, *Sound Effects*.

28 Simon Frith, *The Sociology of Rock*, p. 76.

29 Quoted from a tape transcript of a conversation which the author conducted in London on 20 November 1984.

30 Quoted from *New Musical Express*, 14 November 1985, p. 3.

31 Richard Middleton, *Pop Music & the Blues. A Study of the Relationship and its Significance* (Gollancz) London 1972, p. 128.

32 Alan Durant, *The Conditions of Music* (Macmillan) London 1984, p. 185.

33 Michael Jackson, *Thriller*, CBS Epic 50989 (USA 1983).

34 Quoted from information supplied by the CBS public relations department, New York.

35 Quoted from Peter Bernstein, 'The Record Business. Rocking to the Big Money Beat', *Fortune*, 23 April 1979, p. 60.

36 Cf. Paul Hirsch, *The Structure of the Popular Music Industry* (University of Michigan, Institute for Social Research) Ann Arbor, Mich., 1973, p. 32.

37 Quoted from Kurt Blaukopf, *The Strategies of the Record Industries* (Council for Cultural Co-operation) Strasbourg 1982, p. 17.

38 Quoted from *Sounds*, XI, 1979/8, p. 41.

39 Quoted from a tape transcript of a conversation which the author conducted in London on 26 November 1984.

40 Cf. Paul Hirsch, *The Structure of the Popular Music Industry*, p. 25.

41 Charlie Gillett, ed., *Rock File 2* (Panther Books) St Albans 1974, p. 41.

42 Jon Landau, 'Der Tod von Janis Joplin', in *Let It Rock. Eine Geschichte der Rockmusik von Chuck Berry und Elvis Presley bis zu den Rolling Stones und den Allman Brothers*, ed. F. Schöler (Carl Hanser) Munich, Vienna 1975, p. 177.

7 'ANARCHY IN THE UK': THE PUNK REBELLION

1 Derek Jarman, *Dancing Ledge* (Quartet) London 1984, p. 56.

2 Ulrich Hetscher, 'Schickt die verdammten King Kongs zurück oder macht sie alle', in *Rock gegen Rechts*, ed. Floh de Cologne (Weltkreis) Dortmund 1980, p. 160.

3 Patti Smith, 'Piss Factory/Hey Joe', Sire 1009 (USA 1974).

4 Mat Snow, 'Blitzkrieg Bob', *New Musical Express*, 15 February 1986, p. 11.

5 Quoted from *Sounds* X, 1978/3, p. 6.

6 Quoted from Mike Brake, *The Sociology of Youth Culture and Youth Subcultures. Sex and Drugs and Rock'n'Roll?* (Routledge & Kegan Paul) London, Boston, Henley 1980, pp. 161–2.

7 Sex Pistols, 'Anarchy in the UK', EMI 2506 (GB 1976); © 1976 by Jones, Rotten, Matlock, Cook and Warner Brothers Music Ltd, New York.

8 Quoted from Hollow Skai, *Punk* (Sounds) Hamburg 1981, p. 41.

9 Peter Marsh, 'Dole Queue Rock', *New Society*, 20 January 1977, p. 22.

[10] Simon Frith, 'The Punk Bohemians', *New Society*, 9 March 1978, p. 536.
[11] Peter Weigelt, 'Langeweile', *Asthetik und Kommunikation*, 22–3 (1975), p. 141.
[12] Dick Hebdige, *Subculture*, pp. 106–7.
[13] Quoted from *New Musical Express*, 29 October 1977, p. 25.
[14] Dick Hebdige, *Subculture*, p. 66.
[15] Rudi Thiessen, *It's only rock'n'roll but I like it*, p. 215.
[16] Simon Frith, 'Wir brauchen eine neue Sprache für den Rock der 80er Jahre', in *Rock Session 4. Magazin der populären Musik*, eds. K. Humann and C.-L. Reichert (Rowohlt) Reinbek b. Hamburg 1980, p. 95.
[17] The Clash, 'Garageland', on *The Clash*, CBS Epic 36060 (GB 1977).
[18] The Clash, 'White Riot', on *The Clash*, CBS Epic 36060 (GB 1977); © 1977 by Strummer and Jones.
[19] Simon Frith, 'Post-punk Blues', *Marxism Today*, 27 March 1983, p. 19.
[20] Quoted from *Sniffin' Glue 12*, August/September 1977.
[21] Quoted from Caroline Coon, *1988. The New Wave Punk Rock Explosion* (Omnibus) London, New York, Sydney and Cologne 1982, p. 94.
[22] *Melody Maker*, 7 August 1976, front page.
[23] Quoted from Allan Jones, 'Punk – die verratene Revolution', in *Rock Session 2. Magazin der populären Musik*, eds. J. Gülden and K. Humann (Rowohlt) Reinbek b. Hamburg 1978, p. 17.
[24] Quoted from *Sounds*, 16 October 1976, p. 2.
[25] Quoted from Fred Vermorel and July Vermorel, *The Sex Pistols. The Inside Story* (Star Books) London 1981, p. 112.
[26] Quoted from *Evening Standard*, 17 March 1977, p. 2.
[27] Quoted from *New Musical Express*, 15 February 1986, p. 12.
[28] Alan Durant, 'Rock Revolution or Time-No-Changes. Visions of Change and Continuity in Rock Music', in *Popular Music 5. Continuity and Change*, eds. R. Middleton and D. Horn (Cambridge University Press) Cambridge, London, New York, New Rochelle, Melbourne, Sydney 1985, pp. 118–19.

8 'WILD BOYS': THE AESTHETIC OF THE SYNTHETIC

[1] Iain Chambers, *Urban Rhythms*, p. 199.
[2] Quoted from *Sounds*, XI, 1979/9, p. 43.
[3] Quoted from Dave Laing, 'The Music Industry in Crisis', *Marxism Today*, 25, July 1981, p. 19.
[4] Quoted from Dave Laing, 'The Music Industry in Crisis'.
[5] *UNESCO-Report, Youth in the 1980s* (The UNESCO Press) Paris 1981, p. 17.

6 Quoted from *New Musical Express*, 23 November 1985, p. 2.
7 John Howkins, 'New Technologies, New Politics?', in *BPI Yearbook 1982*, eds. P. Scaping and N. Hunter (British Phonographic Institute) 1982, p. 26.
8 Kevin d'Arcy, 'Wired for Sound and Visions', *Broadcast*, 28 March 1983, p. 32.
9 Andrew Goodwin, 'Popular Music, Video and Community Cable', Sheffield TV Group, *Cable & Community Programming*, Cable Working Papers, no. 3, Sheffield 1983, p. 69.
10 Quoted from Goodwin, 'Popular Music, Video and Community Cable', p. 70.
11 Don Watson, 'T.V.O.P.', *New Musical Express*, 12 October 1985, p. 20.
12 Paul Morley, 'Video and Pop', *Marxism Today*, 27, May 1983, p. 39.
13 Duran Duran, 'Wild Boys', Parlophone DURAN 2 (GB 1984); © 1984 by Duran Duran.
14 See Keith Roe, *Video and Youth. New Patterns of Media Use*, Media Panel Report, no. 18 (Lunds Universitet, Sociologiska Institutionen) Lund 1981.
15 Mark Hustwitt, 'Unsound Visions? Promotional Popular Music Videos in Britain' (paper presented at the Third International Conference on Popular Music Research, Montreal, July 1985) unpublished manuscript, p. 1.
16 Quoted from *New Musical Express*, 22 March 1986, p. 26.
17 Paul Morley, 'Video and Pop', p. 37.
18 Quoted from *New Musical Express*, 11 May 1985, pp. 2–3.
19 Quoted from *New Musical Express*, 30 March 1985, p. 15.
20 Quoted from *Radio Times*, 2–8 January 1982, p. 5.
21 Greil Marcus, 'Speaker to Speaker', *Artforum 11* (1985), p. 9.
22 Quoted from Mark Hustwitt, 'Unsound Visions?', p. 1.

9 POSTSCRIPT: 'THE TIMES THEY ARE A-CHANGING'

1 Bertolt Brecht, 'Der Dreigroschenprozess. Ein soziologisches Experiment', in *Schriften zur Literatur und Kunst*, I (Aufbau-Verlag) Berlin and Weimar 1966, p. 255.

Bibliography

Abrams, Mark, *The Teenage Consumer* (London Press Exchange) London 1959

Ackerman, Paul and Lee Zhito, eds., *The Complete Report of the First International Music Industry Conference* (Billboard Publishing) New York 1969

Adler, Bill, *Love Letters to the Beatles* (Blond & Briggs) London 1964

Alberoni, Fred, 'The Powerless "Elite". Theory and Sociological Research on the Phenomenon of the Stars', in *Sociology of Mass Communication*, ed. D. McQuil (Faber & Faber) London 1972, 75–98

Anderson, Bruce, Peter Hesbacher, K. Peter Etzkorn and R. Serge Denisoff, 'Hit Record Trends 1940–1977', *Journal of Communication*, 32 (1980/2), 31–43

Anson, Robert S., *Gone Crazy and Back Again. The Rise and Fall of the Rolling Stones Generation* (Doubleday) New York 1981

Barnard, Jermone, 'Teen-age Culture. An Overview', *Annals*, no. 338, November 1961, 1–12

Barnes, Richard, *Mods!* (Eel Pie) London 1979

Barthes, Roland, *Mythologies* (Paladin) London, 1973

Bartnick, Norbert and Frieda Bordon, *Keep On Rockin'. Rockmusik zwischen Protest und Profit* (Beltz) Weinheim, Basel 1981

Beckett, Alan, 'Stones', *New Left Review*, 47 (1968), 24–9

Beishuizen, Piet, ed., *The Industry of Human Happiness* (International Federation of the Phonographic Industry) London 1959

Belsito, Peter and Bob Davis, *Hardcore California. A History of Punk and New Wave* (Last Grasp of San Francisco) Berkeley, Cal., 1983

Belz, Carl, *The Story of Rock* (Oxford University Press) New York 1972

Benson, Dennis C., *The Rock Generation* (Abington) Nashville, Tenn., 1976

Berman, Marshall, 'Sympathy for the Devil', *New American Review*, 19 (1974), 23–76

Bernstein, Peter, 'The Record Business. Rocking to the Big Money Beat', *Fortune*, 23 April 1979, 59–68

196

Bigsby, C. W. E., ed., *Superculture. American Popular Culture and Europe* (Paul Elek) London 1975
Approaches to Popular Culture (Edward Arnold) London 1976
Birch, Ian, 'Punk Rock', in *The Rock Primer*, ed. J. Collis (Penguin) Harmondsworth 1980, 274–80
Birchall, Ian, 'The Decline and Fall of British Rhythm & Blues', in *The Age of Rock. Sounds of the American Cultural Revolution*, ed. J. Eisen (Vintage Books) New York 1969, 94–102
Bird, Brian, *Skiffle*, (Robert Hale) London 1958
Blackburn, Robin and Tariq Ali, 'Lennon. The Working Class Hero Turns Red', *Ramparts Magazine*, July 1971, 43–9
Blackford, Andy, *Disco Dancing Tonight. Clubs, Dances, Fashion, Music* (Octopus Books) London 1979
Blacknell, Steve, *The Story of Top Of The Pops* (Patrick Stephens: BBC Publications) London 1985
Blair, Dike and Elizabeth Anscomb, *Punk. Punk Rock, Style, Stance, People, Stars* (Urizen) New York 1978
Blankertz, Stefan and Götz Alsmann, *Rock'n'Roll Subversiv* (Büchse der Pandora) Wetzlar 1979
Blaukopf, Kurt, *Neue musikalische Verhaltensweisen der Jugend* (*Musikpädagogik. Forschung und Lehre*, ed. S. Abel-Struth, V) (Schott) Mainz 1974
The Strategies of the Record Industries (Council for Cultural Co-operation) Strasbourg 1982
The Phonogram in Cultural Communication. A Report on a Research Project Undertaken by MEDIACULT (Springer) Vienna, New York 1982
Booth, Stanley, *Dance with the Devil. The Rolling Stones and Their Times* (Random House) New York 1984
Boston, Virginia, *Punk Rock* (Penguin) New York 1978
Brake, Mike, 'Hippies and Skinheads. Sociological Aspects of Sub-cultures', PhD thesis, London School of Economics 1977
'The Skinheads. An English Working Class Subculture', *Youth and Society*, 6 (1977/2), 24–36
The Sociology of Youth Culture and Youth Subcultures. Sex and Drugs and Rock'n'Roll? (Routledge & Kegan Paul) London, Boston, Henley 1980
Comparative Youth Culture (Routledge & Kegan Paul) London, Boston, Henley 1985
Brecht, Bertolt, 'Der Dreigroschenprozess. Ein soziologisches Experiment', in *Schriften zur Literatur und Kunst*, I (Aufbau-Verlag) Berlin and Weimar 1966
Briggs, Asa, *The Birth of Broadcasting. The History of Broadcasting in the United Kingdom*, I (Oxford University Press) London 1961
The Golden Age of Wireless. The History of Broadcasting in the United Kingdom, II (Oxford University Press) London 1965

Governing the BBC (BBC Publications) London 1979

Brown, Peter and Steven Gaines, *The Love You Make. An Insider's Story of the Beatles* (McGraw Hill) New York 1983

Brown, Ray and Alison Ewbank, 'The British Music Industry 1984' (paper from XIV.IAMCR Conference, Prague, August 1984), unpublished manuscript

Burchill, Julie and Tony Parsons, *'The Boy Looked at Johnny'. The Obituary of Rock'n'Roll* (Pluto Press) London 1978

Bygrave, Mike, *Rock* (Watts) New York, 1978

Cable, Michael, *The Pop Industry Inside Out* (W. H. Allen) London 1977

Carey, James T., 'Changing Patterns in the Popular Song', *American Journal of Sociology*, 74 (1969), 720–31

Carter, Angela, 'Notes for a Theory of Sixties Style', *New Society*, 14 December 1967, 803–7

'Year of the Punk', *New Society*, 22 December 1977, 834–9

Castner, Thilo, 'Pop-Art und Beat-Kultur', *Wirtschaft und Erziehung*, 19 (1967/8), 357–61

Chambers, Iain, 'It's More Than a Song to Sing – Music, Cultural Analysis and the Blues', *Anglistica*, 22 (1979/1), 18–31

'Rethinking Popular Culture', *Screen Education*, 36 (1980), 113–17

'Some Critical Tracks', in *Popular Music 2. Theory and Method*, eds. R. Middleton and D. Horn (Cambridge University Press) Cambridge, London, New York, New Rochelle, Melbourne, Sydney 1982, 19–38

'Pop Music, Popular Culture and the Possible', in *Popular Music Perspectives 2. Papers from The Second International Conference on Popular Music Research, Reggio Emilia 1983*, ed. D. Horn (IASPM) Göteborg, Exeter, Ottawa, Reggio Emilia 1985, 445–50

Urban Rhythms. Pop Music and Popular Culture (Macmillan) Hampshire 1985

'Popular Culture, Popular Knowledge', *OneTwoThreeFour. A Rock'-n'Roll Quarterly*, no. 2, Summer 1985, 9–19

Chapple, Steve and Reebee Garofalo, *Rock'n'Roll Is Here to Pay. The History & Politics of the Music Industry* (Nelson-Hall) Chicago, 1977

Chester, Andrew, 'For a Rock Aesthetic', *New Left Review*, 59 (1970), 83–7

'Second Thoughts on a Rock Aesthetic. The Band', *New Left Review*, 62 (1970), 75–82

Clarke, John, 'The Skinheads and the Study of Youth Culture', Stencilled Occasional Papers, Sub and Popular Culture Series, SP no. 23 (University of Birmingham, Centre for Contemporary Cultural Studies) Birmingham 1974

'Style', in *Resistance through Rituals. Youth Subcultures in Post-war Britain*, eds. S. Hall and T. Jefferson (Hutchinson) London 1976, 175–191

Clarke, John et al., *Jugendkultur als Widerstand. Milieus, Rituale, Provokationen* (Syndicat) Frankfurt (Main) 1979

Clarke, John, Stuart Hall, Tony Jefferson and Brian Roberts, 'Subcultures, Cultures and Class', in *Resistance through Rituals. Youth Subcultures in Post-war Britain* eds. S. Hall and T. Jefferson (Hutchinson) London 1976, 9–74

Clarke, John and Tony Jefferson, 'The Politics of Popular Culture. Culture and Sub-culture', Stencilled Occasional Papers, Sub and Popular Culture Series, SP no. 14 (University of Birmingham, Centre for Contemporary Cultural Studies) Birmingham 1973

Clarke, Mike, 'On the Concept of Subculture', *British Journal of Sociology*, 25 (1974/4), 428–41

Clarke, Paul, '"A Magic Science". Rock Music as a Recording Art', in *Popular Music 3. Producers and Markets*, eds. R. Middleton and D. Horn (Cambridge University Press) Cambridge, London, New York, New Rochelle, Melbourne, Sydney 1985, 195–214

Coffman, James T., '"Everybody Knows This Is Nowhere". Role Conflict and the Rock Musician', *Popular Music and Society*, 1 (1971), 20–32

Cohen, Phil, 'Sub-cultural Conflict and Working Class Community', Working Papers in Cultural Studies, no. 2 (University of Birmingham, Centre for Contemporary Cultural Studies) Birmingham 1972

Cohen, Stanley, *Folk Devils and Moral Panics. The Creation of Mods and Rockers* (MacGibbon and Kee) London 1972, (Martin Robertson) Oxford 1980

Cohen, Stanley and Laurie Taylor, *Ausbruchsversuche. Identität und Widerstand in der modernen Lebenswelt* (Suhrkamp) Frankfurt (Main) 1977

Coleman, Arthur, *The Adolescent Society* (Free Press Glencoe) Chicago 1961

Collier, James L., *Making Music for Money* (Watts) New York 1976

Cook, Bruce, *The Beat Generation* (Charles Scribner's Sons) New York 1971

Cooke, Lez, 'Popular Culture and Rock Music', *Screen/Screen Education* 24 (1983), 46–58

Coon, Caroline, *1988. The New Wave Punk Rock Explosion* (Omnibus) London, New York, Sydney, Cologne 1982

Core, Peter, *Camp. The Lie That Tells the True* (Plexus) London 1984

Corrigan, Paul and Simon Frith, 'The Politics of Youth Culture', in *Resistance through Rituals. Youth Subcultures in Post-war Britain*, eds. S. Hall and T. Jefferson (Hutchinson) London 1976, 321–42

Cowan, Philip, *Behind the Beatles Songs* (Polyantric Press) London 1978

Cubitt, Sean, ' "Maybellene". Meaning and the Listening Subject', in *Popular Music 4. Performers and Audiences*, eds. R. Middleton and D. Horn (Cambridge University Press) Cambridge, London, New York, New Rochelle, Melbourne, Sydney 1984, 207–24

Cutler, Chris, 'Technology, Politics and Contemporary Music. Necessity and Choice in Musical Forms', in *Popular Music 4. Performers and Audiences*, eds. R. Middleton and D. Horn (Cambridge University Press) Cambridge, London, New York, New Rochelle, Melbourne, Sydney 1984, 279–300

    File Under Popular. Theoretical and Critical Writings on Music (November Books) London 1985

Dalton, David, *The Rolling Stones. The First Twenty Years* (Knopf) New York 1981

Dancis, Bernard, 'Safety Pins and Class Struggle. Punk Rock and the Left', *Socialist Review* 39 (1978), 58–83

Daney, Malcolm, *Summer in the City. Rock Music and Way of Life* (Lion Publishing) Berkhamsted 1978

D'Arcy, Kevin, 'Wired for Sound and Visions', *Broadcast*, 28 March 1983, 31–9

Davies, E., 'Psychological Characteristics of Beatle Mania', *Journal of the History of Ideas*, 30 (1969), 273–80

Davies, Hunter, *The Beatles* (Mayflower) London 1969, (revised edition, Dell Publishing) New York 1978

Davis, Clive, 'Creativity within the Corporation', in *The Music Industry. Markets and Methods for the Seventies* (Billboard Publishing) New York 1970, 285–91

    Clive. Inside the Record Business (William Morrow) New York 1975

Davis, Julie, ed., *Punk* (Millington) London 1977

Denisoff, R. Serge, 'The Evolution of Pop Music Broadcasting 1920–1972', *Popular Music and Society*, 3 (1973), 202–26

    Solid Gold. The Popular Record Industry (Transaction) New Brunswick, N.J., 1975

Denisoff, R. Serge and Mark H. Levine, 'The One-Dimensional Approach to Popular Music. A Research Note', *Journal of Popular Culture*, 6 (1971), 911–19

Denisoff, R. Serge and Richard Peterson, eds., *The Sounds of Social Change. Studies in Popular Culture* (Rand McNally) Chicago 1972

Denyer, Ralph, 'Chris Tsangarides Interview. The Producer Series', *Studio Sound* (July 1985), 82–8

Denzin, Norman K., 'Problems in Analysing Elements of Mass Culture. Notes on the Popular Song and Other Artistic Productions', *American Journal of Sociology*, 75 (1970), 1035–8

Dickstein, Morris, *Gates of Eden. American Culture in the Sixties* (Basic Books) New York 1977

Diederichsen, Diedrich, Dick Hebdige, and Olaph-Dante Marx, *Schocker. Stile und Moden der Subkultur* (Rowohlt) Reinbek b. Hamburg 1983

Dijkstra, Bram, 'Nichtrepressive rhythmische Strukturen in einigen Formen der afroamerikanischen und westindischen Musik', in *Die Zeichen. Neue Aspekte der musikalischen Asthetik II*, ed. H. W. Henze (Fischer) Frankfurt (Main) 1981, 60–97

Dimaggio, Paul, 'Market Structure, the Creative Process and Popular Culture. Toward an Organizational Reinterpretation of Mass Culture Theory', *Journal of Popular Culture*, 11 (1977), 436–52

Dollase, Rainer, Michael Rüsenberg and Hans J. Stollenwerk, *Rock People oder die befragte Szene* (Fischer) Frankfurt (Main) 1975
'Kommunikation zwischen Rockmusikern und Publikum', *jazzforschung/jazz research*, 9 (1977), 89–108
'Rockmusik und Massenkultur', *jazzforschung/jazz research*, 11 (1979), 197–208

Duncan, Robert, *The Noise. Notes from a Rock'n'Roll Era* (Ticknor & Fields) New York 1984

Durant, Alan, *The Conditions of Music* (Macmillan) London 1984
'Rock Revolution or Time-No-Changes. Visions of Change and Continuity in Rock Music', in *Popular Music 5. Continuity and Change*, eds. R. Middleton and D. Horn (Cambridge University Press) Cambridge, London, New York, New Rochelle, Melbourne, Sydney 1985, 97–122

Eberly, Philip K., *Music in the Air. America's Changing Tastes in Popular Music 1920–1980* (Hastings) New York 1982

Eisen, Jonathan, ed., *The Age of Rock. Sounds of the American Cultural Revolution* (Vintage Books) New York 1969
The Age of Rock 2. Sights and Sounds of the American Cultural Revolution (Vintage Books) New York 1970

Elliott, Dave, *The Rock Music Industry* (Popular Culture, Block 6, Unit 24, Science, Technology and Popular Culture 1) (Open University Press) Walton Hall, Milton Keynes 1982

EMI, World Record Markets (Westerham Press) London 1971

Epstein, Brian, *A Cellarful of Noise* (Pyramid) New York 1964, (Pierian Press) Ann Arbor, Mich., 1984

Eriksen, Norman, 'Popular Culture and Revolutionary Theory. Understanding Punk Rock', *Theoretical Review*, 18 (1980), 13–55

Ewbank, Alison, 'Youth and the Music Industry in Britain' (paper from Wingspread Conference on Youth and the International Music Industry, Racine, Wisc., 1983), unpublished manuscript

Fass, Pauline S., *The Damned and the Beautiful. American Youth in the 1900's* (Oxford University Press) New York 1977

Fiske, John, 'Videoclippings', *Australian Journal of Cultural Studies*, 2 (1984/1), 111–14

Fletcher, Colin L., 'Beats and Gangs on Merseyside', in *Youth in New Society*, ed. T. Raison (Hart-Davis) London 1964, 22–64

Fletcher, Peter, *Roll Over Rock* (Stainer & Bell) London 1981

Floh de Cologne, ed., *Rock gegen Rechts* (Weltkreis) Dortmund 1980

Fong-Torres, Ben, ed., *The Rolling Stone Interviews, Vol. II* (Warner Books) New York 1973

Frith, Simon, 'Rock and Popular Culture', *Socialist Revolution*, 31 (1977), 97–112

The Sociology of Rock, (Constable) London 1978

'The Punk Bohemians', *New Society*, 9 March 1978, 535–6

'Zur Ideologie des Punk', in *Rock Session 2. Magazin der populären Musik*, eds. J. Gülden and K. Humann (Rowohlt) Reinbek b. Hamburg 1978, 25–32

'Music for Pleasure', *Screen Education*, 34 (1980), 50–61

'Wir brauchen eine neue Sprache für den Rock der 80er Jahre', in *Rock Session 4. Magazin der populären Musik*, eds. K. Humann and C.-L. Reichert (Rowohlt) Reinbek b. Hamburg 1980, 94–104

Sounds Effects. Youth, Leisure and the Politics of Rock'n'Roll, (Pantheon) New York 1981

'The Art of Posing', *New Society*, 23 April 1981, 146–7

'"The Magic That Can Set You Free". The Ideology of Folk and the Myth of the Rock Community', in *Popular Music 1. Folk or Popular? Distinctions, Influences, Continuities*, eds. R. Middleton and D. Horn (Cambridge University Press) Cambridge, London, New York, New Rochelle, Melbourne, Sydney 1981, 159–68

'Youth in the Eighties. A Dispossessed Generation', *Marxism Today*, 25 (November 1981), 12–15

'John Lennon', *Marxism Today*, 25 (January 1981), 23–5

'The Sociology of Rock. Notes from Britain', in *Popular Music Perspectives. Papers from The First International Conference on Popular Music Research*, eds. D. Horn and Ph. Tagg, Amsterdam 1981 (IASPM) Göteborg, Exeter 1982, 142–54

'Post-punk Blues', *Marxism Today*, 27 (March 1983), 18–23

'Popular Music 1950–1980', in *Making Music*, ed. G. Martin (Muller) London 1983, 18–48

Frith, Simon and Howard Horne, 'Doing the Art School Bob. Oder: Ein kleiner Ausflug an die wahren Quellen', in *Rock Session 6. Magazin der populären Musik*, eds. K. Humann and C.-L. Reichert (Rowohlt) Reinbek b. Hamburg 1983, 279–96

'Welcome to Bohemia!', Warwick Working Papers in Sociology (University of Warwick) Coventry 1984

Frith, Simon and Angela McRobbie, 'Rock and Sexuality', *Screen Education*, 29 (1978), 3–19

Gamble, Arthur, *The Conservative Nation* (Routledge & Kegan Paul) London, Boston, Henley 1974
Britain in Decline (Macmillan) London 1981

Gans, Herbert J., *Popular Culture and High Culture. An Analysis and Evaluation of Taste* (Basic Books) New York 1974

Garbarini, Vic and Brian Cullman, *Strawberry Fields Forever. John Lennon Remembered* (Bantam) New York 1980

Garnham, Nicholas, 'A Contribution to the Political Economy of Mass Communications', *Media, Culture and Society*, 1 (1979/2), 123–46

Gayle, Addison, *The Black Aesthetic* (Doubleday) New York 1971

Gehr, Richard, 'The MTV Aesthetic', *Film Comment* (November 1983), 37–40

Gillett, Charlie, 'Big Noise from Across the Water – the American Influence on British Popular Music' (paper from Smithsonian Conference 'The United States in the World', Washington 1978), unpublished manuscript
The Sound of the City. The Rise of Rock and Roll (revised edition, Souvenir) London 1983

Gillett, Charlie, ed., *Rock File 2* (Panther Books) St Albans 1974

Gleason, Ralph J., 'Like A Rolling Stone', in *The Age of Rock. Sounds of the American Cultural Revolution*, ed. J. Eisen (Vintage Books) New York 1969, 64–81

Goodwin, Andrew, 'Popular Music, Video and Community Cable', Sheffield TV Group, *Cable & Community Programming*, Cable Working Papers, no. 3, Sheffield 1983, 54–100

Greene, Bob, *Million Dollar Baby* (New American Library) New York 1975

Griffin, Alistair, *On the Scene at the Cavern* (Hamish Hamilton) London 1964

Grissim, John, *Country Music. White Man's Blues* (Paperback Library) New York 1970

Gronow, Pekka, 'The Record Industry. The Growth of a Mass Medium', in *Popular Music 3. Producers and Markets*, eds. R. Middleton and D. Horn (Cambridge University Press) Cambridge, London, New York, New Rochelle, Melbourne, Sydney 1983, 53–76

Groschopp, Horst, 'Zur Kritik der Subkultur-Theorien in der BRD', *Weimarer Beiträge*, 23 (1977/12), 20–52

Gross, Michael and Maxim Jakubowski, 'Inside the Industry. The Art of Making Records Made Simple', in their *The Rock Year Book 1981* (Grove Press) New York 1981, 209–11

Grossberg, Lawrence, 'Experience, Signification and Reality. The Boundaries of Cultural Semiotics', *Semiotica*, 41 (1982), 73–106

'The Politics of Youth Culture. Some Observations on Rock and Roll in American Culture', *Social Text*, 8 (1983/4), 104–26

'The Social Meaning of Rock'n'Roll', *OneTwoThreeFour. A Rock-'n'Roll Quarterly*, 1 (Summer 1984), 13–21

' "I'd Rather Feel Bad Than Not Feel Anything At All" '. Rock and Roll, Pleasure and Power', *Enclitic*, 8 (1984/1–2), 95–111

'Another Boring Day in Paradise. Rock and Roll and the Empowerment of Everyday Life', in *Popular Music 4. Performers and Audiences*, eds. R. Middleton and D. Horn (Cambridge University Press) Cambridge, London, New York, New Rochelle, Melbourne, Sydney 1984, 225–60

'If Rock and Roll Communicates, Then Why Is It So Noisy? Pleasure and the Popular', in *Popular Music Perspectives 2. Papers from The Second International Conference on Popular Music Research. Reggio Emilia 1983*, ed. D. Horn (IASPM) Göteborg, Exeter, Ottawa, Reggio Emilia 1985, 451–63

'Is There Rock After Punk?', *Critical Studies in Mass Communication*, 3 (1986), 50–74

'Rock and Roll in Search of an Audience or Taking Fun (too?) Seriously', unpublished manuscript

A Social History of Rock Music. From the Greasers to Glitter Rock (David McKay) New York 1976

Guralnick, Peter, *Feel Like Going Home. Portraits in Blues and Rock-'n'Roll* (Vintage Books) New York 1981

Haberman, Jim, 'New York – No Wave', *Sounds*, 11 (1979/11), 36–42

Haley, William, *The Responsibilities of Broadcasting* (BBC Publications) London 1948

Hall, Stuart, 'The Hippies. An American Moment', Stencilled Occasional Papers, Sub and Popular Culture Series, SP no. 16, (University of Birmingham, Centre for Contemporary Cultural Studies) Birmingham 1968; also in *Student Power*, ed. J. Nagel (Merlin Press) London 1969, 112–28

'Cultural Studies. Two Paradigma', *Media, Culture and Society*, 4 (1982/2), 57–72

Hall, Stuart and Paddy Whannel, *The Popular Arts* (Hutchinson) London 1964

Hall, Stuart and Tony Jefferson, eds., *Resistance through Rituals. Youth Subcultures in Post-War Britain* (Hutchinson) London 1976

Hall, Stuart, Dorothy Hobston, Andrew Loure and Paul Willis, eds., *Culture, Media, Language. Working Papers in Cultural Studies, 1972–1979* (Hutchinson) London 1980

Hardy, Phil, 'The British Record Industry', IASPM UK Working Paper 3 (IASPM British Branch Committee) London [1984]

Harker, Dave, *One For the Money. Politics and Popular Song* (Hutchinson) London, Melbourne, Sydney, Auckland, Johannesburg 1980

Harmon, James E., 'Meaning in Rock Music. Notes Toward a Theory of Communication', *Popular Music and Society*, 2 (1972), 18–32

Harris, Maz, *Bikers* (Faber & Faber) London 1985

Harry, Bill, *Mersey Beat. The Beginnings of The Beatles* (Omnibus) London, New York, Cologne, Sydney 1977

Hartwig, Helmut, *Jugendkultur – Ästhetische Praxis in der Pubertät* (Rowohlt) Reinbek b. Hamburg 1980

Hatch, Tony, *So You Want to Be in the Music Business* (Everest Books) London 1976

Hebdige, Dick, 'The Style of the Mods', Stencilled Occasional Papers, Sub and Popular Culture Series, SP no. 20 (University of Birmingham, Centre for Contemporary Cultural Studies) Birmingham 1973

Subculture. The Meaning of Style (Methuen) London, New York 1979

'The Meaning of Mod', in *Resistance through Rituals. Youth Subcultures in Post-war Britain*, eds. S. Hall and T. Jefferson (Hutchinson) London 1977, 87–98

'Object as Image. The Italian Scooter Cycle', *Block 5*, Middlesex Polytechnic 1981, 44–64

'Towards a Cartography of Taste, 1935–1962', in *Popular Culture: Past and Present*, eds. B. Waites, T. Bennett and G. Martin (Open University Press / Croom Helm) London 1982, 194–218

'In Poor Taste', *Block 8*, Middlesex Polytechnic 1983, 54–68

'Posing ... Threats, Striking ... Poses. Youth, Surveillance and Display', *Substance* 37/38 (1983), 68–88

Hellman, Heikki and Martti Soramäki, 'Video-Commercial Structures and Cultural Changes' (paper from XIV. IAMCR Conference, Prague 1984), unpublished manuscript

Henderson, Bill, *How to Run Your Own Rock & Roll Band* (CBS Publications, Popular Library) New York 1977

Hennessey, Mike, 'PolyGram Restructures for the 1980s', *Billboard*, 12 July 1980, 4, 62

Hennion, Antoine, 'The Production of Success. An Anti-Musicology of the Pop Song', in *Popular Music 3. Producers and Markets*, eds. R. Middleton and D. Horn (Cambridge University Press) Cambridge, London, New York, New Rochelle, Melbourne, Sydney 1983, 159–94

Herman, Gary, *The Who* (Studio Vista) London 1971

Hetscher, Ulrich, 'Schickt die verdammten King Kongs zurück oder macht sie alle', in *Rock gegen Rechts*, ed. Floh de Cologne (Weltkreis) Dortmund 1980, 137–69

Heubner, Thomas, *Die Rebellion der Betrogenen. Rocker, Popper, Punks und Hippies – Modewellen und Protest in der westlichen Welt!* (Verlag Neues Leben) Berlin 1986

Hey, Ken, '"I'll Give It a 95". An Approach to the Study of Early Rock'n'Roll', *Popular Music and Society*, 3 (1974), 315–28

Hill, Leslie, 'An Insight into the Finances of the Record Industry', *The Three Banks Review* (National and Commercial Banking Group Ltd, London), 118 (June 1978), 28–42

Hirsch, Paul, 'Sociological Approaches to the Pop Music Phenomenon', *American Behaviour Scientist*, 14 (1971/3), 371–88

The Structure of the Popular Music Industry (University of Michigan, Institute for Social Research) Ann Arbor, Mich., 1973

Hirsch, Paul and Jon Robinsohn, 'It's the Sound That Does It', *Psychology Today*, 3 (1969), 42–5

Hodge, Robert, 'Video Clips as a Revolutionary Form', *Australian Journal of Cultural Studies*, 2 (1984/1), 115–20

Hoffman, Abbie, *Woodstock Nation. A Talk-Rock Album* (Pocket) New York 1971

Hoffmann, Raoul, *Zwischen Galaxis & Underground. Die neue Popmusik* (Deutscher Taschenbuch Verlag) Munich 1971

Horowitz, David, Michael P. Lerner and Craig Pyes, eds., *Counterculture and Revolution* (Random House) New York 1973

Howkins, John, 'New Technologies, New Politics?', in *BPI Yearbook 1982*, eds. P. Scaping and N. Hunter (British Phonographic Institute) London 1982, 23–35

Howlett, Kevin, *The Beatles at the Beeb. The Story of Their Radio Career 1962–1965* (BBC Publications) London [1982]

Hoyland, John, 'An Open Letter to John Lennon', *Black Dwarf*, 27 October 1968

Hudson, Jan, *The Sex and Savagery of Hells Angels* (New American Library) New York 1967

Hustwitt, Mark, 'Rocker Boy Blues. The Writing on Pop', *Screen/Screen Education*, 25 (1984), 89–98

'Unsound Visions? Promotional Popular Music Videos in Britain' (paper from III International Conference on Popular Music Research, Montreal, July 1985) unpublished manuscript

Jacobs, Norman, ed., *Culture for the Millions? Mass Media in Modern Society* (Beacon) Boston 1959

Jacques, Martin, 'Trends in Youth Culture. Some Aspects', *Marxism Today*, 17 (June 1973), 268–80

Jahn, Mike, *Rock. From Elvis Presley to the Rolling Stones* (Time Books) New York 1973

Jarman, Derek, *Dancing Ledge* (Quartet) London 1984

Jaspers, Tony, *Understanding Pop* (SCM Press) London 1972

Jefferson, Tony, 'The Teds. A Political Resurrection', Stencilled Occasional Papers, Sub and Popular Culture Series, SP no. 22 (University of Birmingham, Centre for Contemporary Cultural Studies) Birmingham 1973

Jefferson, Tony and John Clarke, 'Working Class Youth Cultures', Stencilled Occasional Papers, Sub and Popular Culture Series, SP no. 18 (University of Birmingham, Centre for Contemporary Cultural Studies) Birmingham 1973

Jenkinson, Phillip and Alan Warner, *Celluloid Rock. Twenty Years of Movie Rock* (Lorimer) London 1975

John Lennon erinnert sich (Release) Hamburg, no date

John, Mike, *Rock. A Social History of the Music, 1945–1972* (Quadrangle) New York 1973

Johnson, Derek, *Beat Music* (Hansen) Kopenhagen, (Chester) London 1969

Johnson, P., 'The Menace of Beatleism', *New Statesman* 28 (February 1964), 17

Jones, Allan, 'Punk – die verratene Revolution', in *Rock Session 2. Magazin der populären Musik*, eds. J. Gülden and K. Humann (Rowohlt) Reinbek b. Hamburg 1978, 5–24

Jones, Bryan, 'The Politics of Popular Culture', Stencilled Occasional Papers, Sub and Popular Culture Series, SP no. 12 (University of Birmingham, Centre for Contemporary Cultural Studies) Birmingham 1972

Jones, Nick, 'Well, What Is Pop Art?', *Melody Maker*, 3 July 1965, 11

Kalkkinen, Marja-Leena and Raija Sarkkinen, 'The International Entertainment Industry and the New Media' (paper from XIV. IAMCR Conference; Prague 1984), unpublished manuscript

Kneif, Tibor, *Rockmusik. Ein Handbuch zum kritischen Verständnis* (Rowohlt) Reinbek b. Hamburg 1982

Kozak, Roman, 'CBS Redirecting A&R Emphasis', *Billboard* (17 December 1977), 8, 93

'Yetnikoff Vows CBS Records to Up Profits', *Billboard* (17 March 1979), 3, 9

Laing, Dave, *The Sound of Our Time* (Sheed & Ward) London 1969

'Interpreting Punk Rock', *Marxism Today*, 22 (April 1978), 123–8

'Music Video: The Music Industry in Crisis', *Marxism Today*, 25 (July 1981), 19–21

'Industrial Product or Cultural Form', *Screen/Screen Education*, 26 (1985), 78–83

One Chord Wonders. Power and Meaning in Punk Rock (Open University Press) Milton Keynes, Philadelphia 1985

Laing, Dave, Karl Dallas, Robin Denselow and Robert Shelton, *The Electric Muse. The Story of Folk into Rock* (Eyre Methuen) London 1975

Lamont, Richard, 'Mixing the Media', *Studio Sound* (July 1985), 64–70

Landau, Jon, 'Rock'n'Radical?', *Daily World* (22 February 1969), 18

'Rock 1970 – It's too Late to Stop Now', in *American Music. From Storyville to Woodstock*, ed. Ch. Nanry (Rutgers University Press) New Brunswick, N.J., 1972, 238–66

It's too Late to Stop Now. A Rock'n'Roll Journal (Straight Arrow Books) San Francisco 1972

'Der Tod von Janis Joplin', in *Let It Rock. Eine Geschichte der Rockmusik von Chuck Berry und Elvis Presley bis zu den Rolling Stones und den Allman Brothers*, ed. F. Schöler (Carl Hanser) Munich, Vienna 1975, 177–80

Lasch, Christopher, *The Culture of Narcissism* (Pantheon) New York 1979

Laurie, Peter, *Teenage Revolution* (Blond & Briggs) London 1965

Lefébvre, Henri, *Critique de la vie quotidienne, Fondements d'une sociologie de la quotidienneté*, II (L'Arche Editeur) Paris 1961

Leigh, Spencer, *Paul Simon. Now and Then* (Raven Books) Liverpool 1973

Let's Go Down the Cavern. The Story of Liverpool's Merseybeat (Vermilion) London 1984

Leimbacher, Ed, 'The Crash of The Jefferson Airplane', *Ramparts Magazine* (January 1970), 8–21

Lennon, John, *Spaniard in the Works* (Cape) London 1965

In His Own Write (Cape) London 1968

'A Very Open Letter to John Hoyland from John Lennon', *Black Dwarf* (10 January 1969)

Lewis, George, 'Popular Music and Research Design. Methodological Alternatives', *Popular Music and Society*, I (1972), 108–15

Lindner, Rolf, *Punk Rock oder: Der vermarktete Aufruhr* (Fischer) Frankfurt (Main) 1977

Lipsitz, George, *Class and Culture in Cold War America. 'A Rainbow at Midnight'* (Bergin & Garvey) South Hadley, Mass., 1982

London, Herbert J., *Closing the Circle. A Cultural History of the Rock Revolution* (Nelson-Hall) Chicago 1984

Lull, James, 'Popular Music. Resistance to New Wave', *Journal of Communication*, 32 (1982/1), 121–31

'Thrashing in the Pit. A Ethnography of San Francisco Punk Sub-culture', in Th. R. Lindlof, *Natural Audiences* (Abley Publishing) Norwood, N.J., 1986, 32–79

Luthe, Heinz O., 'Recorded Music and the Music Industry', *International Social Science Journal*, 20 (1968), 656–65

Lydon, Michael, 'Rock for Sale', in *The Age of Rock 2. Sights and Sounds of the American Cultural Revolution*, ed. J. Eisen (Vintage Books) New York 1970, 55–71

Rock Folk. Portraits from the Rock'n'Roll Pantheon (Dutton) New York 1971

Mabey, Richard, *Behind the Scene* (Penguin) Harmondsworth 1968
The Pop Process (Hutchinson) London 1969

Malamud, Bernard, *A New Life* (Chatto & Windus) London 1980

Malone, Bill C., *Country Music USA* (University of Texas Press) Austin, Tex., 1968

Marcus, Greil, *Rock and Roll Will Stand* (Beacon) New York 1969
Mystery Train. Images of America in Rock'n'Roll (Omnibus) London 1977
'Speaker to Speaker', *Artforum 11* (1985), 9

Marks, James and Linda Eastman, *Rock* (Bantam Books) New York 1968

Marsh, Dave, *Before I Get Old. The Story of The Who* (Plexus) London 1983

Marsh, Peter; 'Dole Queue Rock', *New Society*, 20 January 1977, 22–9

Martin, Bernice, *A Sociology of Contemporary Cultural Change* (Blackwell) Oxford 1981
'Pop Music and Youth', *Media Development*, 29 (1982/1), 32–41

Martin, George, *All You Need is Ears* (St Martin's Press) New York 1979

Martin, George, ed., *Making Music* (Muller) London 1983

Masters, Brian, *The Swinging Sixties* (Constable) London 1985

Mattelart, Armand, *Multinational Corporations and the Control of Culture. The Ideological Apparatuses of Imperialism* (Harvester Press) London 1979

May, Chris, *Rock'n'Roll* (Socion Books) London, no date

May, Chris and Ian Phillips, *British Beat* (Socion Books) London, no date

McCabe, Peter and Robert D. Schonfield, *Apple to the Core. The Unmaking of The Beatles* (Sphere) London 1971

McRobbie, Angela, 'Settling Accounts with Subcultures. A Feminist Critique', *Screen Education*, 34 (1980), 37–49

Mellers, Wilfried, *Twilight of the Gods. The Beatles in Retrospect* (Faber) London 1973
A Darker Shade of Pale. A Backdrop to Bob Dylan (Oxford University Press) New York 1985

Melly, George, *Revolt into Style* (Penguin) Harmondsworth 1973

Meltzer, Richard, *The Aesthetics of Rock* (Something Else Press) New York 1970

Meyer, Gust De, 'Minimal and Repetitive Aspects in Pop Music', in *Popular Music Perspectives 2. Papers from The Second International Conference on Popular Music Research, Reggio Emilia 1983*, ed. D. Horn (IASPM), Göteborg, Exeter, Ottawa, Reggio Emilia 1985, 387–96

Middleton, Richard, *Pop Music & The Blues. A Study of the Relationship and Its Significance* (Gollancz) London 1972

210 Bibliography

Miles, Barry, *Beatles in Their Own Words* (Omnibus) London 1978
Miller, Jim, ed., *The Rolling Stone Illustrated History of Rock'n'Roll* (Random House and Rolling Stone Press) New York 1980
Morley, Dave, 'Industrial Conflict and the Mass Media', Stencilled Occasional Papers, Media Series, SP no. 8 (University of Birmingham, Centre for Contemporary Cultural Studies) Birmingham 1974
'Reconceptualizing the Media Audience. Towards an Ethnography of Audiences', Stencilled Occasional Papers, Media Series, SP no. 9 (University of Birmingham, Centre for Contemporary Cultural Studies) Birmingham 1974
Morley, Paul, 'Video and Pop', *Marxism Today*, 27 (May 1983), 37–9
Morse, Bernard, *The Sexual Revolution* (Fawcett Publications) Derby, Conn., 1962
Muldoon, Roland, 'Subculture. The Street-Fighting Pop Group', in *Black Dwarf* (15 October 1968)
Muncie, John, *Pop Culture, Pop Music and Post-war Youth: Subcultures* (Popular Culture, Block 5, Unit 19, Politics, Ideology and Popular Culture 1) (Open University Press) Walton Hall, Milton Keynes 1982
Mungham, Geoff and Geoff Pearson, *Working Class Youth Cultures* (Routledge & Kegan Paul) London, Boston, Henley 1976
Murdock, Graham, 'Besitz und Kontrolle der Massenmedien in Großbritannien heute. Strukturen und Konsequenzen', in *Massenkommunikationsforschung* 1, ed. D. Prokop (Suhrkamp) Frankfurt (Main) 1972, 36–63
'Adolescent Culture and the Mass Media', Stencilled Occasional Papers (University of Leicester, Centre for Mass Communication Research) Leicester 1979
Murdock, Graham and Robin McCron, 'Scoobies, Skins and Contemporary Pop', *New Society* (29 March 1973), 129–31
'Consciousness of Class and Consciousness of Generation', in *Resistance through Rituals. Youth Subcultures in Post-war Britain*, eds. S. Hall and T. Jefferson (Hutchinson) London 1976, 192–208
'Music Classes – Über klassenspezifische Rockbedürfnisse', in R. Lindner, *Punk Rock oder: Der vermarktete Aufruhr* (Fischer) Frankfurt (Main) 1977, 18–30
Murdock, Graham and Guy Phelps, 'Responding to Popular Music. Criteria of Classification and Choice Among English Teenagers', *Popular Music and Society*, 1 (1972), 144–51
Naison, Mark, 'Youth Culture. A Critical View', *Radical America* (September/October 1970), 14–23
Nanry, Charles, ed., *American Music. From Storyville to Woodstock* (Rutgers University Press) New Brunswick, N.J., 1972
Naumann, Michael and Penth, Boris, eds., *Living in a Rock'n'Roll Fantasy* (Asthetik und Kommunikation) Berlin (West) 1979

Neville, Richard, *Playpower* (Paladin) London 1970

Norman, Phillip, *Shout! The Beatles in Their Generation* (Simon & Schuster) New York 1981

Nuttal, Jeff, *Bomb Culture* (Paladin) London 1969

Nye, Russel, *The Unembarrassed Muse. The Popular Arts in America* (Dial) New York 1970

O'Brien, Patrick, 'MTV: Just Like Life', (paper from the International Sociological Association Meeting 'Communication and Life Styles', Ljubljana 1985), unpublished manuscript

O'Neill, William L., *Coming Apart. An Informal History of America in the 1960's* (Times Books) Chicago 1977

Orman, John M., *The Politics of Rock Music* (Nelson-Hall) Chicago 1984

Palmer, Tony, *Born Under a Bad Sign* (William Kimber) London 1970

Pareles, Jon and Patricia Romanowski, *The Rolling Stone Encyclopedia of Rock & Roll* (Rolling Stone Press and Summit Books) New York 1983

Partridge, Richard, 'Merseybeat Memories', *Melody Maker* (25 August 1973), 33, 49

Partridge, William L., *The Hippy Ghetto. The Story of a Subculture* (Holt, Rinehart & Winston) New York 1973

Penth, Boris and Günter Franzen, *Last Exit. Punk: Leben im toten Herz der Städte* (Rowohlt) Reinbek b. Hamburg 1982

Peron, René, 'The Record Industry', in *Communication and Class Struggle*, eds. A. Mattelart and S. Sieglaub, I (International-General) New York 1979, 121–58

Peterson, Richard A. and David G. Berger, 'Entrepreneurship in Organizations. Evidence from the Popular Music Industry', *Administrative Science Quarterly*, 16 (1971/3), 97–106
'Cycles in Symbol Production. The Case of Popular Music', *American Sociological Review*, 40 (1975/2), 158–73

Petrie, Gavin, *Pop Today* (Hamlyn) London 1974

Pichaske, David, *A Generation in Motion. Popular Music and Culture in the Sixties* (Schirmer) New York 1979

Pinto-Duschinsky, Mark, 'Bread and Circuses. The Conservatives in Office, 1951–1964', in *The Age of Affluence*, eds. V. Bodganor and R. Skidelsky (Macmillan) London, New York 1970, 54–67

Pollock, Bruce and John Wagman, *The Face of Rock and Roll. Images of a Generation* (Holt, Rinehart & Winston) New York 1978

Qualen, John, *The Music Industry. The End of Vinyl?* (Comedia) London 1985

Račič, Ladislav, 'On the Aesthetics of Rock-Music', *International Review of the Aesthetics and Sociology of Music*, 12 (1981/2), 199–202

Randle, Bill, 'Theory of Popular Culture', Working Paper (Case-Western Reserve University) 1969

Real, Michael R., 'Popular Music and Cultural Change', *Media Development*, 29 (1982/1), 52–61

Rebstock, André, *Imperialistische Massen-Kultur und 'Pop-Musik'* (Spartakus MSB, Fachgruppe Gestaltung) Hamburg 1972

Rieger, Jon H., 'The Coming Crisis in the Youth Market', *Popular Music and Society*, 4 (1975), 19–35

Riesman, David et al., *The Lonely Crowd. A Study of the Changing American Character* (Yale) New Haven 1961, revised edition

Robinson, Richard, *Rock Revolution* (CBS Publications, Popular Library) New York 1976

Rock, Paul and Stanley Cohen, 'The Teddy Boy', in *The Age of Affluence*, eds. V. Bodganor and R. Skidelsky (Macmillan) London, New York 1970, 122–53

Roe, Keith, *Video and Youth. New Patterns of Media Use*, Media Panel Report no. 18 (Lunds Universitet, Sociologiska Institutionen) Lund 1981

  The Influence of Video Technology in Adolescence, Media Panel Report no. 27 (Lunds Universitet, Sociologiska Institutionen) Lund 1983

Rogers, Dave, *Rock'n'Roll* (Routledge & Kegan Paul) London, Boston, Henley 1982

Röhrling, Helmut, *Wir sind die, vor denen uns unsere Eltern gewarnt haben. Szenen und Personen aus den amerikanischen Sechzigern* (Clemens Zerling) Berlin (West) 1980

Rothenbuhler, Eric W. and John W. Dimmick, 'Popular Music. Contradiction and Diversity in the Industry 1974–1980', *Journal of Communication*, 32 (1982), 143–9

Salzinger, Helmut, *Rock Power oder Wie musikalisch ist die Revolution? Ein Essay über Pop-Musik und Gegenkultur* (Fischer) Frankfurt (Main) 1972

Sanchez, Tony, *Up and Down with The Rolling Stones* (Signet) New York 1980

Sandner, Wolfgang, ed., *Rockmusik. Aspekte zur Geschichte, Ästhetik, Produktion* (Schott) Mainz 1977

Sarlin, Bob, *Turn It Up! (I can't hear the words)* (Coronet) London 1975

Savage, Jon, 'The Punk Process', *The Face* (November 1981), 48–51

Savary, Louis M., *Popular Song & Youth Today* (Association) New York 1971

Scaduto, Anthony, *Bob Dylan. An Intimate Biography*, Grosset & Dunlap) New York 1972

Scaping, Peter, ed., *BPI Yearbook 1979* (British Phonographic Institute) London 1979

Scaping, Peter and Norman Hunter, eds., *BPI Yearbook 1982* (British Phonographic Institute) London 1982

Schafe, William J., *Rock Music. Where It's Been, What It Means, Where It's Going* (Augsburg) Minneapolis, Minn., 1972

Schaffner, Nicholas, *The Beatles Forever* (Pinnacle Books) New York 1978

Schaumburg, Ron, *Growing Up With The Beatles* (Pyramid) New York 1976

Schicke, Charles, *Revolution in Sound. A Biography of the Recording Industry* (Little Brown) Boston 1974

Schmidt, Mathias R., *Bob Dylan und die sechziger Jahre. Aufbruch und Abkehr* (Fischer) Frankfurt (Main) 1983

Sculatti, Gene and Davin Seay, *San Francisco Nights. The Psychedelic Music Trips 1965–1968* (Sidgwick & Jackson) London 1985

Seuss, Jürgen, Gerold Dommermuth and Hans Maier, *Beat in Liverpool* (Europäische Verlagsanstalt) Frankfurt (Main) 1965

Shaw, Arnold, *The Rock Revolution* (Macmillan) London 1969

Shemel, Sidney and M. William Krasilovsky, *The Business of Music* (Watson-Guptill) New York 1971

Shore, Larry, 'The Crossroads of Business and Music. The Music Industry in the United States and Internationally', unpublished manuscript

Shore, Michael, *The Rolling Stone Book of Rock Video* (Quill) New York 1985

Shore, Michael and Dick Clark, *The History of American Bandstand* (Ballantine) New York 1985

Sinclair, John, 'Popmusik ist Revolution', *Sounds*, 1 (1968/12), 106–15 *Music and Politics* (World) New York 1971

Skai, Hollow, *Punk* (Sounds) Hamburg 1981

Sklar, Rick, *Rocking America* (St Martin's Press) New York 1984

Sladek, Isabella, 'Gebrauchsgrafik als Massenkommunikation. Zur Ästhetik der visuellen Rhetorik der kommerziellen Gebrauchsgrafik im Imperialismus', *Bildende Kunst*, I (1985/9), 414–16; II (1985/10), 465–7; III (1985/12), 546–9

Snow, Mat, 'Blitzkrieg Bob', *New Musical Express*, 15 (February 1986), 11

Solothurmann, Jürg, 'Zur Asthetik der afroamerikanischen Musik', *jazzforschung/jazz research*, 9 (1977), 69–88

Soramäki, Martti and Jukka Haarma, *The International Music Industry* (OY, Yleisradio Ab., The Finnish Broadcasting Company, Planning and Research Department) Helsinki 1981

Spitz, Robert S., *The Making of Superstars. The Artists and Executives of the Rock Music World* (Doubleday) New York 1978

Stark, Jürgen and Michael Kurzawa, *Der große Schwindel? Punk – New Wave – Neue Welle* (Verlag Freie Gesellschaft) Frankfurt (Main) 1981

Steele-Perkins, Chris and Richard Smith, *The Teds* (Travelling Light/Exit) London 1979

Stokes, Geoffrey, *Star Making Machinery. Inside the Business of Rock'n'Roll* (Random House) New York 1977

Stratton, Jon, 'Between Two Worlds. Arts and Commerce in the Record Industry', *Sociological Review*, 30 (1982), 267–85

'Capitalism and Romantic Ideology in the Record Business', in *Popular Music 3. Producers and Markets*, eds. R. Middleton and D. Horn (Cambridge University Press) Cambridge, London, New York, New Rochelle, Melbourne, Sydney 1983, 143–58

Struck, Jürgen, *Rock Around the Cinema. Die Geschichte des Rockfilms* (Verlag Monika Nüchtern) Munich 1979

Sutcliffe, Kevin, 'Video Killed the Radio Star', *Camerawork*, 30 (1984), 26–32

Swingewood, Arthur, *The Myth of Mass Culture* (Macmillan) London 1977

Tagg, Philip, *Kojak – 50 Seconds of Television Music. Towards the Analysis of Affect in Popular Music* (Studies from the Department of Musicology, University of Gothenburg) Göteborg 1980

Taylor, Jon and Dave Laing, 'Disco-Pleasure Discourse. On ''Rock and Sexuality'' ', *Screen Education*, 31 (1979), 43–8

Taylor, Ken, *Rock Generation* (Sun Books) Melbourne 1970

The Music Industry. Markets and Methods for the Seventies (Billboard Publishing) New York 1970

Thiessen, Rudi, *It's only rock'n'roll but I like it. Zu Kult und Mythos einer Protestbewegung* (Medusa) West Berlin 1981

Thomson, David, *England in the Twentieth Century* (Pelican) Harmondsworth 1981

Toll, Robert C., *The Entertainment Machine. American Show Business in the Twentieth Century* (Oxford University Press) New York, London 1982

Trow, Mike, *The Pulse of '64. The Mersey Beat* (Vintage Books) New York 1978

Turner, Graeme, 'Video Clips and Popular Music', *Australian Journal of Cultural Studies* I (May 1983), 105–11

UNESCO-Report. Youth in the 1980's (The UNESCO Press) Paris 1981

van der Plas, Wim, 'Can Rock Be Art?', in *Popular Music Perspectives 2. Papers from The Second International Conference on Popular Music Research, Reggio Emilia 1983*, ed. D. Horn (IASPM), Göteborg, Exeter, Ottawa, Reggio Emilia 1985, 397–404

van der Wal, Harm, *The Impact of New Technologies on the Strategies of the Music Industries* (Council for Cultural Co-operation) Strasbourg 1985

Vermorel, Fred and July Vermorel, *The Sex Pistols. The Inside Story* (Star Books) London 1981

Vignolle, Jean Pierre, 'Mixing Genres and Reaching the Public. The Production of Popular Music', *Social Science Information*, 19 (1980/1), 75–105

Vulliamy, Graham, 'A Re-assessment of the Mass Culture Controversy. The Case of Rock Music', *Popular Music and Society*, 4 (1975), 130–55

Waites, Bernard, Tony Bennett and Graham Martin, eds., *Popular Culture: Past and Present* (Open University Press / Croom Helm) London 1982

Wale, Michael, *Vox Pop. Profiles of the Pop Process* (Harrap) London 1971

Wallis, Roger and Krister Malm, *Big Sounds from Small Peoples. The Music Industry in Small Countries* (Constable) London 1984

Watson, Don, 'T.V.O.P.', *New Musical Express* (12 October 1985), 20

Weigelt, Peter, 'Langeweile', *Asthetik und Kommunikation*, 22–3 (1975), 141–56

Whitcomb, Ian, *After the Ball. Pop Music from Rag to Rock* (Allen Lane) London 1972

White, Adam, 'WEA International's Sales to New Peak', *Billboard* (26 April 1980), 56

Wicke, Peter, 'Rockmusik – Aspekte einer Faszination', *Weimarer Beiträge*, 27 (1981/9), 98–126

   'Rock Music. A Musical Aesthetic Study', in *Popular Music 2. Theory and Method*, eds. R. Middleton and D. Horn (Cambridge University Press) Cambridge, London, New York, New Rochelle, Melbourne, Sydney 1982, 219–44

   'Von der Aura der technisch produzierten Klanggestalt', in *Wegzeichen. Studien zur Musikwissenschaft*, eds. J. Mainka and P. Wicke (Verlag Neue Musik) Berlin 1985, 276–88

   'Rock'n'Revolution. Sul significato della musica rock in una cultura di massa progressista', *Musica/Realtà*, 6 (1985/17), 5–12

Wiener, Jon, *Come Together. John Lennon in His Time* (Random House) New York 1984

Williamson, Judith, *Decoding Advertisements. Ideology and Meaning in Advertising* (Marion Boyars) London, New York 1978

Willis, Paul, 'Subcultural Meaning of the Motor Bike', Working Papers in Cultural Studies, no. 1 (University of Birmingham, Centre for Contemporary Cultural Studies) Birmingham 1970

   'Symbolism and Practice. The Social Meaning of Pop Music', Stencilled Occasional Papers, Sub and Popular Culture Series, SP no. 13 (University of Birmingham, Centre for Contemporary Cultural Studies) Birmingham 1974

   Profane Culture (Routledge & Kegan Paul) London, Boston, Henley 1978

Willmott, Peter, *Adolescent Boys of East London* (Penguin) Harmonds-
     worth 1969
Winkler, Peter, 'Wild Boys – Girls Fun' (Paper from International
     Conference on Popular Music Research III, Montreal, July 1985),
     unpublished manuscript
Wolfe, Arnold S., 'Pop on Video. Narrative Modes in the Visualisation
     of Popular Music on "Your Hit Parade" and "Solid Gold"', in
     *Popular Music Perspectives 2. Papers from The Second International
     Conference on Popular Music Research, Reggio Emilia 1983*,
     ed. D. Horn (IASPM), Göteborg, Exeter, Ottawa, Reggio Emilia
     1985, 428–44
     'Rock on Cable. On MTV: Music Television, the First Video Music
     Channel', *Popular Music and Society*, 9 (1983), 41–50
Wooler, Bob, 'Well Now – Dig This!', *Mersey Beat. Merseyside's Own
     Entertainment Paper*, 1, no. 5 (31 August–14 September 1961), 2
York, Peter, *Style Wars* (Sidgwick & Jackson) London 1980
Zimmer, Jochen, *Rocksoziologie. Theorie und Sozialgeschichte der
     Rock-Musik* (VSA) Hamburg 1981

Discography

Antologie Blues/2. Dokumentární nahrávky vybral Paul Oliver, CBS/
    Supraphon 1015 3801-02 ZD (ČSSR 1983)
Beatles, The
    'Love Me Do' / 'P.S. I Love You', Parlophone R 4949 (GB 1962)
    'Roll Over Beethoven', EMI Electrola 1 C 062-04 181 (GB 1963)
    Sgt Pepper's Lonely Hearts Club Band, Parlophone PCS 7027 (GB
    1967)
    'Hey Jude' / 'Revolution', Apple R 5722 (GB 1968)
    The Beatles [*White Album*], Apple PCS 7067/8 (GB 1968)
Berry, Chuck
    'Maybellene', Chess 1604 (USA 1955)
    'Roll Over Beethoven', Chess 1626 (USA 1956)
    'School Day', Chess 1653 (USA 1957)
    'Sweet Little Sixteen', Chess 1693 (USA 1958)
    Chuck Berry, Amiga 855835 (DDR 1981)
Channel, Bruce
    'Hey Baby', Smash 1731 (USA 1962)
Clash, The
    The Clash, CBS Epic 36060 (GB 1977)
Dae, Sonny, and his Knights
    'Rock Around the Clock', Arcade 123 (USA 1953)
Domino, Fats
    'The Fat Man', Imperial 5058 (USA 1950)
Dupree, Champion Jack
    'Junker Blues', Atlantic 40526 (USA 1940)
Duran Duran
    'Wild Boys', Parlophone DURAN 2 (GB 1984)
Dylan, Bob
    The Freewheelin' Bob Dylan, CBS Columbia CS 8786 (USA 1963)
    'The Times They Are A-Changin'', CBS Columbia CS 8905 (USA
    1964)
    Greatest Hits, Amiga 855680 (DDR 1979)
Eagles, The
    Desperado, Asylum 1 C 062-94 386 (USA 1973)

Frankie Goes to Hollywood
  'Relax', ZTT 12 ZTAS 1 (GB 1983)
Haley, Bill, and his Comets
  'Rock Around the Clock', Decca 29124 (USA 1954)
  'Shake, Rattle and Roll', Decca 29204 (USA 1954)
  Bill Haley And His Comets, Amiga 844784 (DDR 1980)
Jackson, Michael
  Thriller, CBS Epic 50989 (USA 1983); Amiga 856105 (DDR 1984)
Lennon, John & Plastic Ono Band
  'Give Peace a Chance', Apple 1813 (GB 1969)
Page, Patti
  'Tennessee Waltz', Mercury 5534 X 45 (USA 1950)
Perkins, Carl
  'Sure to Fall', Sun 5 (USA 1956)
Pink Floyd
  A Saucerful of Secrets, EMI Columbia 6258 (GB 1968)
  The Dark Side of the Moon, Harvest 11163 (GB 1973); Amiga 855667
    (DDR 1979)
Presley, Elvis
  'That's All Right (Mama)' / 'Blue Moon of Kentucky', Sun 209
    (USA 1954)
  'Hound Dog', RCA Victor 47-6604 (USA 1956)
  'Love Me Tender', RCA Victor 47-6643 (USA 1956)
  Elvis Presley, Amiga 855630 (DDR 1978)
Rolling Stones, The
  '(I can't get no) Satisfaction', Decca F 12220 (GB 1965)
  Beggars Banquet, Decca 6.22157 (GB 1968)
  The Rolling Stones, Amiga 855885 (DDR 1982)
Sex Pistols
  'Anarchy in the UK', EMI 2506 (GB 1976)
Simon & Garfunkel
  'The Boxer', CBS Columbia 4-44785 (USA 1969)
  Simon & Garfunkel's Greatest Hits, Amiga 855684 (DDR 1979)
Smith, Patti
  'Piss Factory' / 'Hey Joe', Sire 1009 (USA 1974)
Thornton, Willie Mae
  'Hound Dog', Peacock 1612 (USA 1953)
Turner, Joe
  'Shake, Rattle and Roll', Atlantic 45-1026 (USA 1954)
Who, The
  'My Generation', Brunswick 05944 (GB 1965)
  The Who, Amiga 855803 (DDR 1981)
Zappa, Frank & The Mothers of Invention
  We're Only in It for the Money, Verve V + V6 5045 X (USA 1968)

Index of people and groups

General index